GREEN LANTERN

SECRET ORIGIN

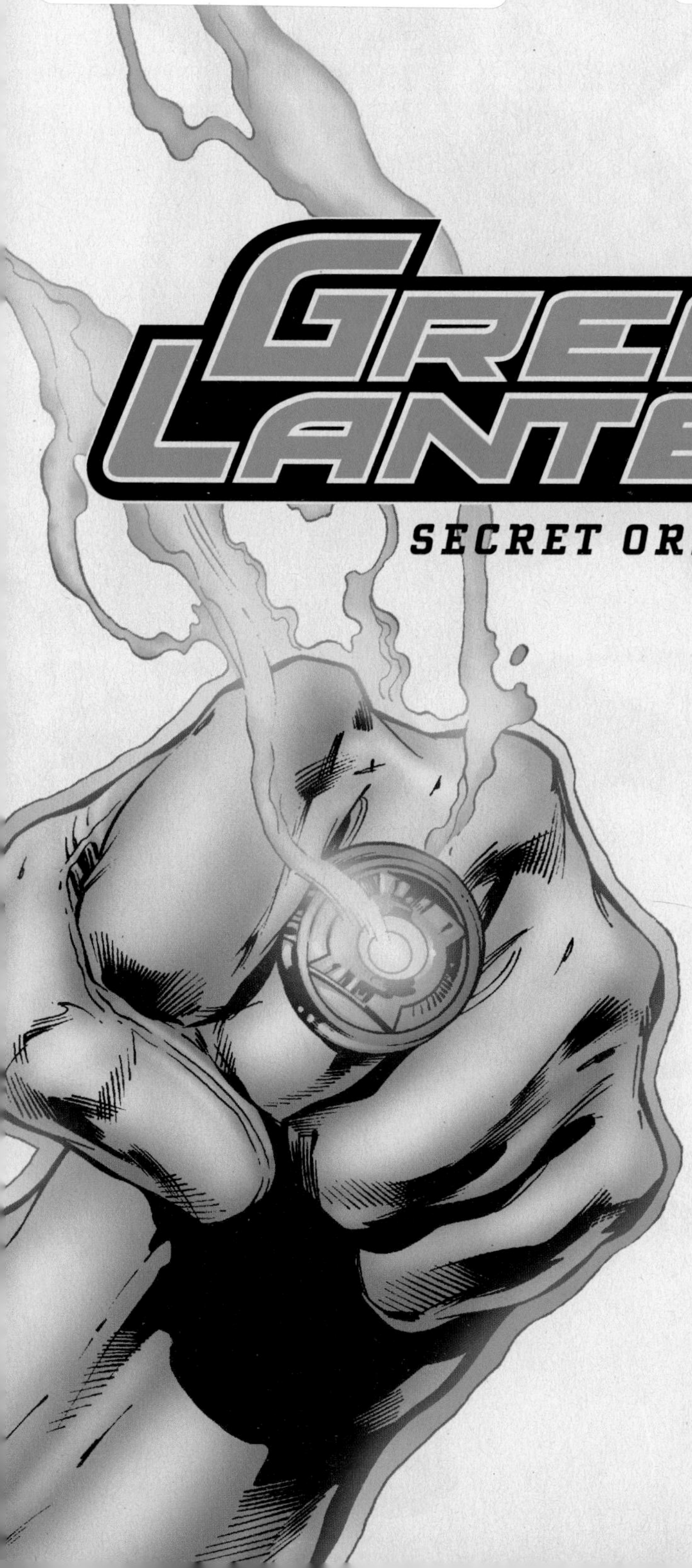

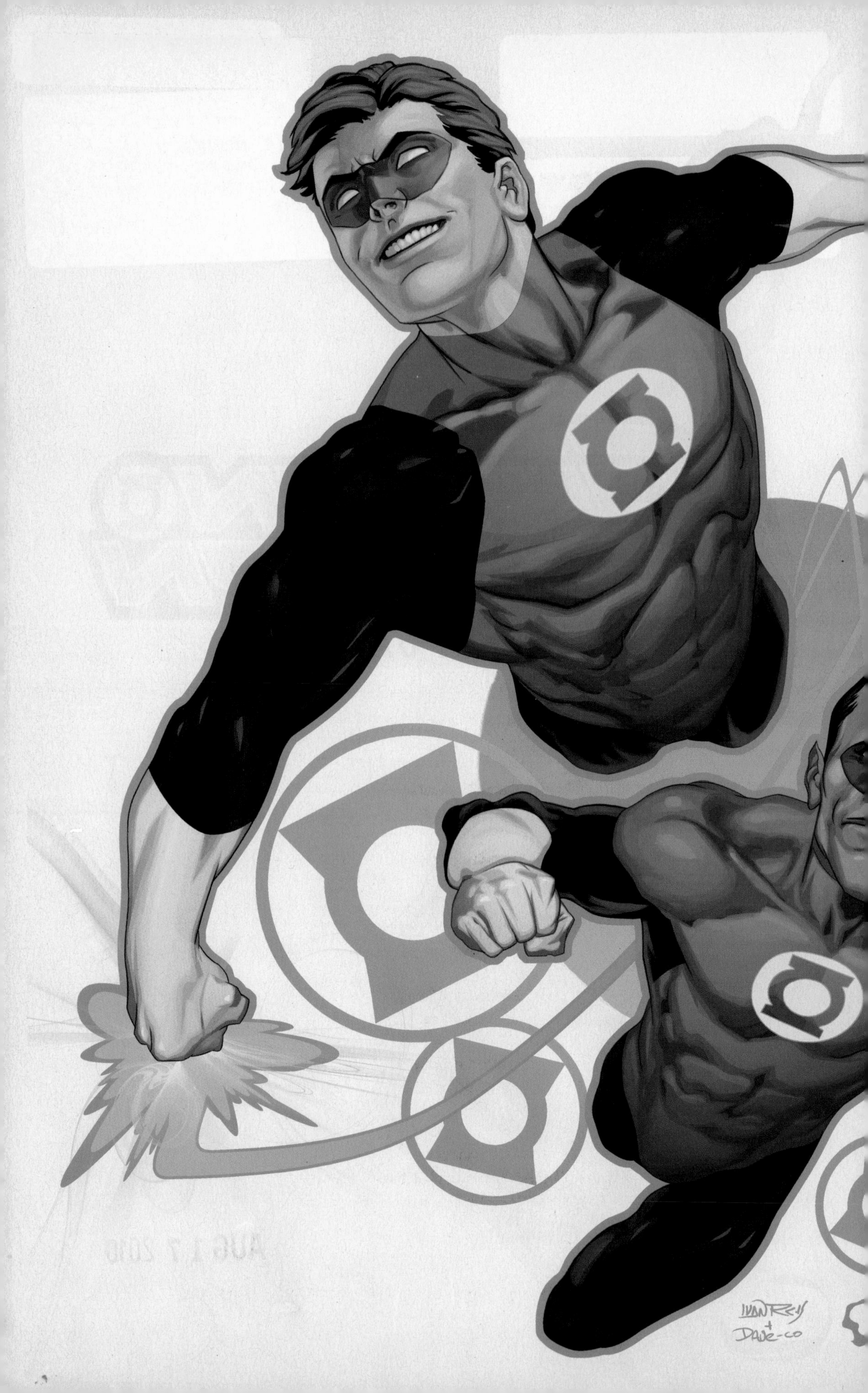

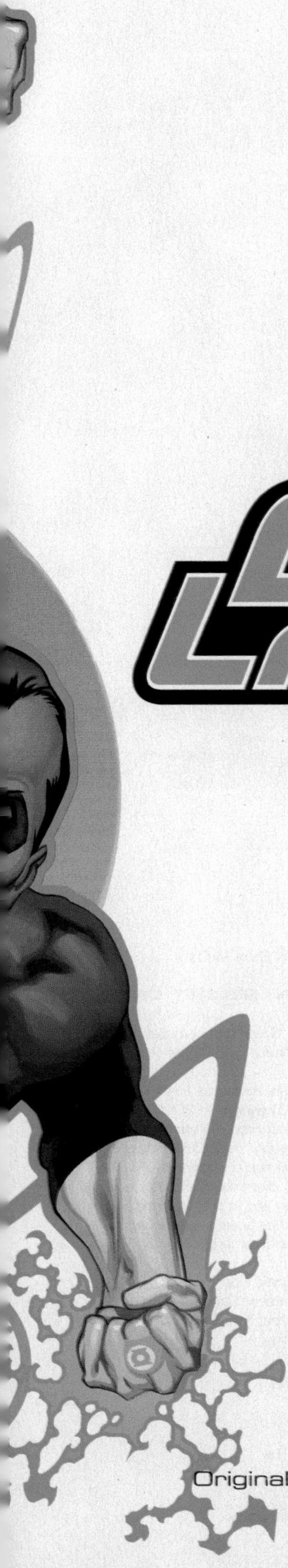

GREEN LANTERN

SECRET ORIGIN

Geoff Johns
Writer

Ivan Reis
Penciller

Oclair Albert
Inker

Randy Mayor
Colors

Rob Leigh
Letters

With
Julio Ferreira Partial Inker Book 3
Ivan Reis Partial Inker Book 6

Original Series Covers by **Ivan Reis** and **Dave McCaig**

DC COMICS

Dan DiDio Senior VP-Executive Editor
Eddie Berganza Editor-original series
Adam Schlagman Assistant Editor-original series
Bob Joy Editor-collected edition
Robbin Brosterman Senior Art Director
Paul Levitz President & Publisher
Georg Brewer VP-Design & DC Direct Creative
Richard Bruning Senior VP-Creative Director
Patrick Caldon Executive VP-Finance & Operations
Chris Caramalis VP-Finance
John Cunningham VP-Marketing
Terri Cunningham VP-Managing Editor
Amy Genkins Senior VP-Business & Legal Affairs
Alison Gill VP-Manufacturing
David Hyde VP-Publicity
Hank Kanalz VP-General Manager, WildStorm
Jim Lee Editorial Director-WildStorm
Gregory Noveck Senior VP-Creative Affairs
Sue Pohja VP-Book Trade Sales
Steve Rotterdam Senior VP-Sales & Marketing
Cheryl Rubin Senior VP-Brand Management
Alysse Soll VP-Advertising & Custom Publishing
Jeff Trojan VP-Business Development, DC Direct
Bob Wayne VP-Sales

Cover art by Ivan Reis and Dave McCaig

GREEN LANTERN: SECRET ORIGIN

Published by DC Comics. Cover and compilation
Copyright © 2008 DC Comics. All Rights Reserved.

Originally published in single magazine form in
GREEN LANTERN 29-35 Copyright © 2008
DC Comics. All Rights Reserved. All characters,
their distinctive likenesses and related elements
featured in this publication are trademarks of
DC Comics. The stories, characters and incidents
featured in this publication are entirely fictional.
DC Comics does not read or accept unsolicited
submissions of ideas, stories or artwork.

DC Comics, 1700 Broadway, New York, NY 10019
A Warner Bros. Entertainment Company
Printed by Worldcolor Press, Inc., Dubuque, IA. USA.
6/16/10. Second Printing.

ISBN: 978-1-4012-2017-4

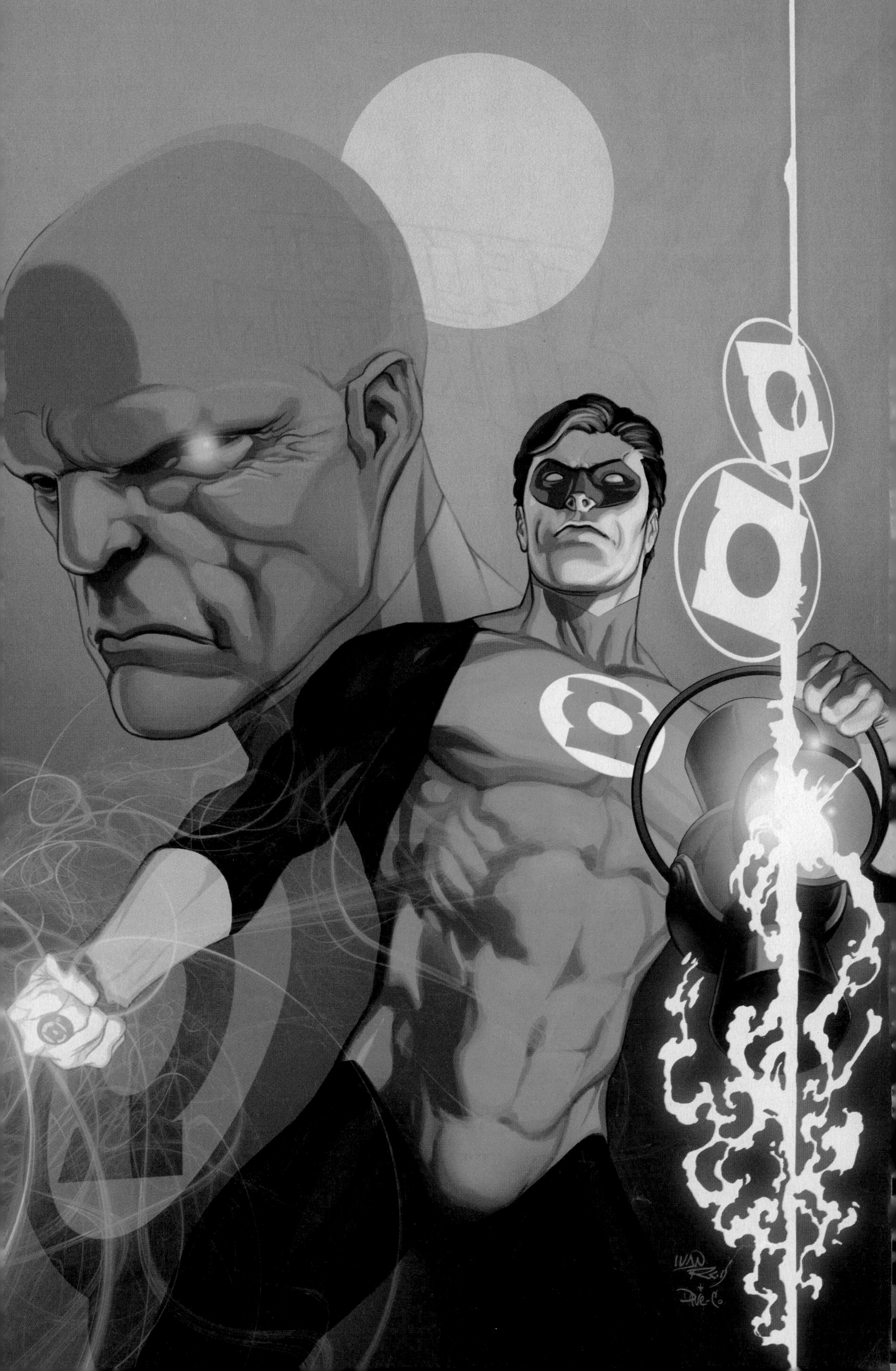

SECRET ORIGIN

BOOK ONE

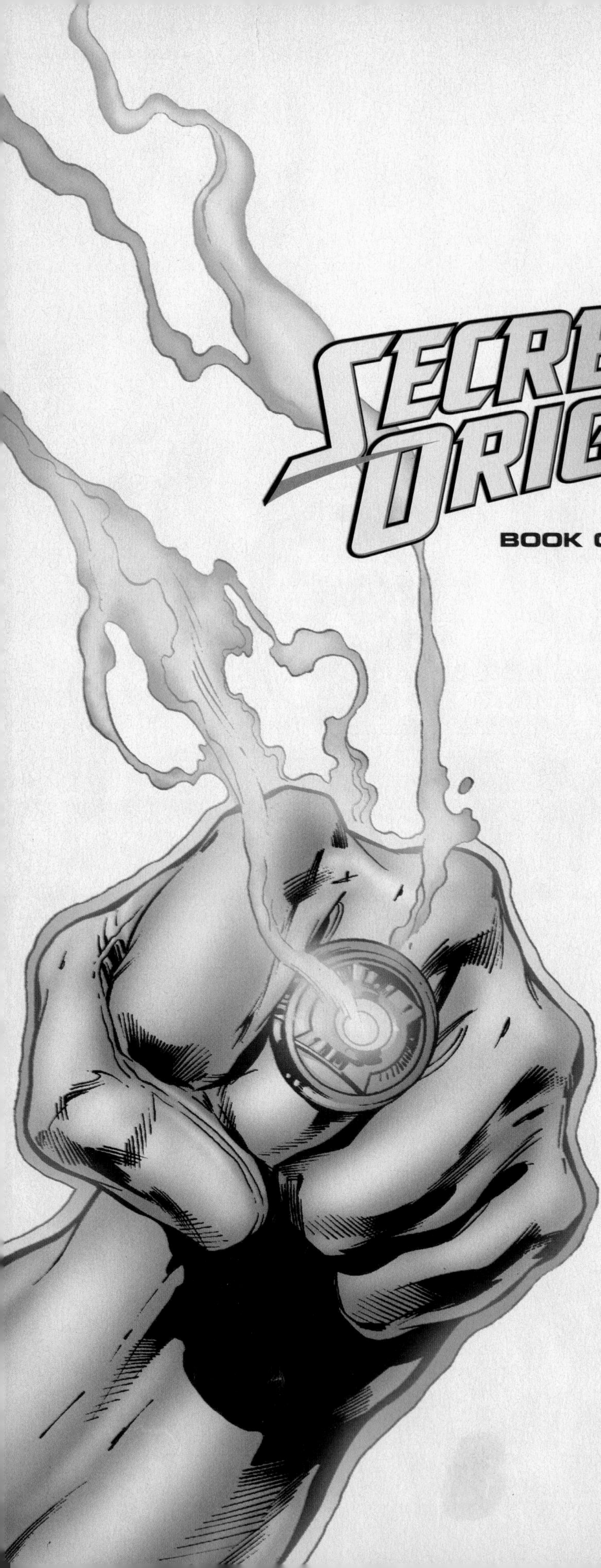

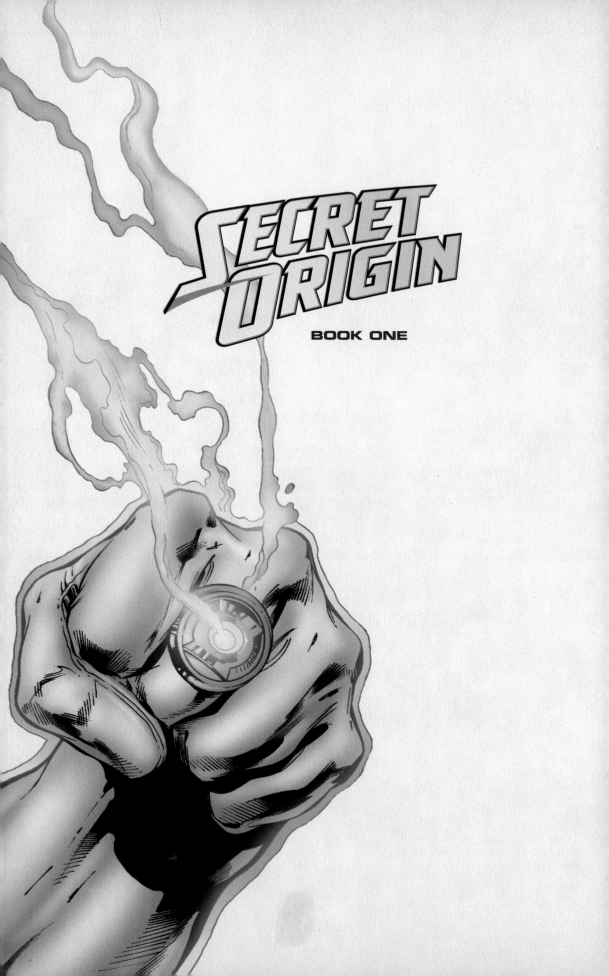

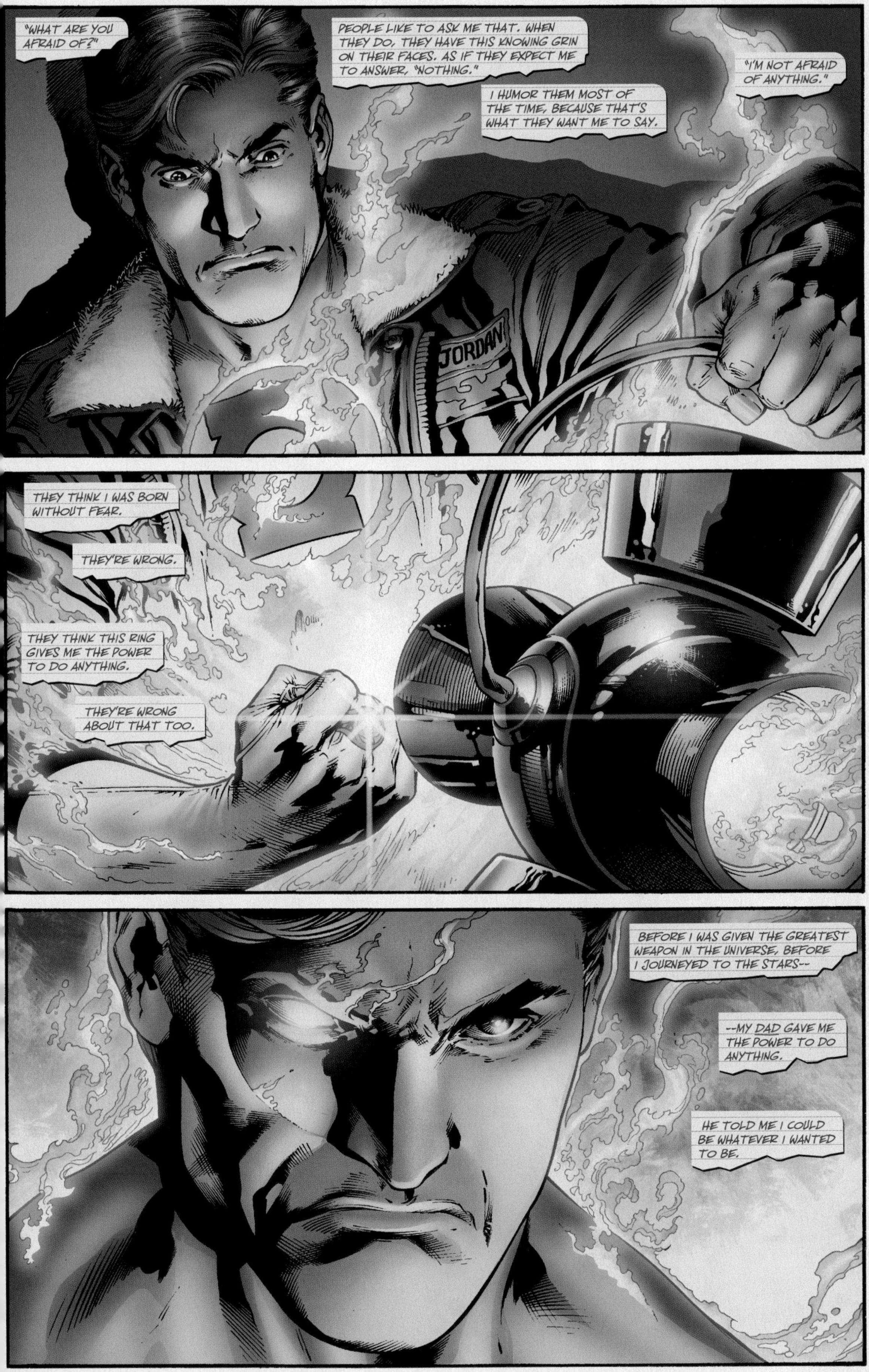
"WHAT ARE YOU AFRAID OF?"
PEOPLE LIKE TO ASK ME THAT. WHEN THEY DO, THEY HAVE THIS KNOWING GRIN ON THEIR FACES. AS IF THEY EXPECT ME TO ANSWER, "NOTHING."
I HUMOR THEM MOST OF THE TIME, BECAUSE THAT'S WHAT THEY WANT ME TO SAY.
"I'M NOT AFRAID OF ANYTHING."
JORDAN
THEY THINK I WAS BORN WITHOUT FEAR.
THEY'RE WRONG.
THEY THINK THIS RING GIVES ME THE POWER TO DO ANYTHING.
THEY'RE WRONG ABOUT THAT TOO.
BEFORE I WAS GIVEN THE GREATEST WEAPON IN THE UNIVERSE, BEFORE I JOURNEYED TO THE STARS--
--MY DAD GAVE ME THE POWER TO DO ANYTHING.
HE TOLD ME I COULD BE WHATEVER I WANTED TO BE.

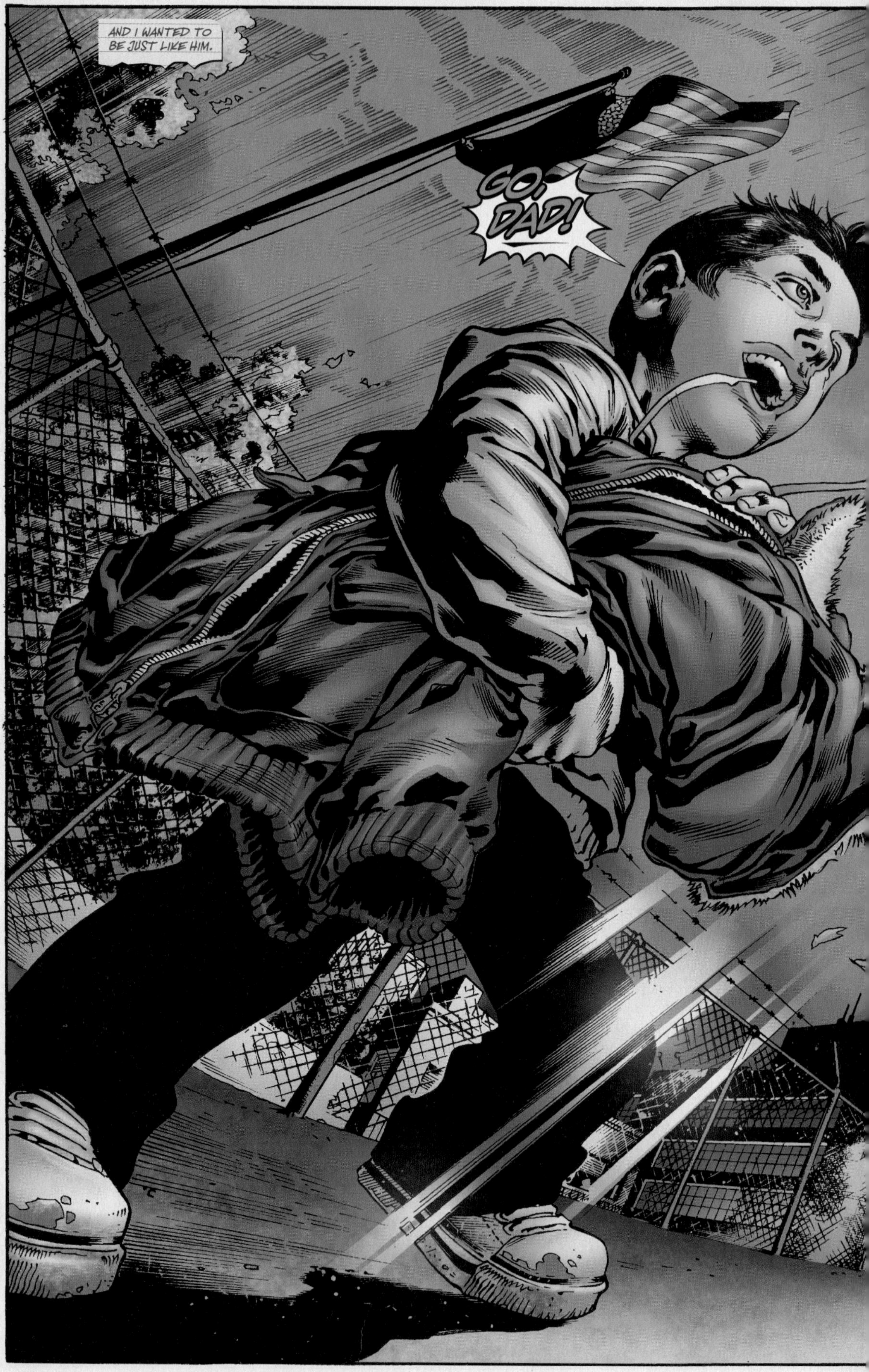
AND I WANTED TO BE JUST LIKE HIM.
GO, DAD!

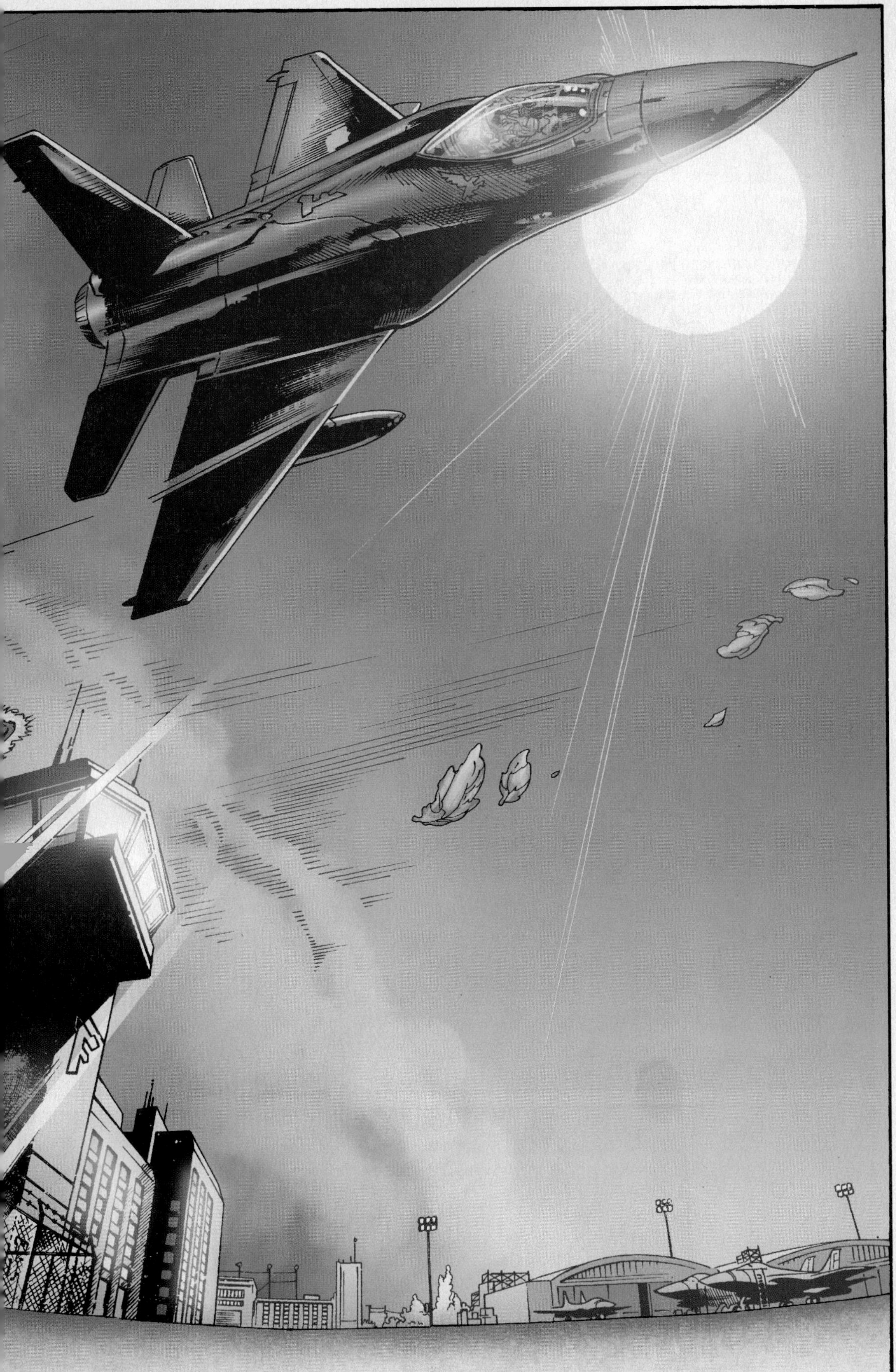

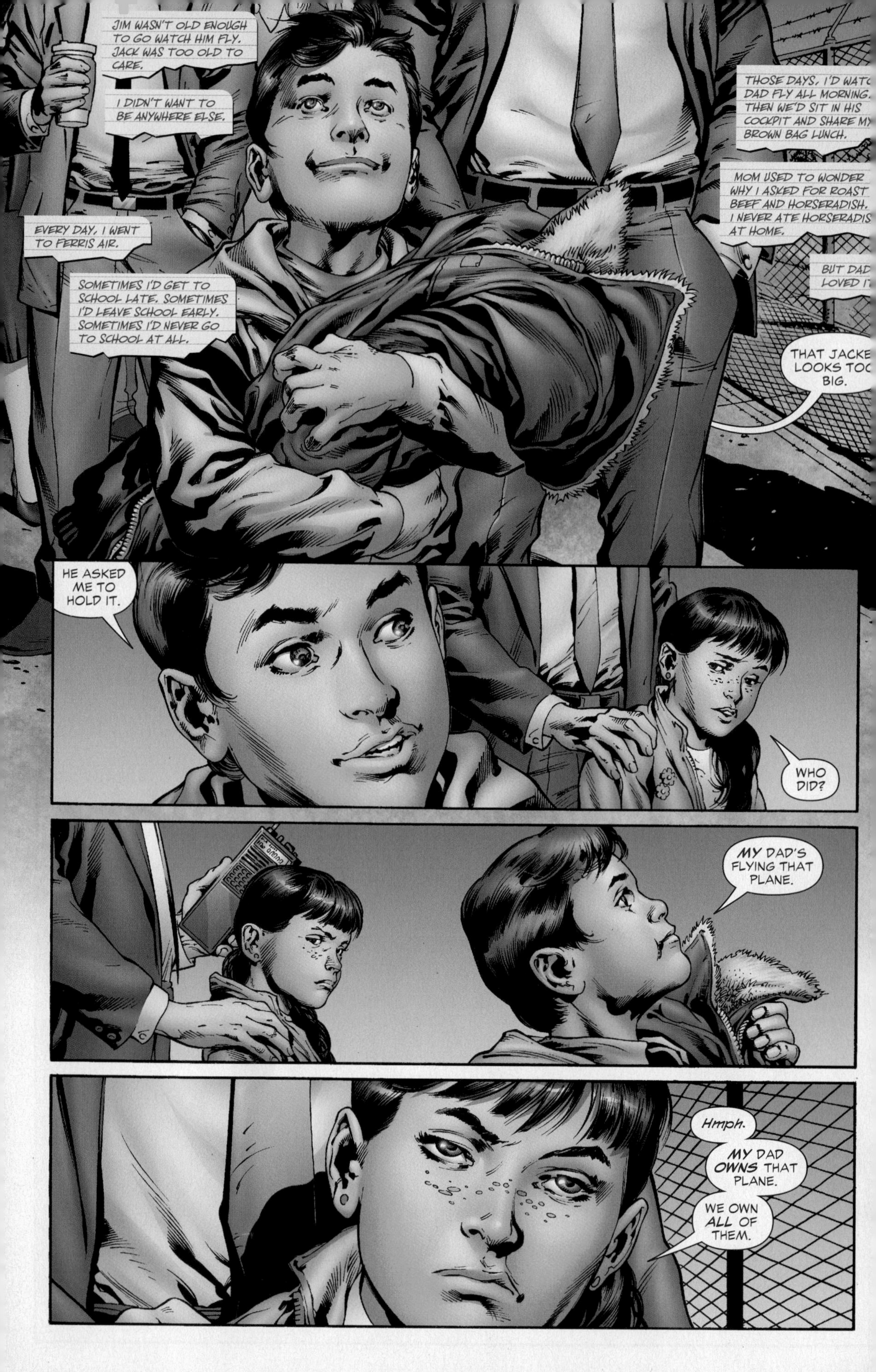

JIM WASN'T OLD ENOUGH TO GO WATCH HIM FLY. JACK WAS TOO OLD TO CARE.
I DIDN'T WANT TO BE ANYWHERE ELSE.
EVERY DAY, I WENT TO FERRIS AIR.
SOMETIMES I'D GET TO SCHOOL LATE. SOMETIMES I'D LEAVE SCHOOL EARLY. SOMETIMES I'D NEVER GO TO SCHOOL AT ALL.
THOSE DAYS, I'D WATC DAD FLY ALL MORNING. THEN WE'D SIT IN HIS COCKPIT AND SHARE MY BROWN BAG LUNCH.
MOM USED TO WONDER WHY I ASKED FOR ROAST BEEF AND HORSERADISH. I NEVER ATE HORSERADIS AT HOME.
BUT DAD LOVED IT
THAT JACKE LOOKS TOO BIG.
HE ASKED ME TO HOLD IT.
WHO DID?
MY DAD'S FLYING THAT PLANE.
Hmph.
MY DAD OWNS THAT PLANE.
WE OWN ALL OF THEM.

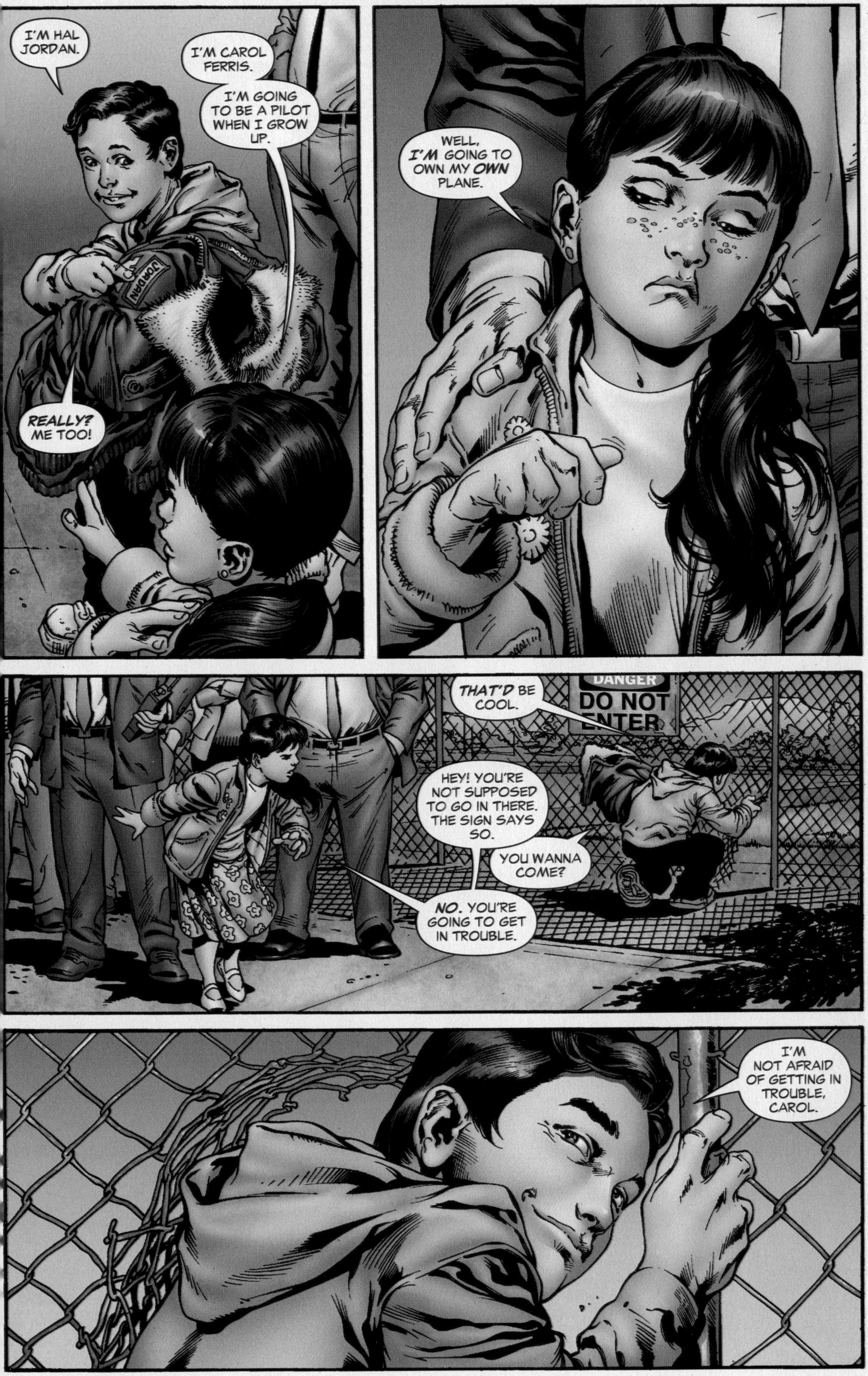
I'M HAL JORDAN.
I'M CAROL FERRIS.
I'M GOING TO BE A PILOT WHEN I GROW UP.
REALLY? ME TOO!
JORDAN
WELL, I'M GOING TO OWN MY OWN PLANE.
THAT'D BE COOL.
DANGER
DO NOT ENTER
HEY! YOU'RE NOT SUPPOSED TO GO IN THERE. THE SIGN SAYS SO.
YOU WANNA COME?
NO. YOU'RE GOING TO GET IN TROUBLE.
I'M NOT AFRAID OF GETTING IN TROUBLE, CAROL.

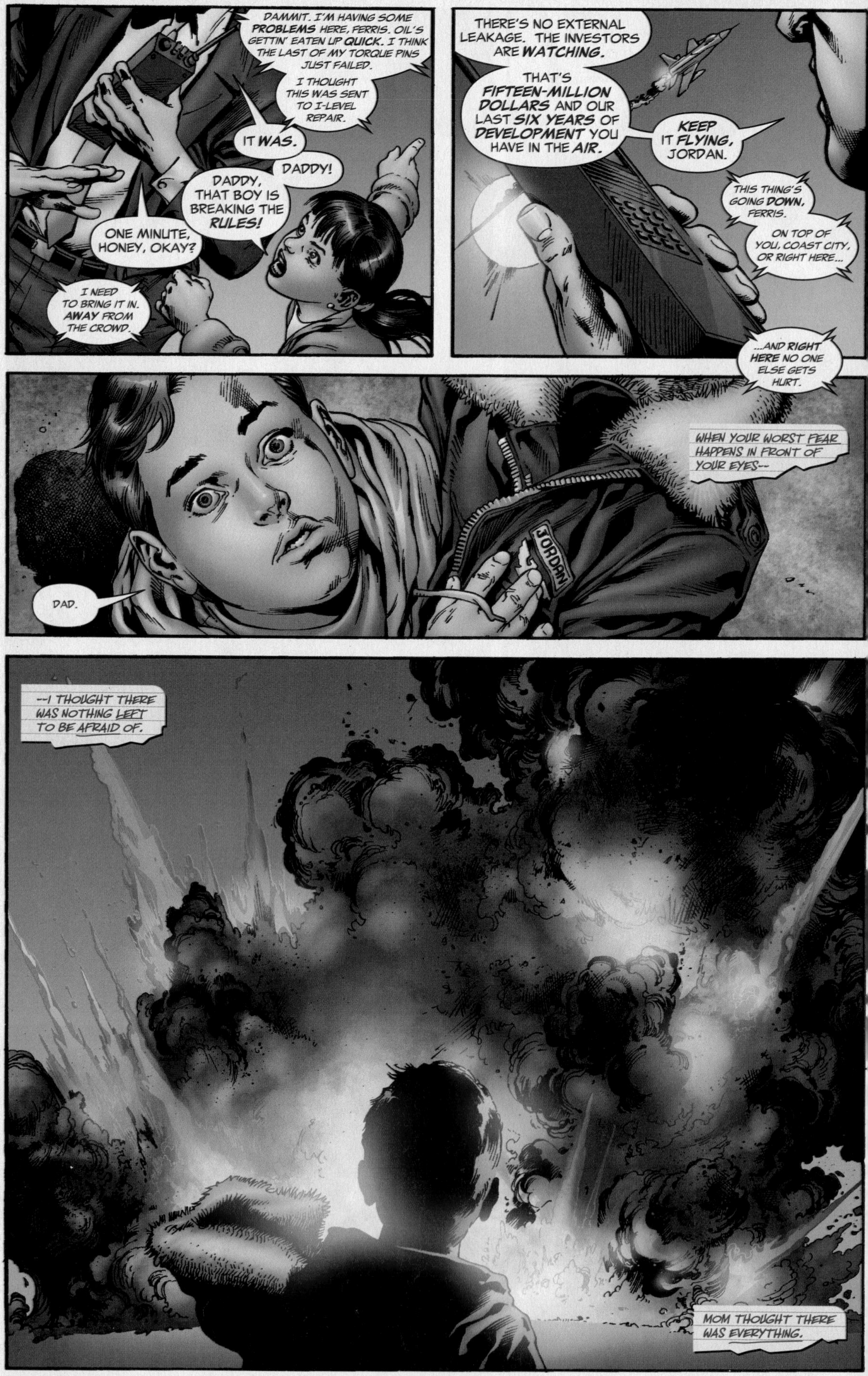
DAMMIT. I'M HAVING SOME PROBLEMS HERE, FERRIS. OIL'S GETTIN' EATEN UP QUICK. I THINK THE LAST OF MY TORQUE PINS JUST FAILED.
I THOUGHT THIS WAS SENT TO I-LEVEL REPAIR.
IT WAS.
DADDY!
DADDY, THAT BOY IS BREAKING THE RULES!
ONE MINUTE, HONEY, OKAY?
I NEED TO BRING IT IN. AWAY FROM THE CROWD.
THERE'S NO EXTERNAL LEAKAGE. THE INVESTORS ARE WATCHING.
THAT'S FIFTEEN-MILLION DOLLARS AND OUR LAST SIX YEARS OF DEVELOPMENT YOU HAVE IN THE AIR.
KEEP IT FLYING, JORDAN.
THIS THING'S GOING DOWN, FERRIS.
ON TOP OF YOU, COAST CITY, OR RIGHT HERE...
...AND RIGHT HERE NO ONE ELSE GETS HURT.
WHEN YOUR WORST FEAR HAPPENS IN FRONT OF YOUR EYES--
JORDAN
DAD.
--I THOUGHT THERE WAS NOTHING LEFT TO BE AFRAID OF.
MOM THOUGHT THERE WAS EVERYTHING.

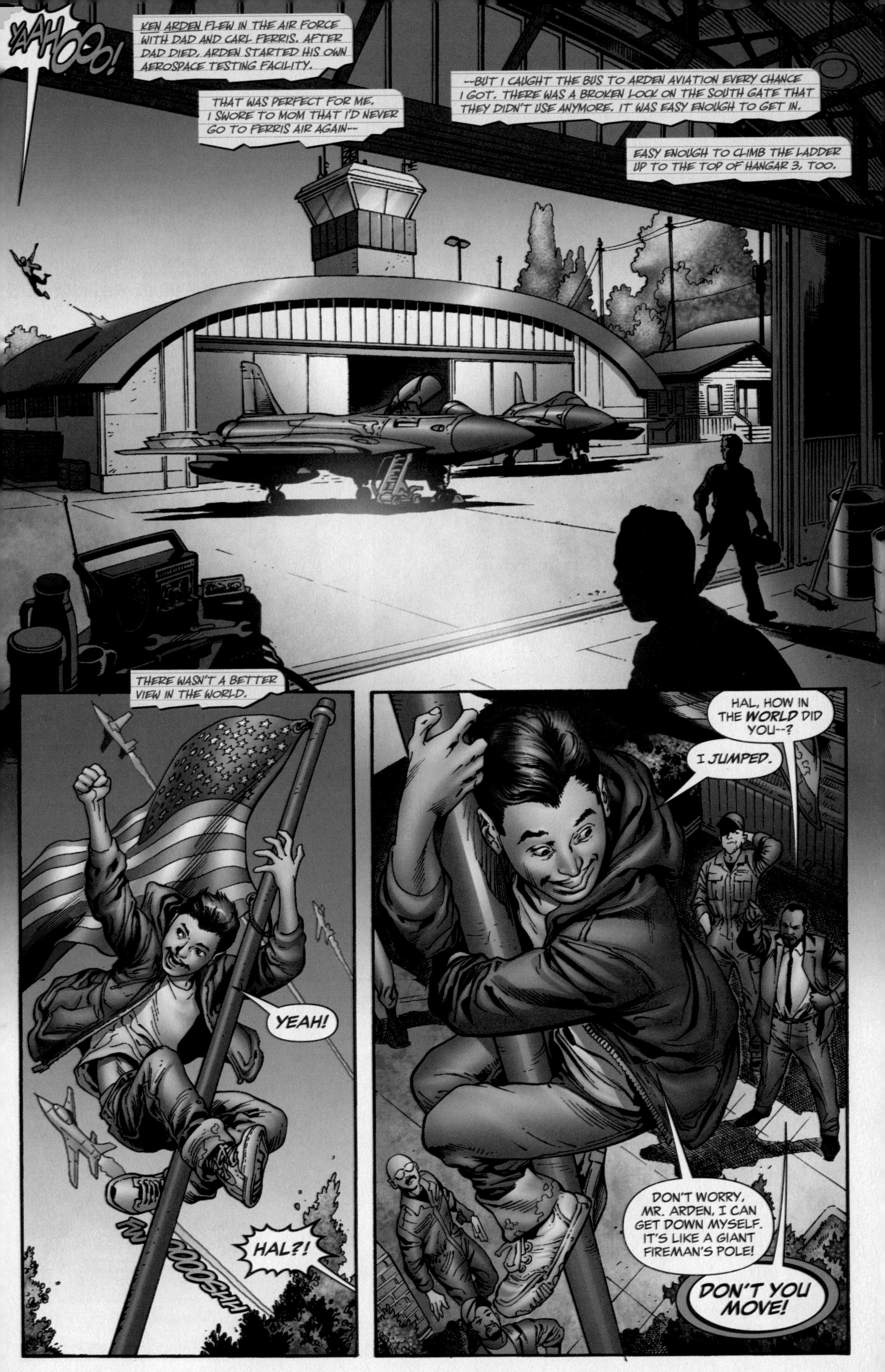
YAAHOOO!
KEN ARDEN FLEW IN THE AIR FORCE WITH DAD AND CARL FERRIS. AFTER DAD DIED, ARDEN STARTED HIS OWN AEROSPACE TESTING FACILITY.
THAT WAS PERFECT FOR ME. I SWORE TO MOM THAT I'D NEVER GO TO FERRIS AIR AGAIN--
--BUT I CAUGHT THE BUS TO ARDEN AVIATION EVERY CHANCE I GOT. THERE WAS A BROKEN LOCK ON THE SOUTH GATE THAT THEY DIDN'T USE ANYMORE. IT WAS EASY ENOUGH TO GET IN.
EASY ENOUGH TO CLIMB THE LADDER UP TO THE TOP OF HANGAR 3, TOO.
THERE WASN'T A BETTER VIEW IN THE WORLD.
YEAH!
HAL?!
FWOOOOSH
HAL, HOW IN THE WORLD DID YOU--?
I JUMPED.
DON'T WORRY, MR. ARDEN, I CAN GET DOWN MYSELF. IT'S LIKE A GIANT FIREMAN'S POLE!
DON'T YOU MOVE!

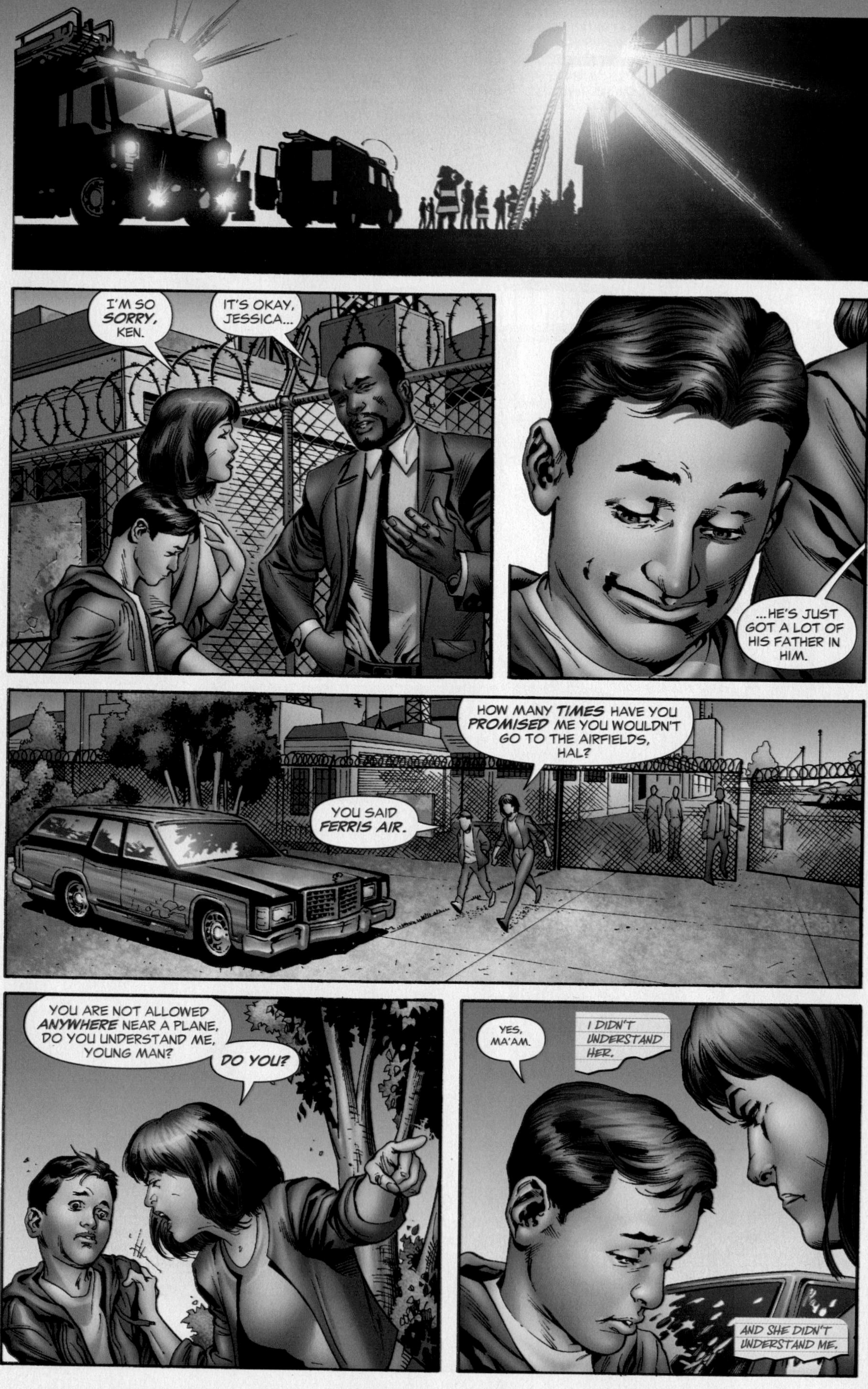
I'M SO SORRY, KEN.
IT'S OKAY, JESSICA...
...HE'S JUST GOT A LOT OF HIS FATHER IN HIM.
HOW MANY TIMES HAVE YOU PROMISED ME YOU WOULDN'T GO TO THE AIRFIELDS, HAL?
YOU SAID FERRIS AIR.
YOU ARE NOT ALLOWED ANYWHERE NEAR A PLANE, DO YOU UNDERSTAND ME, YOUNG MAN?
DO YOU?
YES, MA'AM.
I DIDN'T UNDERSTAND HER.
AND SHE DIDN'T UNDERSTAND ME.

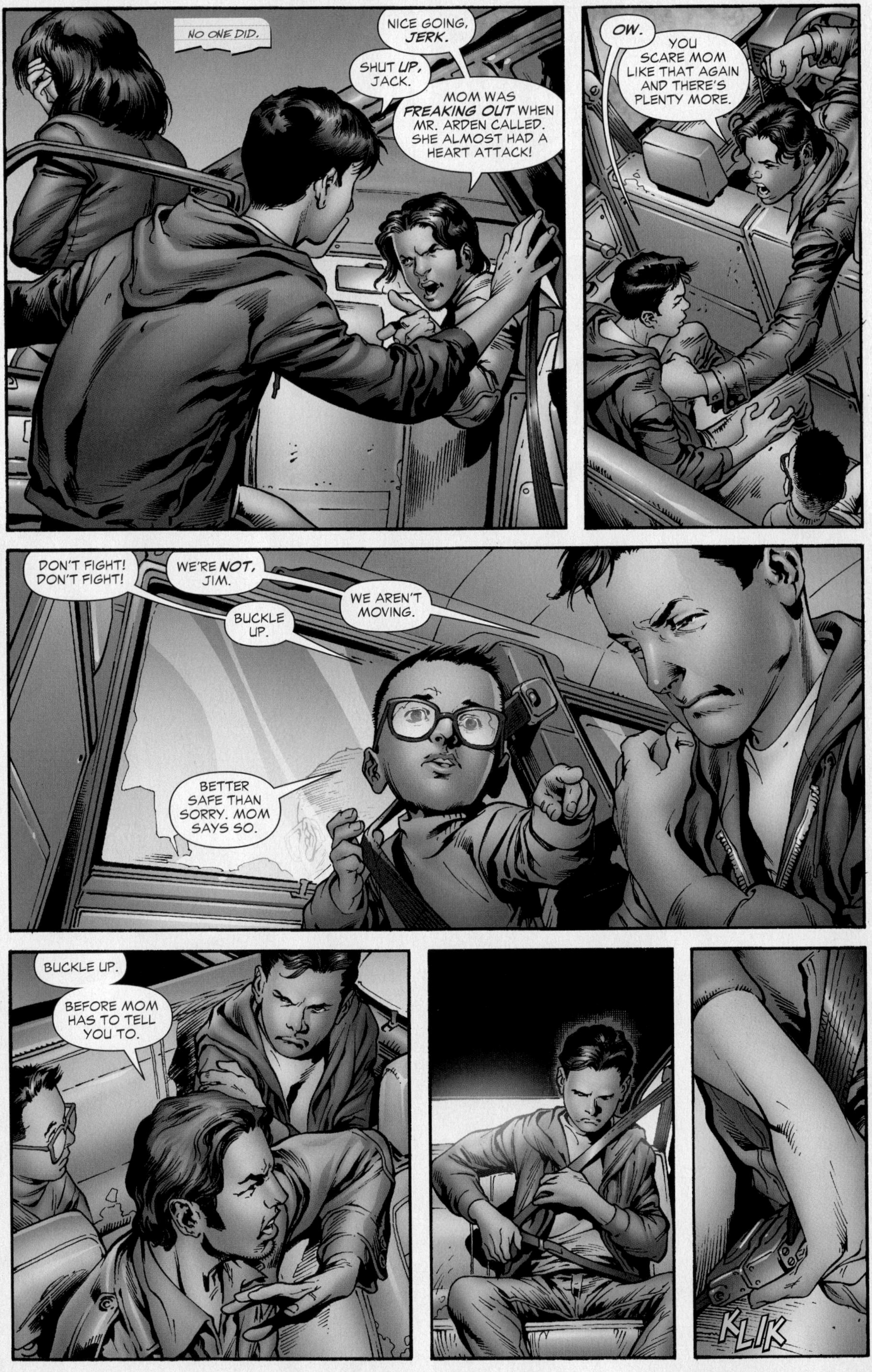

NO ONE DID.
NICE GOING, JERK.
SHUT UP, JACK.
MOM WAS FREAKING OUT WHEN MR. ARDEN CALLED. SHE ALMOST HAD A HEART ATTACK!
OW.
YOU SCARE MOM LIKE THAT AGAIN AND THERE'S PLENTY MORE.
DON'T FIGHT! DON'T FIGHT!
WE'RE NOT, JIM.
WE AREN'T MOVING.
BUCKLE UP.
BETTER SAFE THAN SORRY. MOM SAYS SO.
BUCKLE UP.
BEFORE MOM HAS TO TELL YOU TO.
KLIK

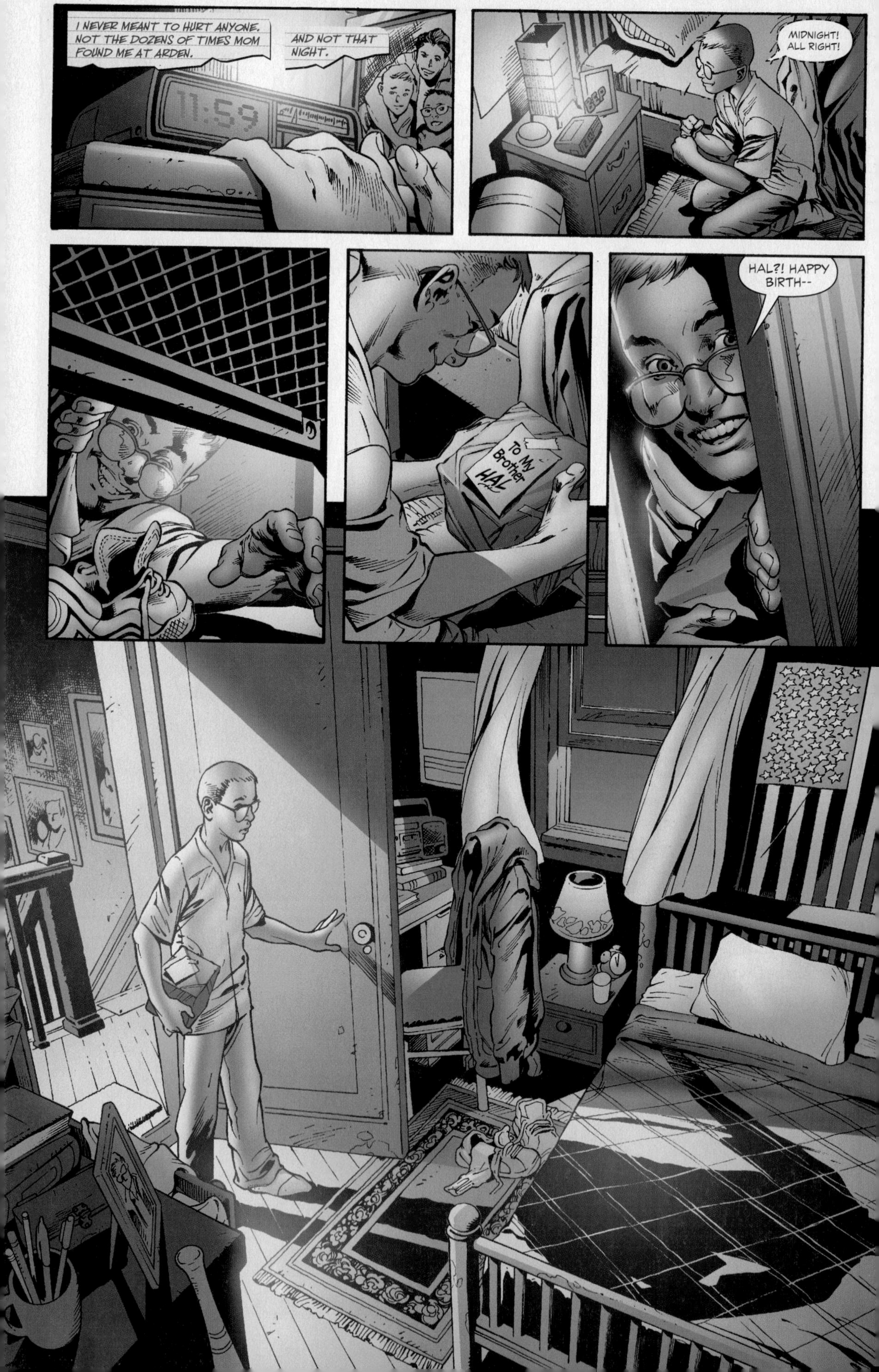
I NEVER MEANT TO HURT ANYONE. NOT THE DOZENS OF TIMES MOM FOUND ME AT ARDEN.
AND NOT THAT NIGHT.
11:59
MIDNIGHT! ALL RIGHT!
To My Brother HAL
HAL?! HAPPY BIRTH--

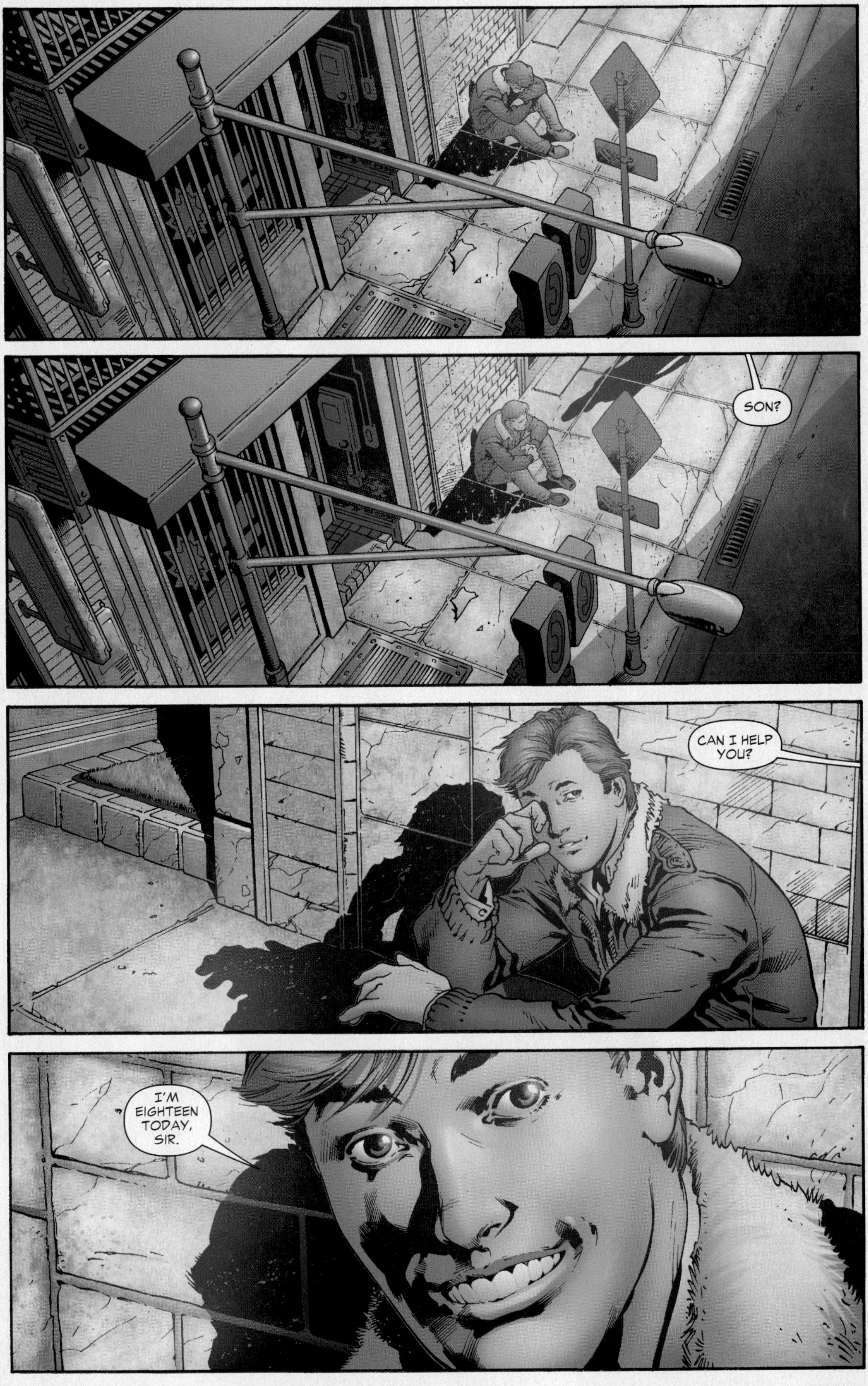
SON?
CAN I HELP YOU?
I'M EIGHTEEN TODAY, SIR.

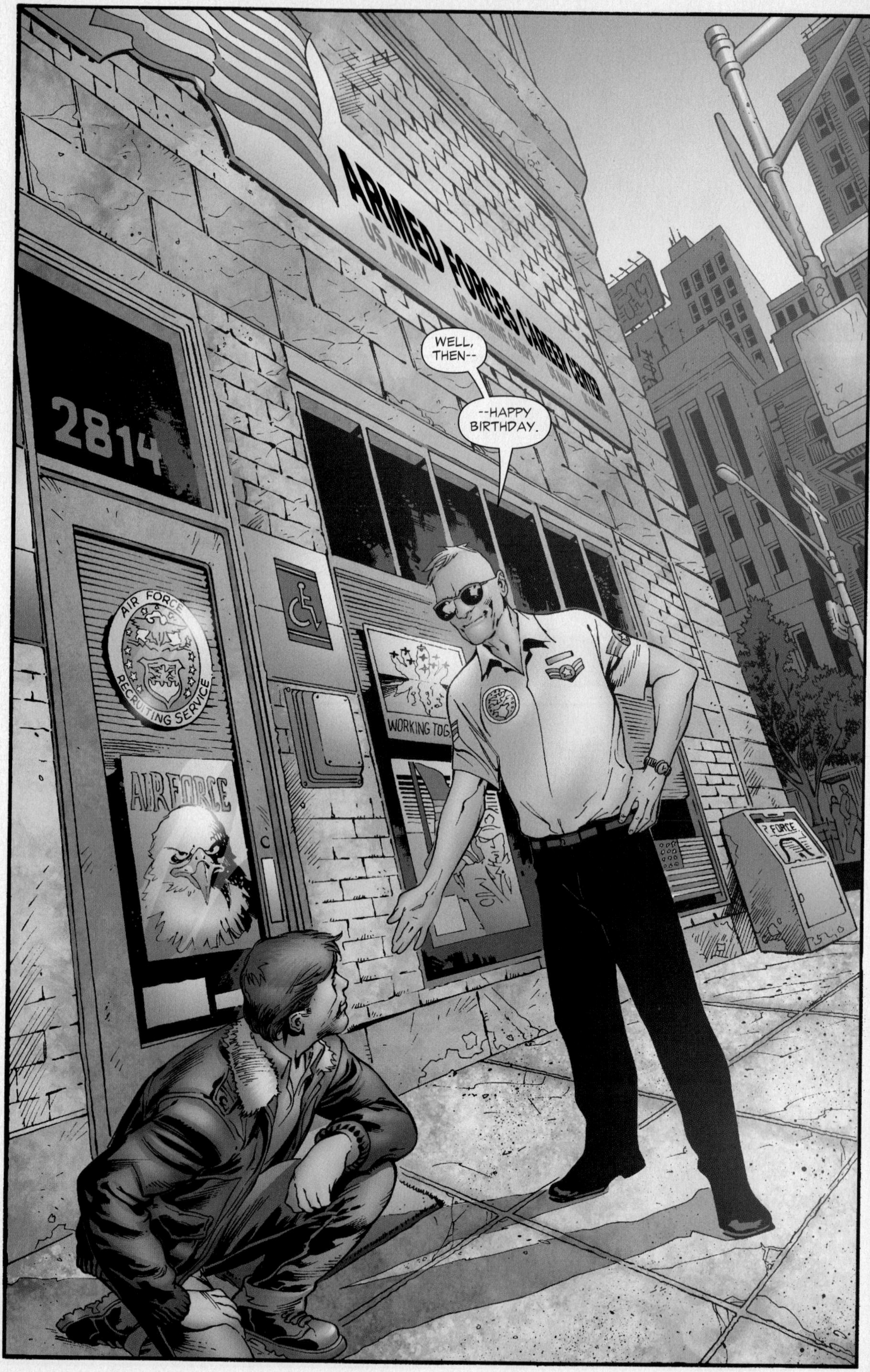
ARMED FORCES CAREER CENTER
US ARMY
US MARINE CORPS
WELL, THEN--
--HAPPY BIRTHDAY.
2814
AIR FORCE RECRUITING SERVICE
AIR FORCE
WORKING TOG

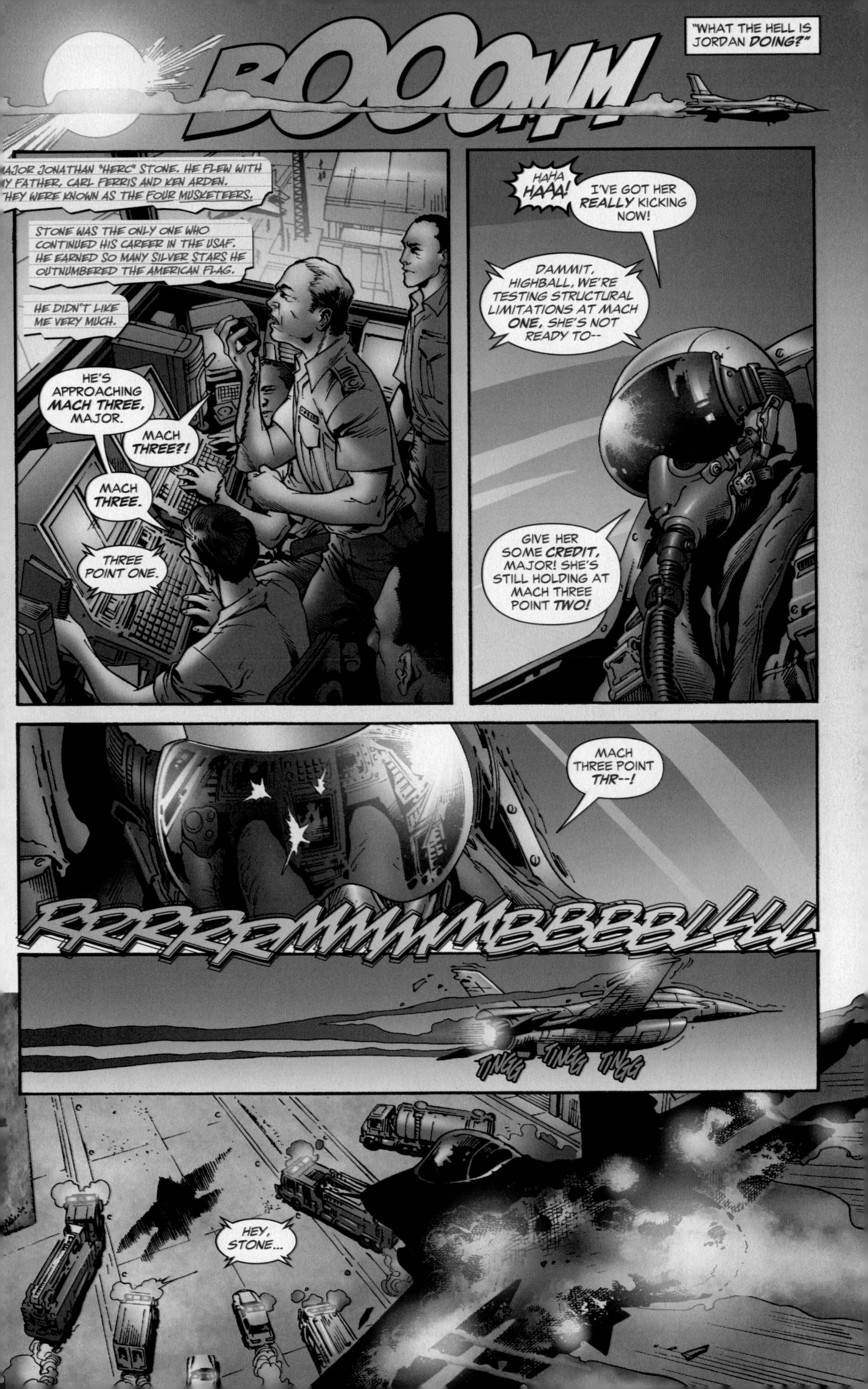
"WHAT THE HELL IS JORDAN DOING?"
BOOOMM
MAJOR JONATHAN "HERC" STONE. HE FLEW WITH MY FATHER, CARL FERRIS AND KEN ARDEN. THEY WERE KNOWN AS THE FOUR MUSKETEERS.
STONE WAS THE ONLY ONE WHO CONTINUED HIS CAREER IN THE USAF. HE EARNED SO MANY SILVER STARS HE OUTNUMBERED THE AMERICAN FLAG.
HE DIDN'T LIKE ME VERY MUCH.
HE'S APPROACHING MACH THREE, MAJOR.
MACH THREE?!
MACH THREE.
THREE POINT ONE.
HAHA HAAA!
I'VE GOT HER REALLY KICKING NOW!
DAMMIT, HIGHBALL, WE'RE TESTING STRUCTURAL LIMITATIONS AT MACH ONE. SHE'S NOT READY TO--
GIVE HER SOME CREDIT, MAJOR! SHE'S STILL HOLDING AT MACH THREE POINT TWO!
MACH THREE POINT THR--!
RRRRRMMMMMBBBBBLLLL
TINGG TINGG TINGG
HEY, STONE...

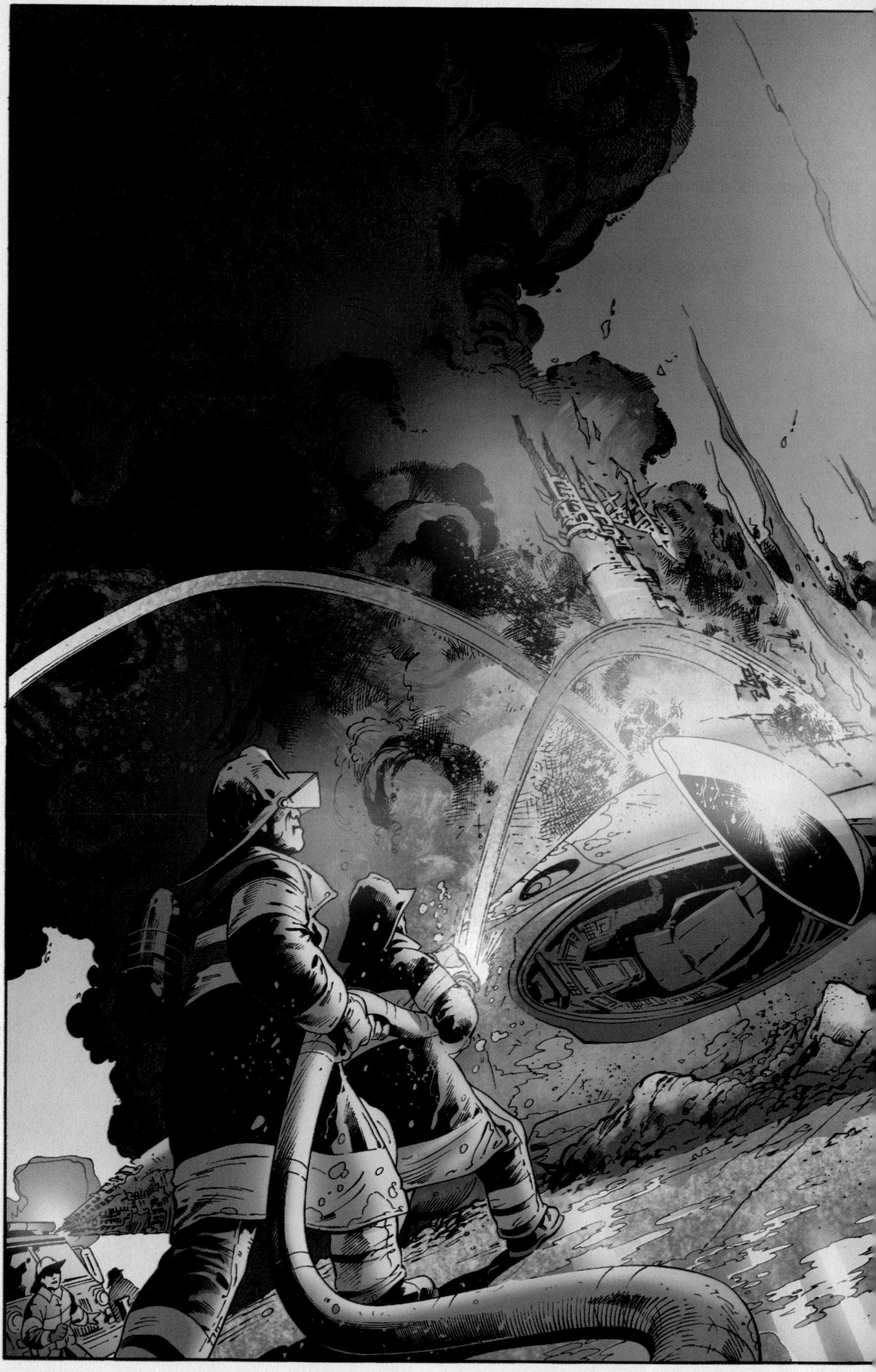

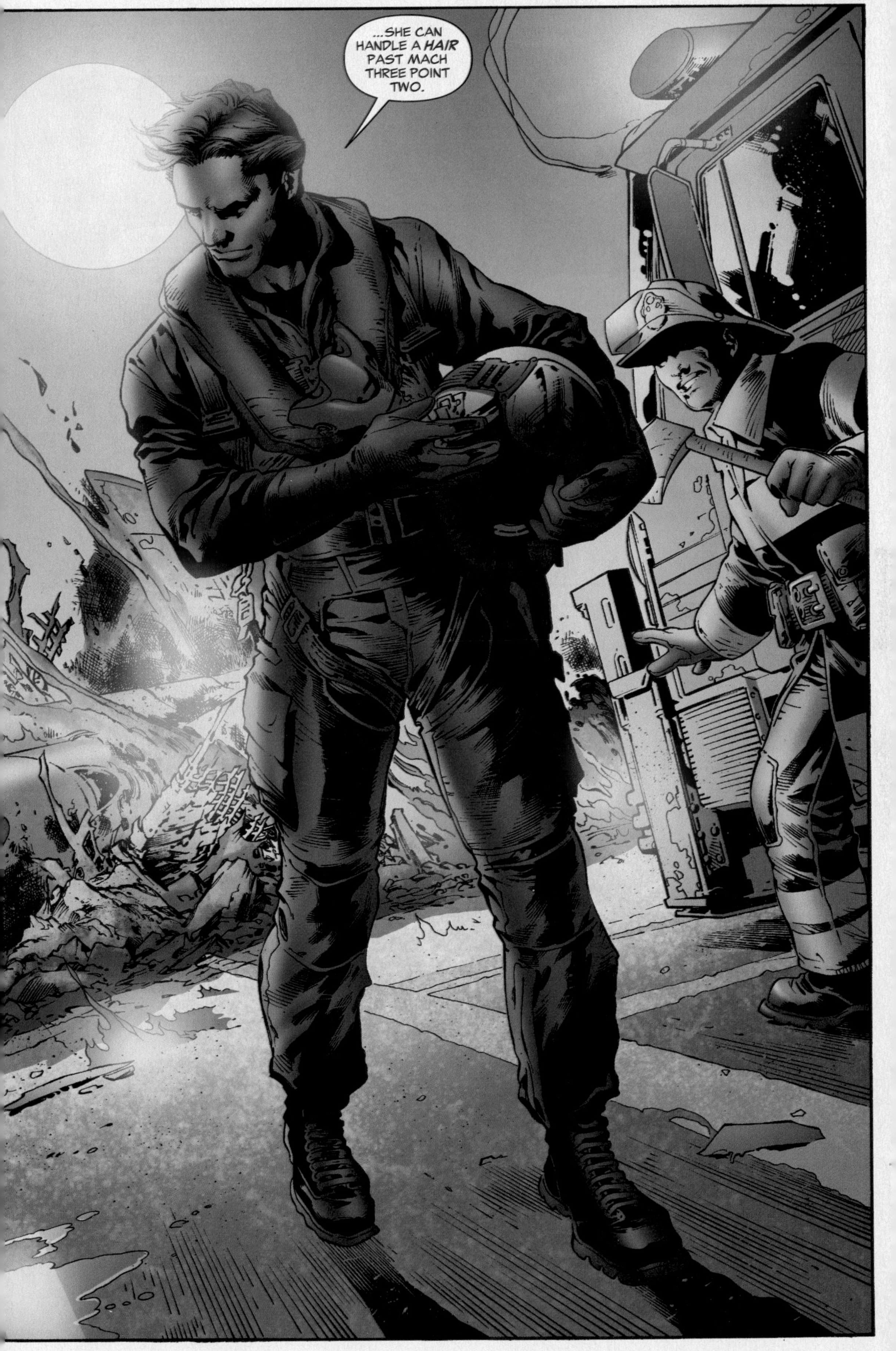
...SHE CAN HANDLE A HAIR PAST MACH THREE POINT TWO.

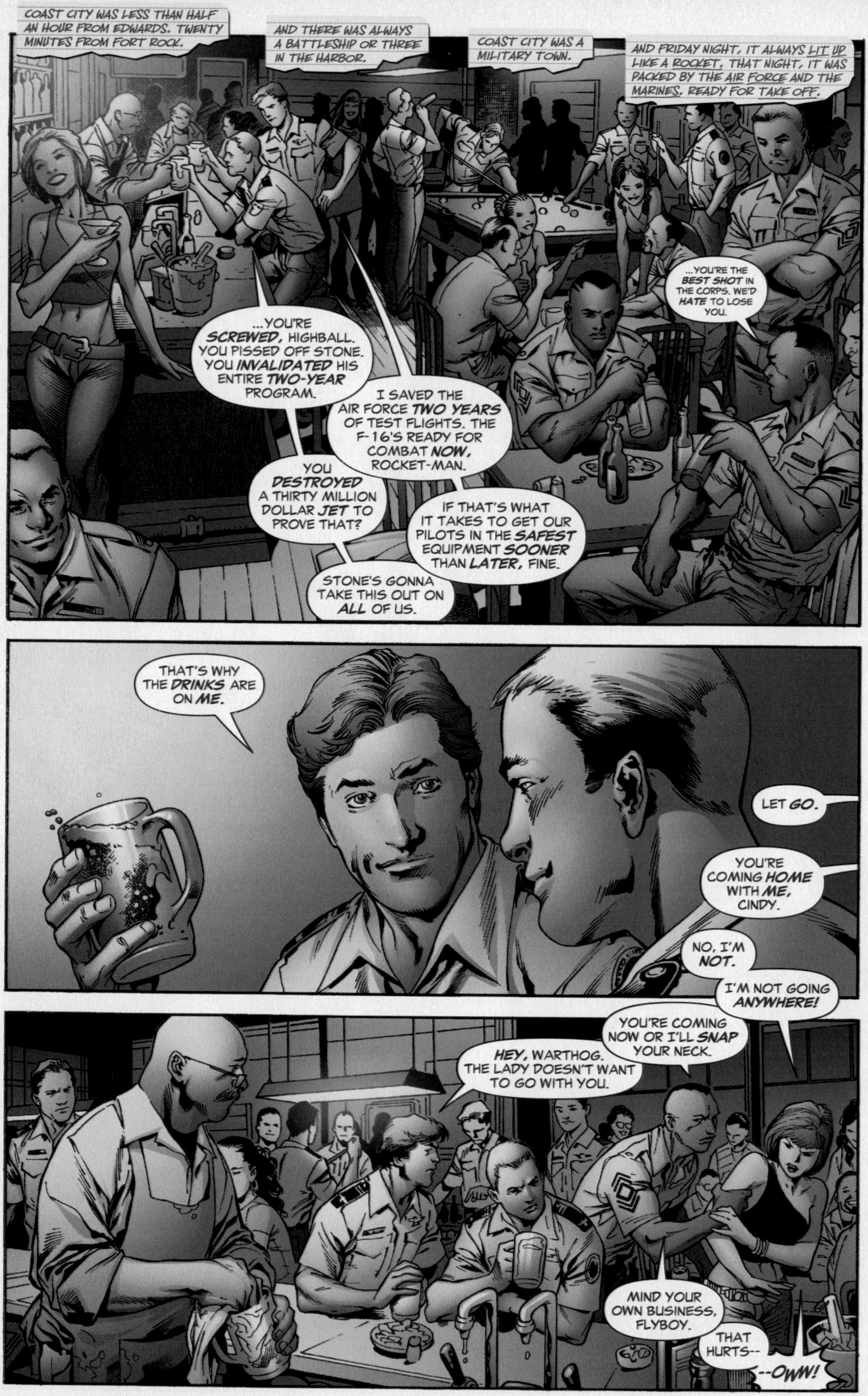
COAST CITY WAS LESS THAN HALF AN HOUR FROM EDWARDS. TWENTY MINUTES FROM FORT ROCK.
AND THERE WAS ALWAYS A BATTLESHIP OR THREE IN THE HARBOR.
COAST CITY WAS A MILITARY TOWN.
AND FRIDAY NIGHT, IT ALWAYS LIT UP LIKE A ROCKET. THAT NIGHT, IT WAS PACKED BY THE AIR FORCE AND THE MARINES, READY FOR TAKE OFF.
...YOU'RE SCREWED, HIGHBALL. YOU PISSED OFF STONE. YOU INVALIDATED HIS ENTIRE TWO-YEAR PROGRAM.
I SAVED THE AIR FORCE TWO YEARS OF TEST FLIGHTS. THE F-16'S READY FOR COMBAT NOW, ROCKET-MAN.
YOU DESTROYED A THIRTY MILLION DOLLAR JET TO PROVE THAT?
IF THAT'S WHAT IT TAKES TO GET OUR PILOTS IN THE SAFEST EQUIPMENT SOONER THAN LATER, FINE.
STONE'S GONNA TAKE THIS OUT ON ALL OF US.
...YOU'RE THE BEST SHOT IN THE CORPS. WE'D HATE TO LOSE YOU.
THAT'S WHY THE DRINKS ARE ON ME.
LET GO.
YOU'RE COMING HOME WITH ME, CINDY.
NO, I'M NOT.
I'M NOT GOING ANYWHERE!
YOU'RE COMING NOW OR I'LL SNAP YOUR NECK.
HEY, WARTHOG. THE LADY DOESN'T WANT TO GO WITH YOU.
MIND YOUR OWN BUSINESS, FLYBOY.
THAT HURTS--
--OWW!

YOU SEE THAT, STEWART?

THAT *JET JOCKEY* JUST KNOCKED DOWN ONE OF *OURS.*

HERE WE GO.

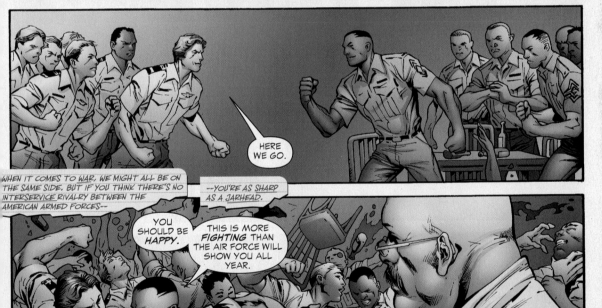

HERE WE GO.

WHEN IT COMES TO *WAR,* WE MIGHT ALL BE ON THE SAME SIDE, BUT IF YOU THINK THERE'S NO INTERSERVICE RIVALRY BETWEEN THE AMERICAN ARMED FORCES--

--YOU'RE AS *SHARP* AS A *JARHEAD.*

YOU SHOULD BE *HAPPY.*

THIS IS MORE *FIGHTING* THAN THE AIR FORCE WILL SHOW YOU ALL YEAR.

THEN I BETTER MAKE IT *COUNT.*

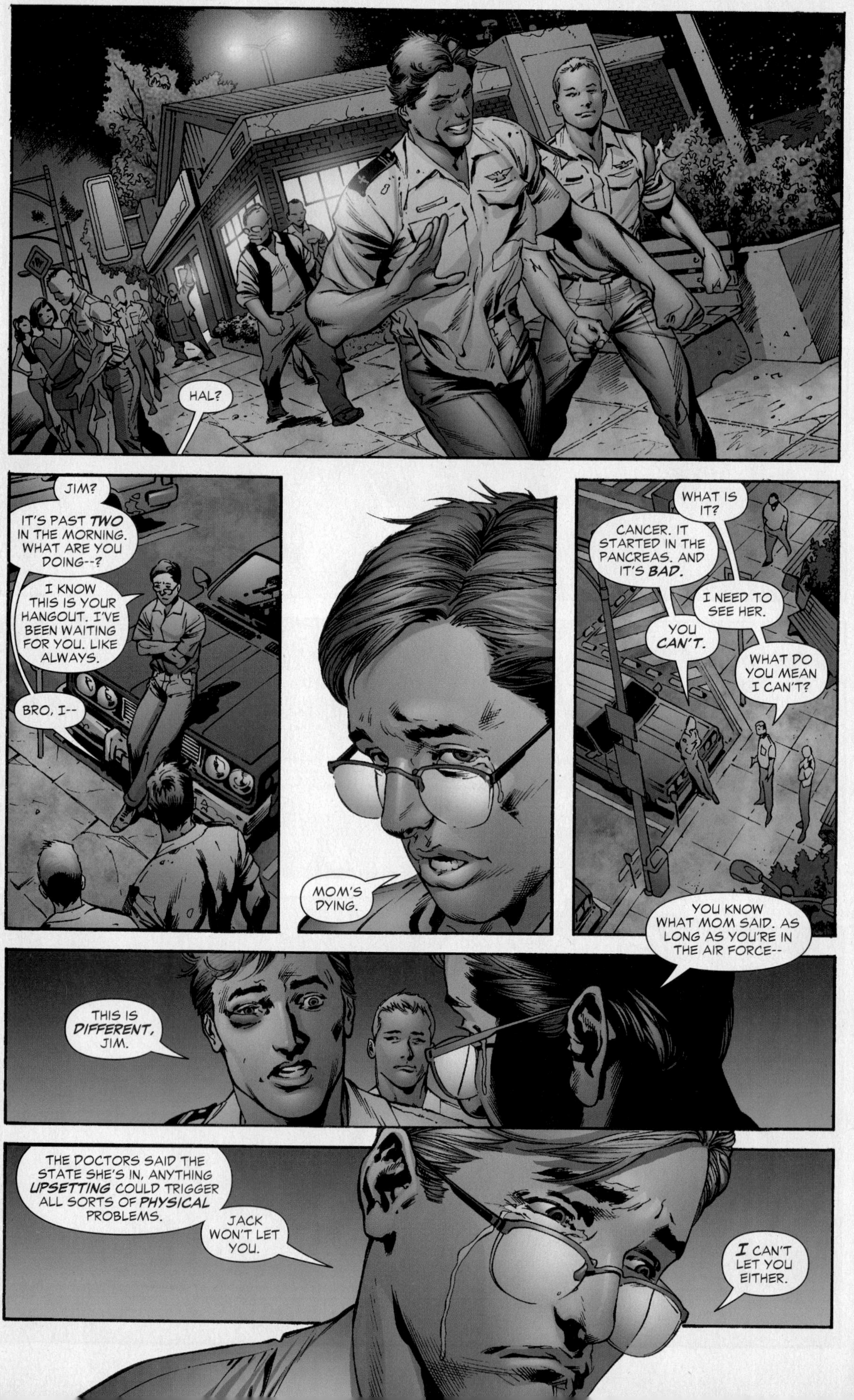
HAL?
JIM?
IT'S PAST TWO IN THE MORNING. WHAT ARE YOU DOING--?
I KNOW THIS IS YOUR HANGOUT. I'VE BEEN WAITING FOR YOU. LIKE ALWAYS.
BRO, I--
MOM'S DYING.
WHAT IS IT?
CANCER. IT STARTED IN THE PANCREAS. AND IT'S BAD.
I NEED TO SEE HER.
YOU CAN'T.
WHAT DO YOU MEAN I CAN'T?
YOU KNOW WHAT MOM SAID. AS LONG AS YOU'RE IN THE AIR FORCE--
THIS IS DIFFERENT, JIM.
THE DOCTORS SAID THE STATE SHE'S IN, ANYTHING UPSETTING COULD TRIGGER ALL SORTS OF PHYSICAL PROBLEMS.
JACK WON'T LET YOU.
I CAN'T LET YOU EITHER.

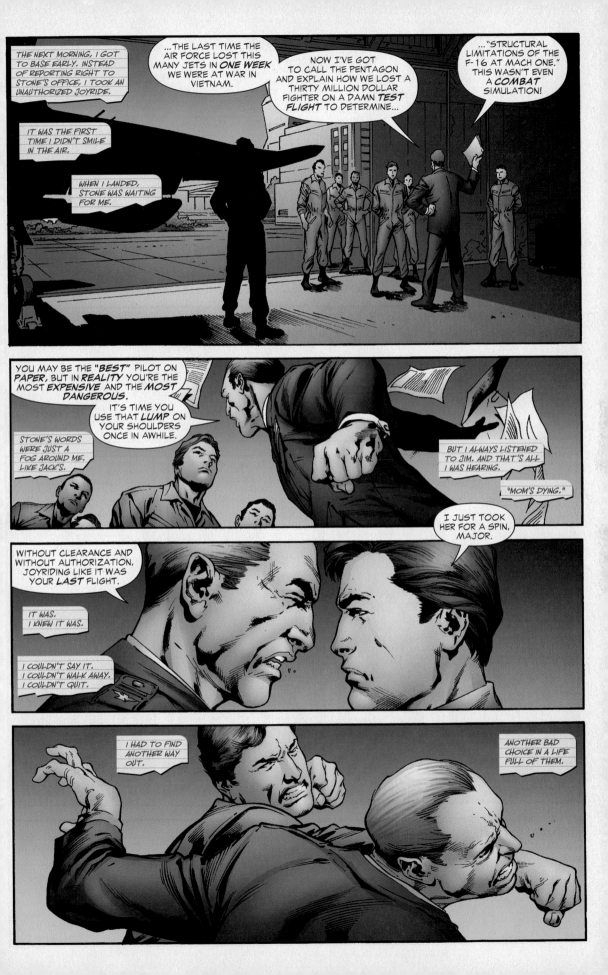

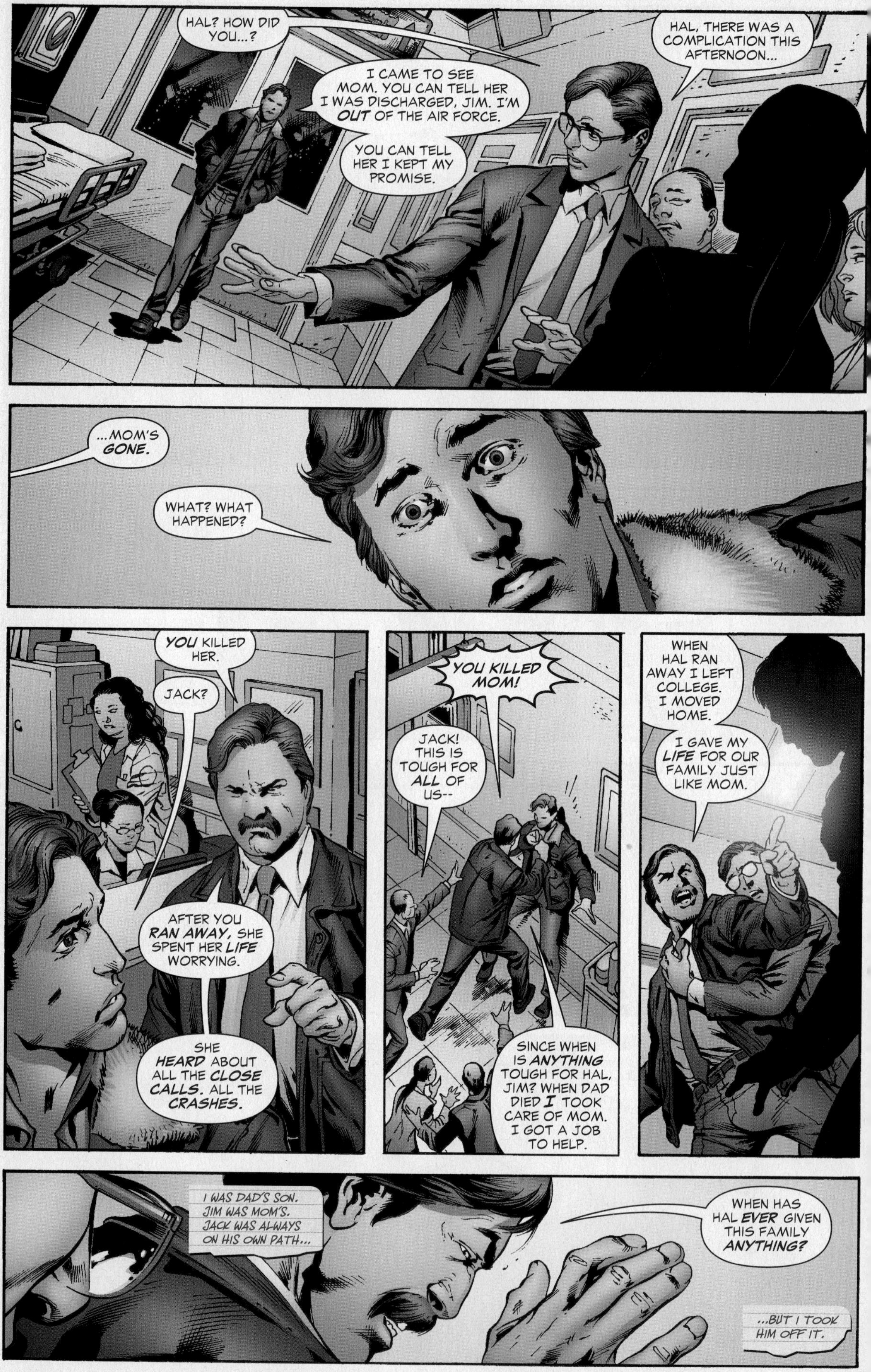
HAL? HOW DID YOU...?
I CAME TO SEE MOM. YOU CAN TELL HER I WAS DISCHARGED, JIM. I'M OUT OF THE AIR FORCE.
YOU CAN TELL HER I KEPT MY PROMISE.
HAL, THERE WAS A COMPLICATION THIS AFTERNOON...
...MOM'S GONE.
WHAT? WHAT HAPPENED?
YOU KILLED HER.
JACK?
AFTER YOU RAN AWAY, SHE SPENT HER LIFE WORRYING.
SHE HEARD ABOUT ALL THE CLOSE CALLS. ALL THE CRASHES.
YOU KILLED MOM!
JACK! THIS IS TOUGH FOR ALL OF US--
SINCE WHEN IS ANYTHING TOUGH FOR HAL, JIM? WHEN DAD DIED I TOOK CARE OF MOM. I GOT A JOB TO HELP.
WHEN HAL RAN AWAY I LEFT COLLEGE. I MOVED HOME.
I GAVE MY LIFE FOR OUR FAMILY JUST LIKE MOM.
I WAS DAD'S SON. JIM WAS MOM'S. JACK WAS ALWAYS ON HIS OWN PATH...
WHEN HAS HAL EVER GIVEN THIS FAMILY ANYTHING?
...BUT I TOOK HIM OFF IT.

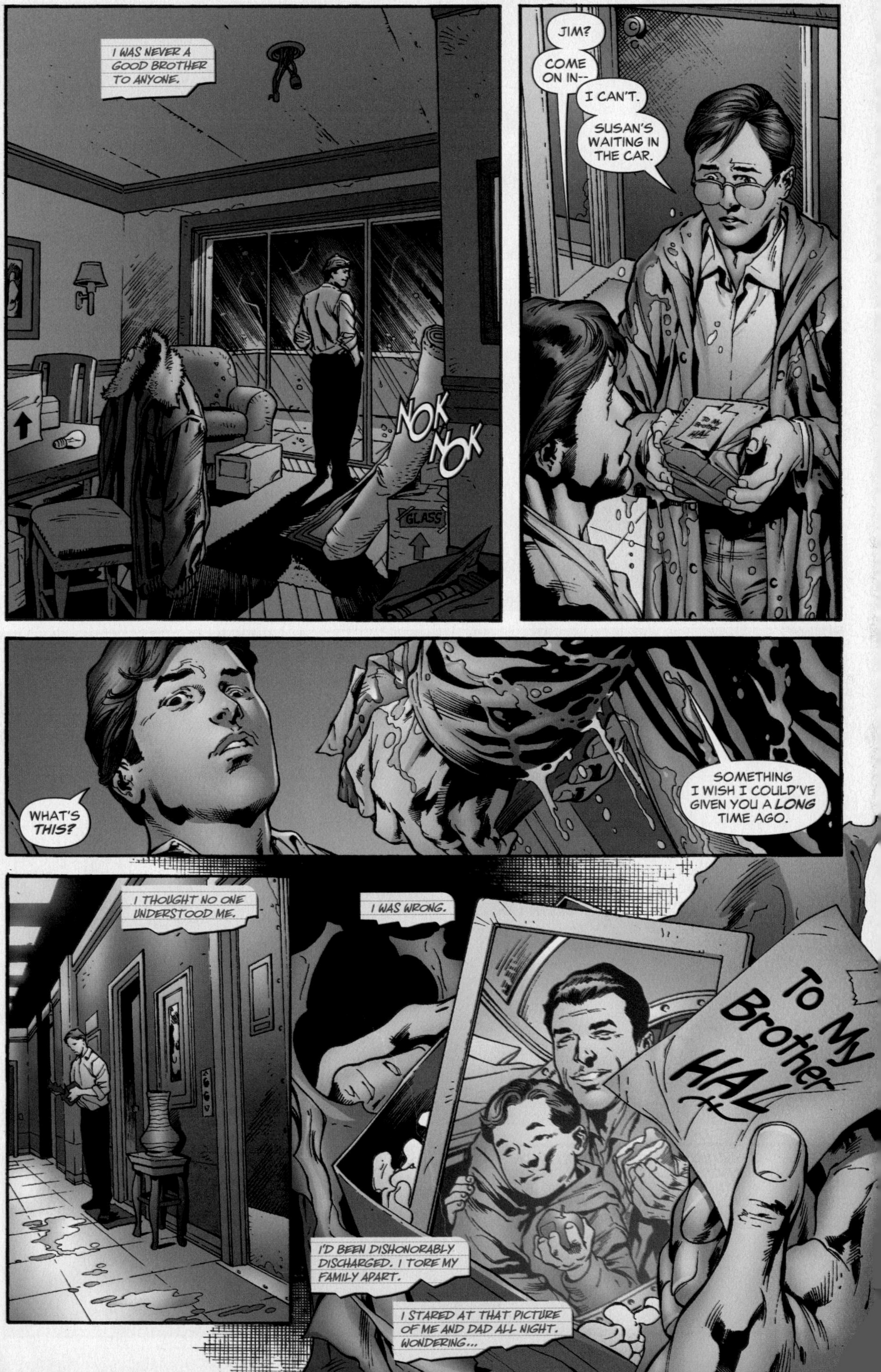

I WAS NEVER A GOOD BROTHER TO ANYONE.
NOK NOK
JIM?
COME ON IN--
I CAN'T.
SUSAN'S WAITING IN THE CAR.
To My Brother HAL
WHAT'S THIS?
SOMETHING I WISH I COULD'VE GIVEN YOU A LONG TIME AGO.
I THOUGHT NO ONE UNDERSTOOD ME.
I WAS WRONG.
To My Brother HAL
I'D BEEN DISHONORABLY DISCHARGED. I TORE MY FAMILY APART.
I STARED AT THAT PICTURE OF ME AND DAD ALL NIGHT. WONDERING...

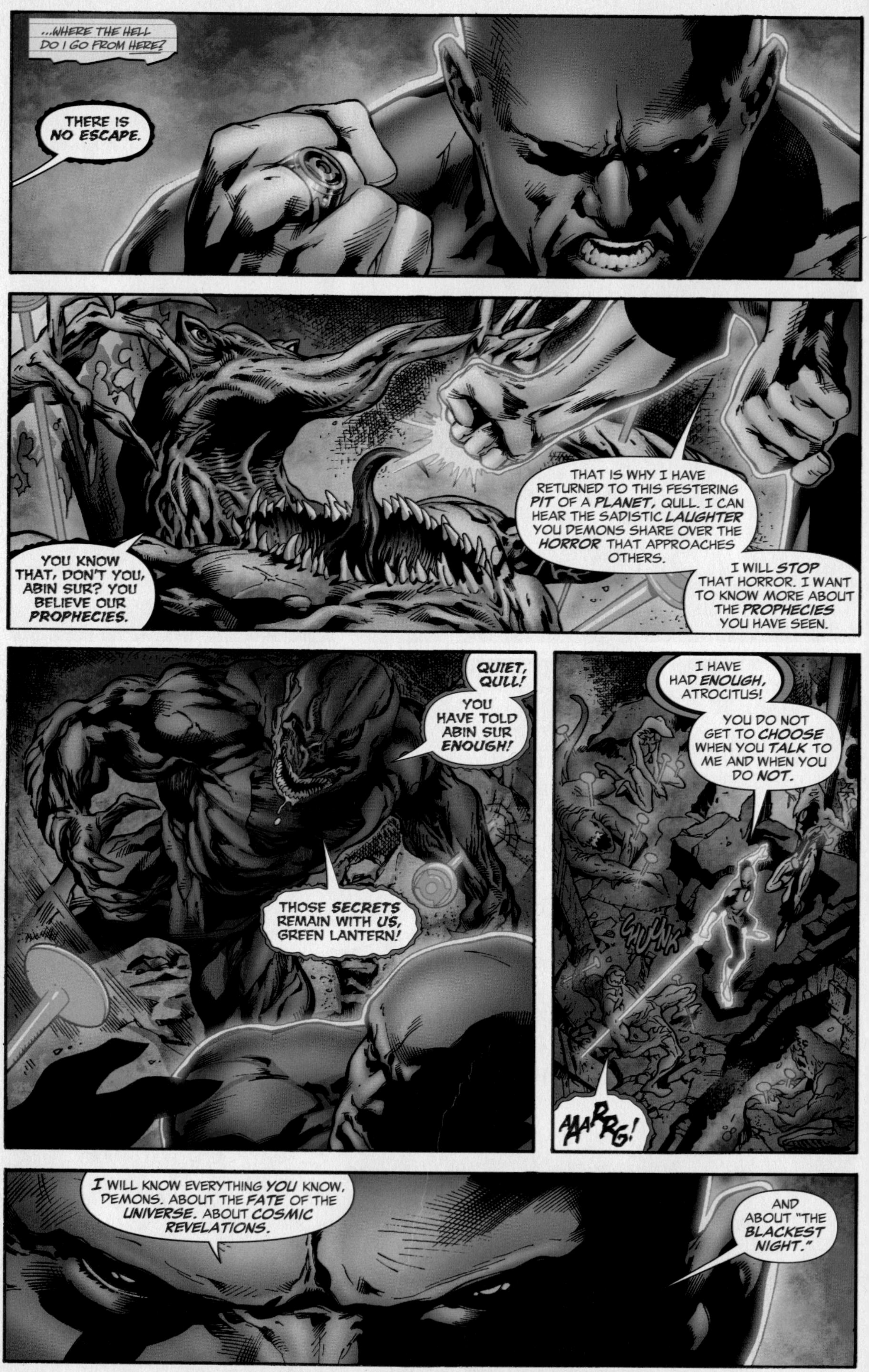
...WHERE THE HELL DO I GO FROM HERE?
THERE IS NO ESCAPE.
YOU KNOW THAT, DON'T YOU, ABIN SUR? YOU BELIEVE OUR PROPHECIES.
THAT IS WHY I HAVE RETURNED TO THIS FESTERING PIT OF A PLANET, QULL. I CAN HEAR THE SADISTIC LAUGHTER YOU DEMONS SHARE OVER THE HORROR THAT APPROACHES OTHERS.
I WILL STOP THAT HORROR. I WANT TO KNOW MORE ABOUT THE PROPHECIES YOU HAVE SEEN.
QUIET, QULL!
YOU HAVE TOLD ABIN SUR ENOUGH!
THOSE SECRETS REMAIN WITH US, GREEN LANTERN!
I HAVE HAD ENOUGH, ATROCITUS!
YOU DO NOT GET TO CHOOSE WHEN YOU TALK TO ME AND WHEN YOU DO NOT.
CHUNK
AAARRG!
I WILL KNOW EVERYTHING YOU KNOW, DEMONS. ABOUT THE FATE OF THE UNIVERSE. ABOUT COSMIC REVELATIONS.
AND ABOUT "THE BLACKEST NIGHT."

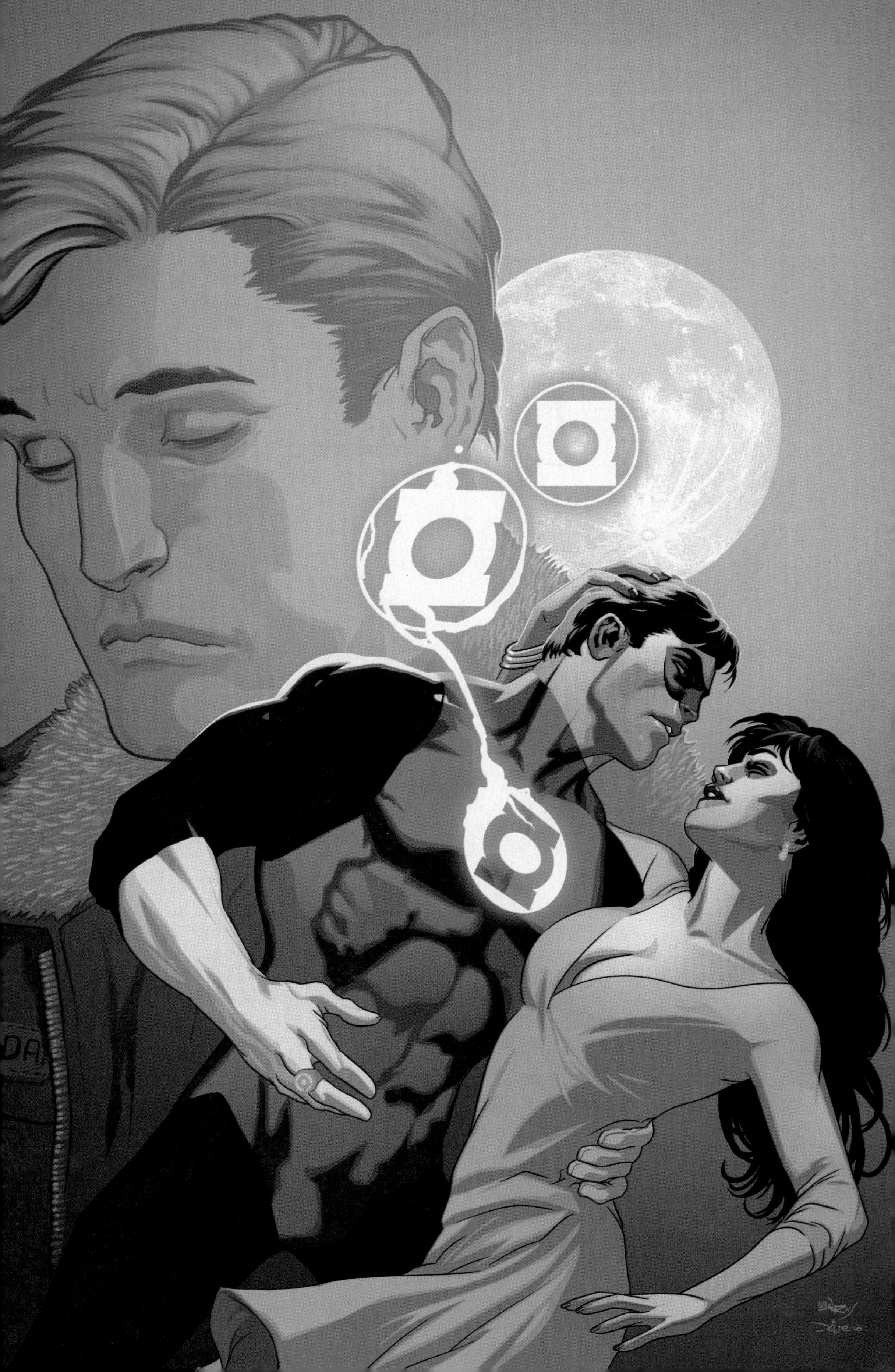

SECRET ORIGIN

BOOK TWO

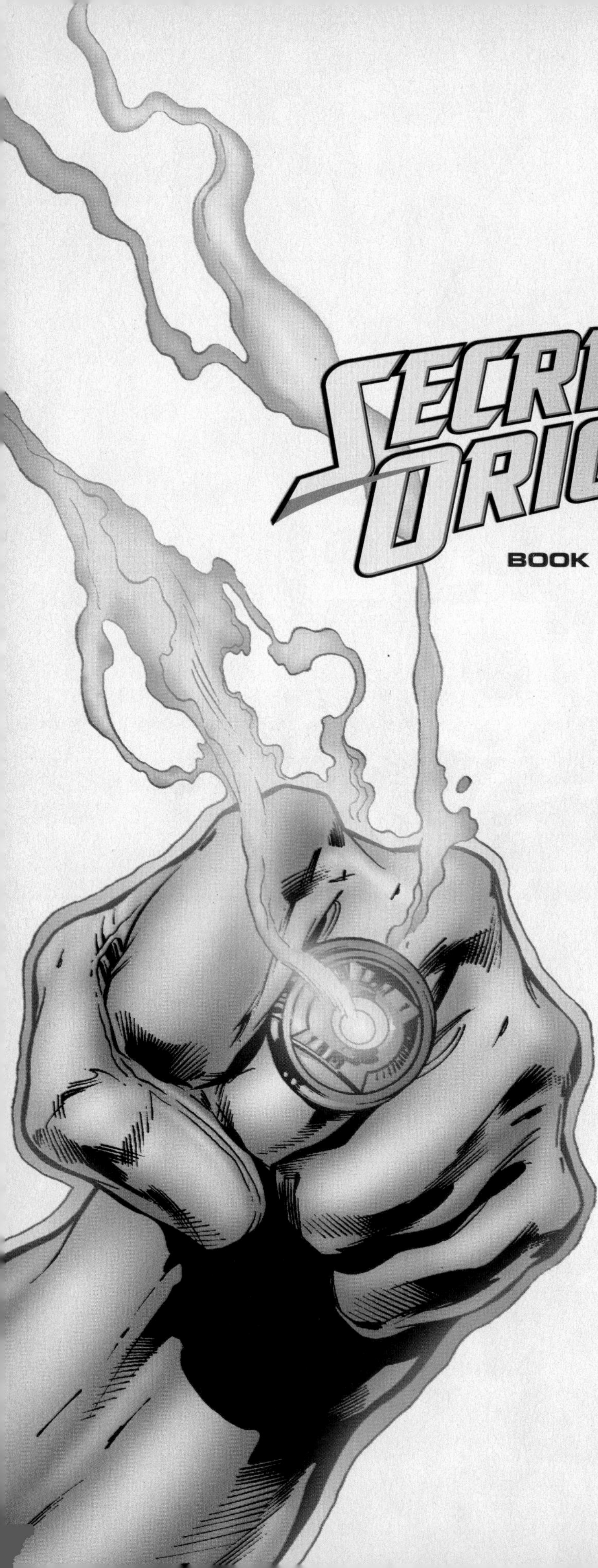

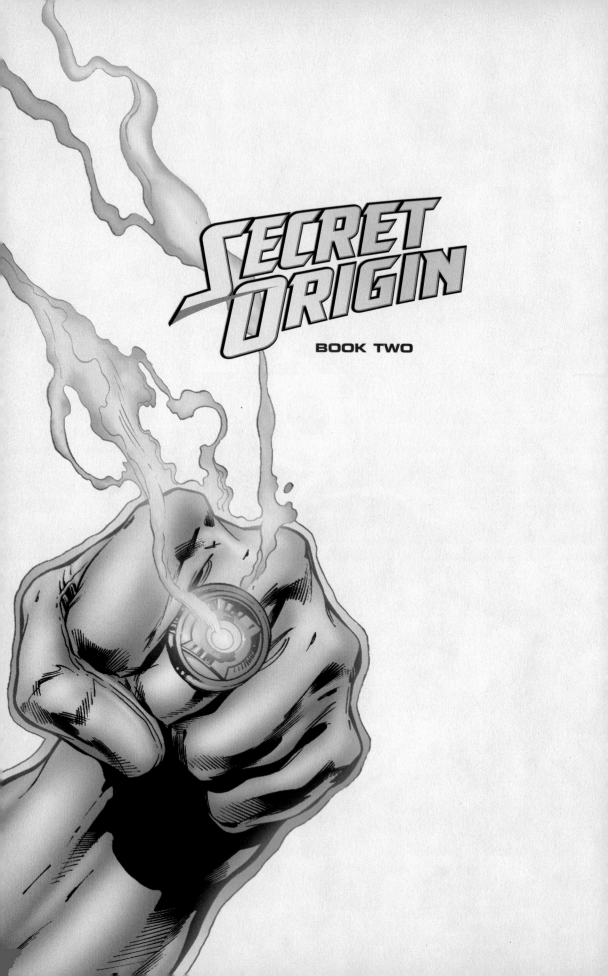

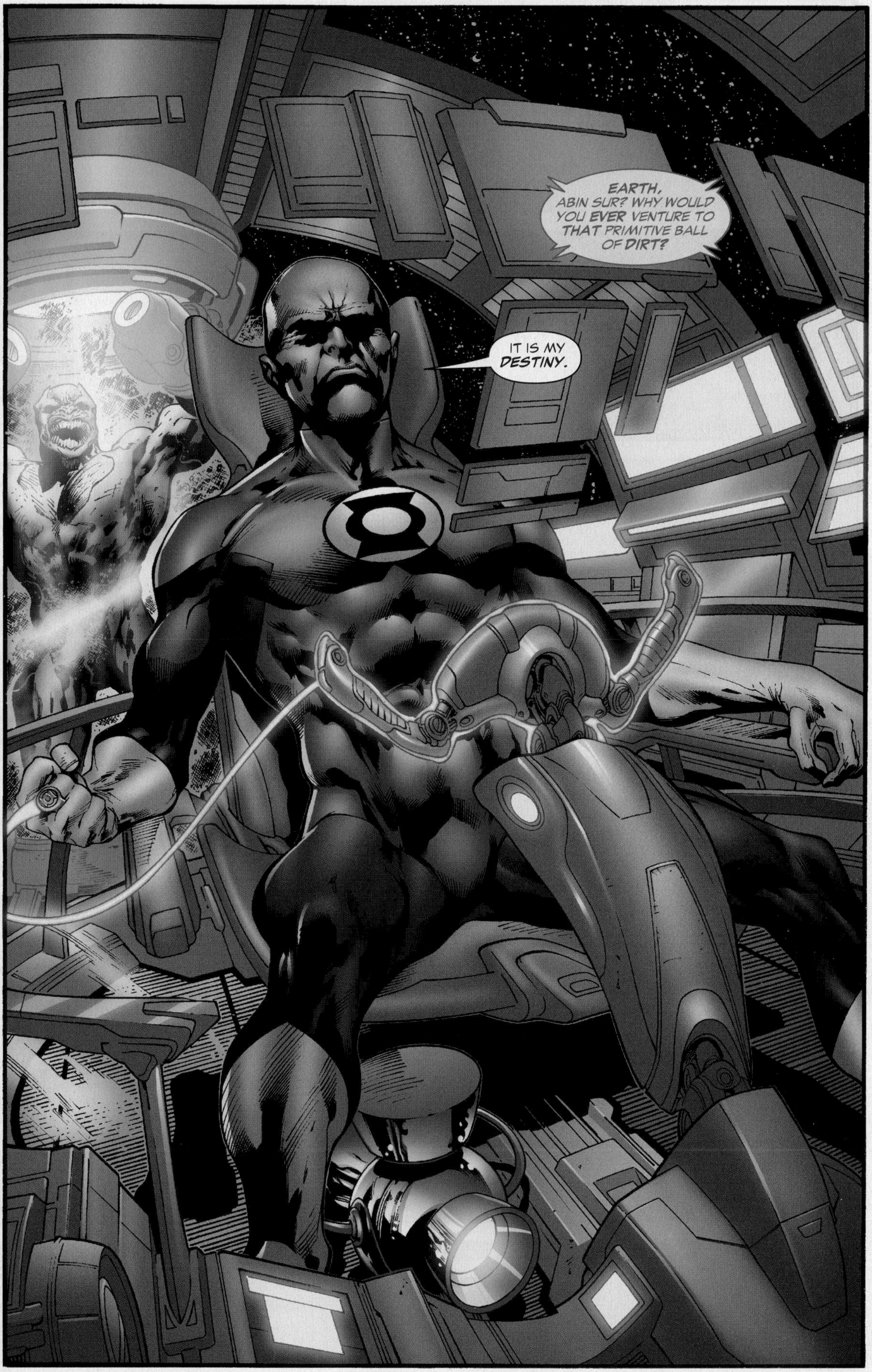
EARTH, ABIN SUR? WHY WOULD YOU EVER VENTURE TO THAT PRIMITIVE BALL OF DIRT?
IT IS MY DESTINY.

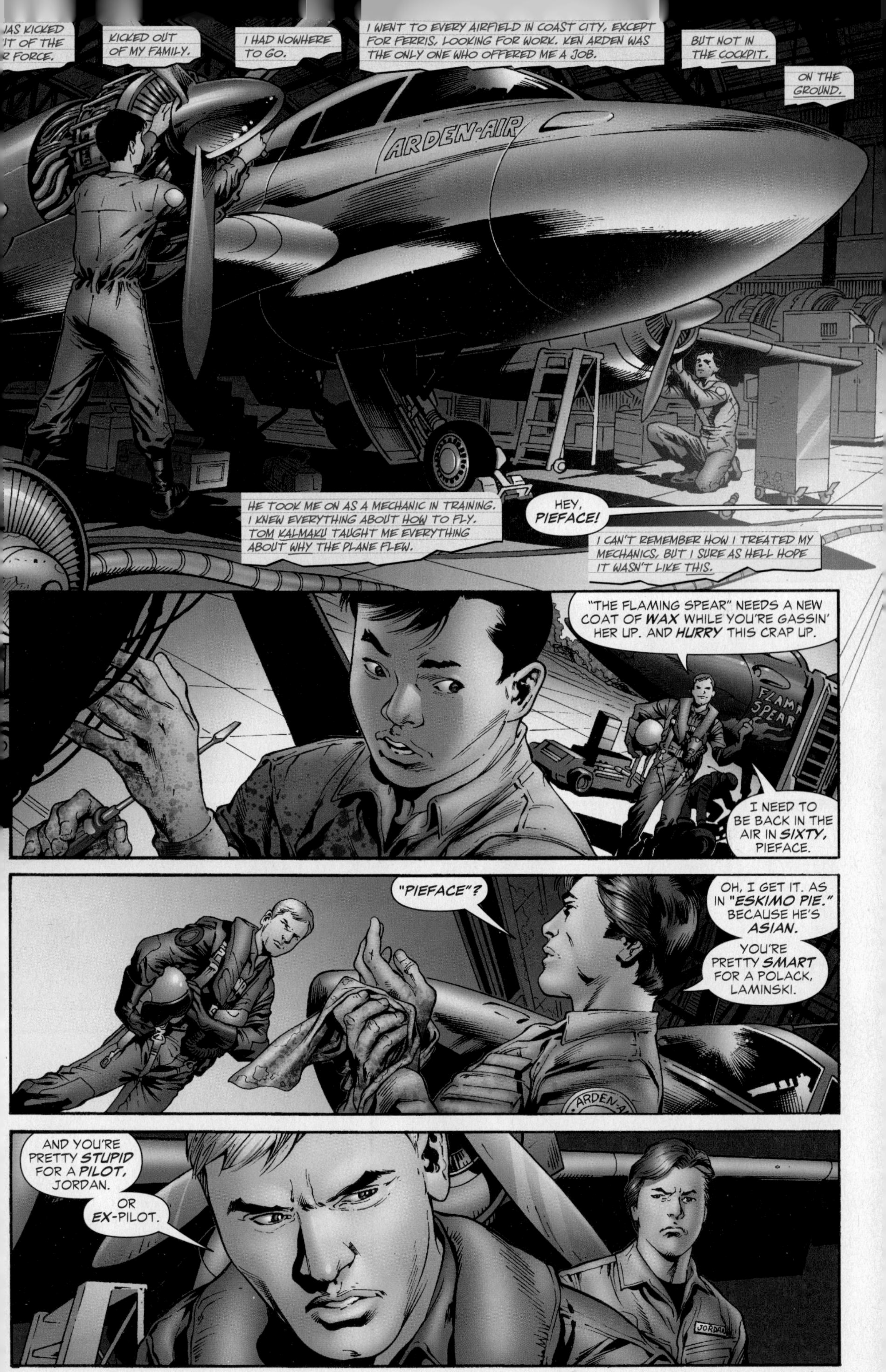

WAS KICKED OUT OF THE AIR FORCE.
KICKED OUT OF MY FAMILY.
I HAD NOWHERE TO GO.
I WENT TO EVERY AIRFIELD IN COAST CITY, EXCEPT FOR FERRIS, LOOKING FOR WORK. KEN ARDEN WAS THE ONLY ONE WHO OFFERED ME A JOB.
BUT NOT IN THE COCKPIT.
ON THE GROUND.
ARDEN-AIR
HE TOOK ME ON AS A MECHANIC IN TRAINING. I KNEW EVERYTHING ABOUT HOW TO FLY. TOM KALMAKU TAUGHT ME EVERYTHING ABOUT WHY THE PLANE FLEW.
HEY, PIEFACE!
I CAN'T REMEMBER HOW I TREATED MY MECHANICS, BUT I SURE AS HELL HOPE IT WASN'T LIKE THIS.
"THE FLAMING SPEAR" NEEDS A NEW COAT OF WAX WHILE YOU'RE GASSIN' HER UP. AND HURRY THIS CRAP UP.
I NEED TO BE BACK IN THE AIR IN SIXTY, PIEFACE.
"PIEFACE"?
OH, I GET IT. AS IN "ESKIMO PIE." BECAUSE HE'S ASIAN.
YOU'RE PRETTY SMART FOR A POLACK, LAMINSKI.
AND YOU'RE PRETTY STUPID FOR A PILOT, JORDAN.
OR EX-PILOT.
JORDAN

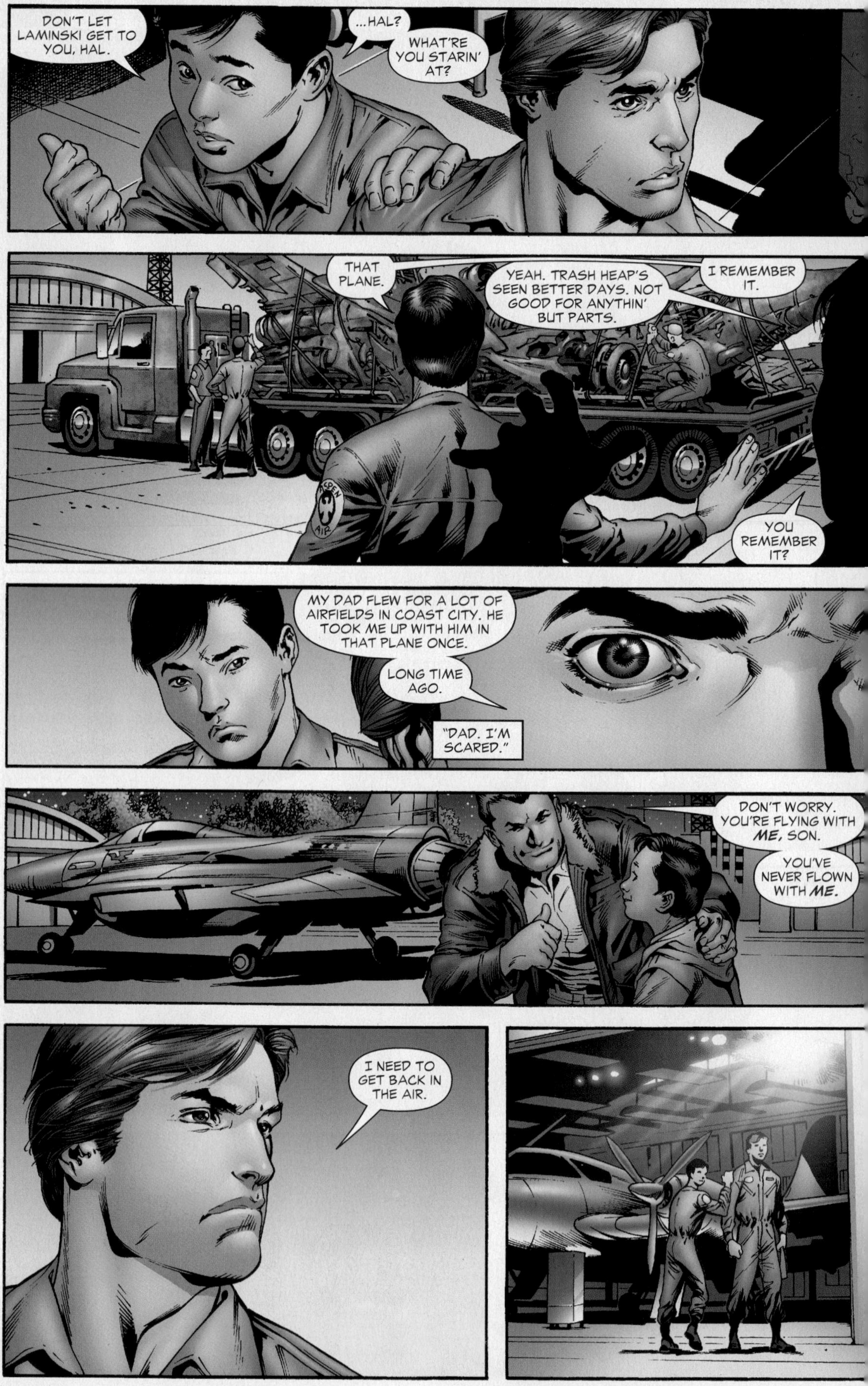
DON'T LET LAMINSKI GET TO YOU, HAL.
...HAL?
WHAT'RE YOU STARIN' AT?
THAT PLANE.
YEAH. TRASH HEAP'S SEEN BETTER DAYS. NOT GOOD FOR ANYTHIN' BUT PARTS.
I REMEMBER IT.
YOU REMEMBER IT?
MY DAD FLEW FOR A LOT OF AIRFIELDS IN COAST CITY. HE TOOK ME UP WITH HIM IN THAT PLANE ONCE.
LONG TIME AGO.
"DAD. I'M SCARED."
DON'T WORRY. YOU'RE FLYING WITH ME, SON.
YOU'VE NEVER FLOWN WITH ME.
I NEED TO GET BACK IN THE AIR.

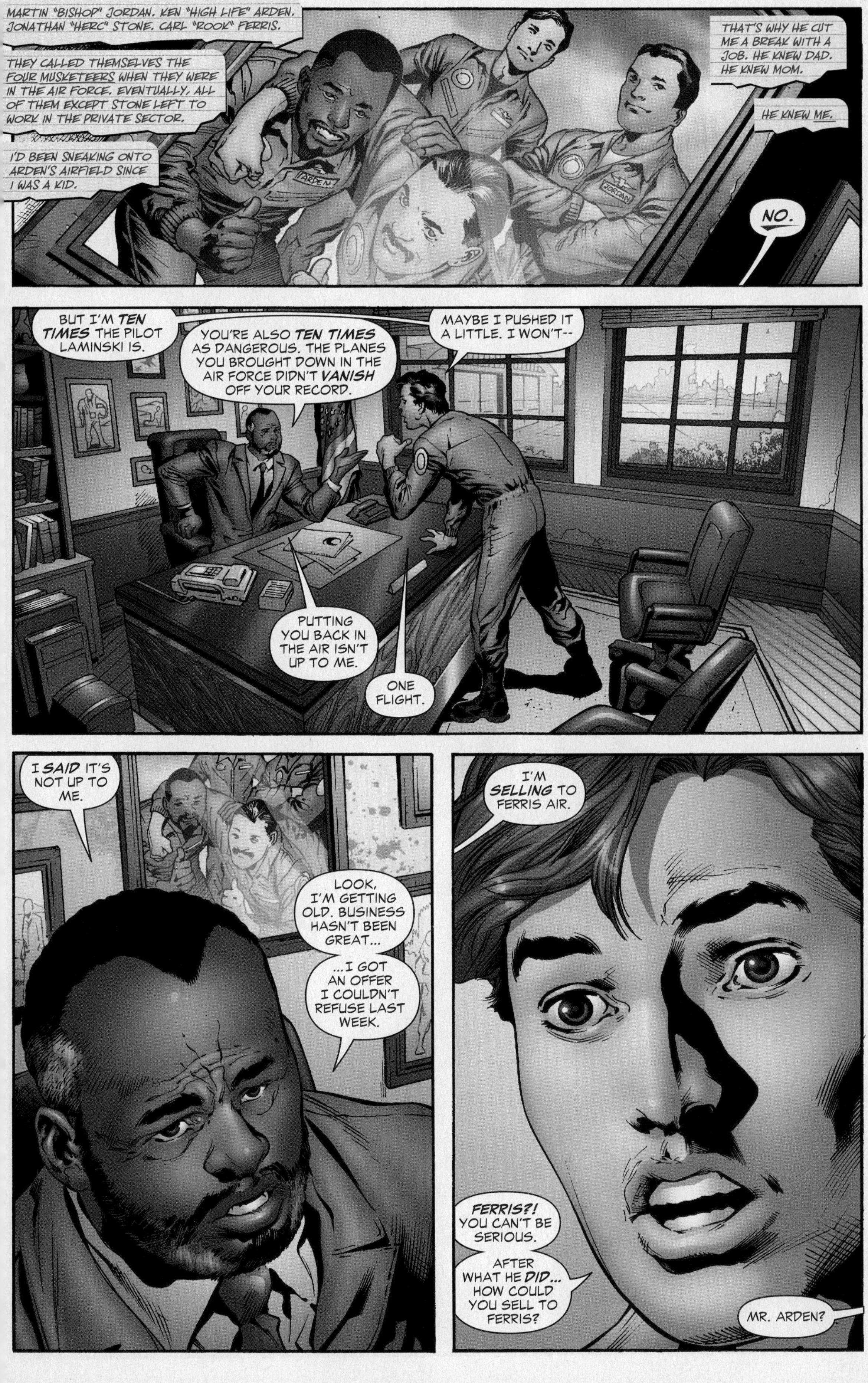
MARTIN "BISHOP" JORDAN. KEN "HIGH LIFE" ARDEN. JONATHAN "HERC" STONE. CARL "ROOK" FERRIS.
THEY CALLED THEMSELVES THE FOUR MUSKETEERS WHEN THEY WERE IN THE AIR FORCE. EVENTUALLY, ALL OF THEM EXCEPT STONE LEFT TO WORK IN THE PRIVATE SECTOR.
I'D BEEN SNEAKING ONTO ARDEN'S AIRFIELD SINCE I WAS A KID.
ARDEN
JORDAN
THAT'S WHY HE CUT ME A BREAK WITH A JOB. HE KNEW DAD. HE KNEW MOM.
HE KNEW ME.
NO.
BUT I'M TEN TIMES THE PILOT LAMINSKI IS.
YOU'RE ALSO TEN TIMES AS DANGEROUS. THE PLANES YOU BROUGHT DOWN IN THE AIR FORCE DIDN'T VANISH OFF YOUR RECORD.
MAYBE I PUSHED IT A LITTLE. I WON'T--
PUTTING YOU BACK IN THE AIR ISN'T UP TO ME.
ONE FLIGHT.
I SAID IT'S NOT UP TO ME.
LOOK, I'M GETTING OLD. BUSINESS HASN'T BEEN GREAT...
...I GOT AN OFFER I COULDN'T REFUSE LAST WEEK.
I'M SELLING TO FERRIS AIR.
FERRIS?! YOU CAN'T BE SERIOUS.
AFTER WHAT HE DID... HOW COULD YOU SELL TO FERRIS?
MR. ARDEN?

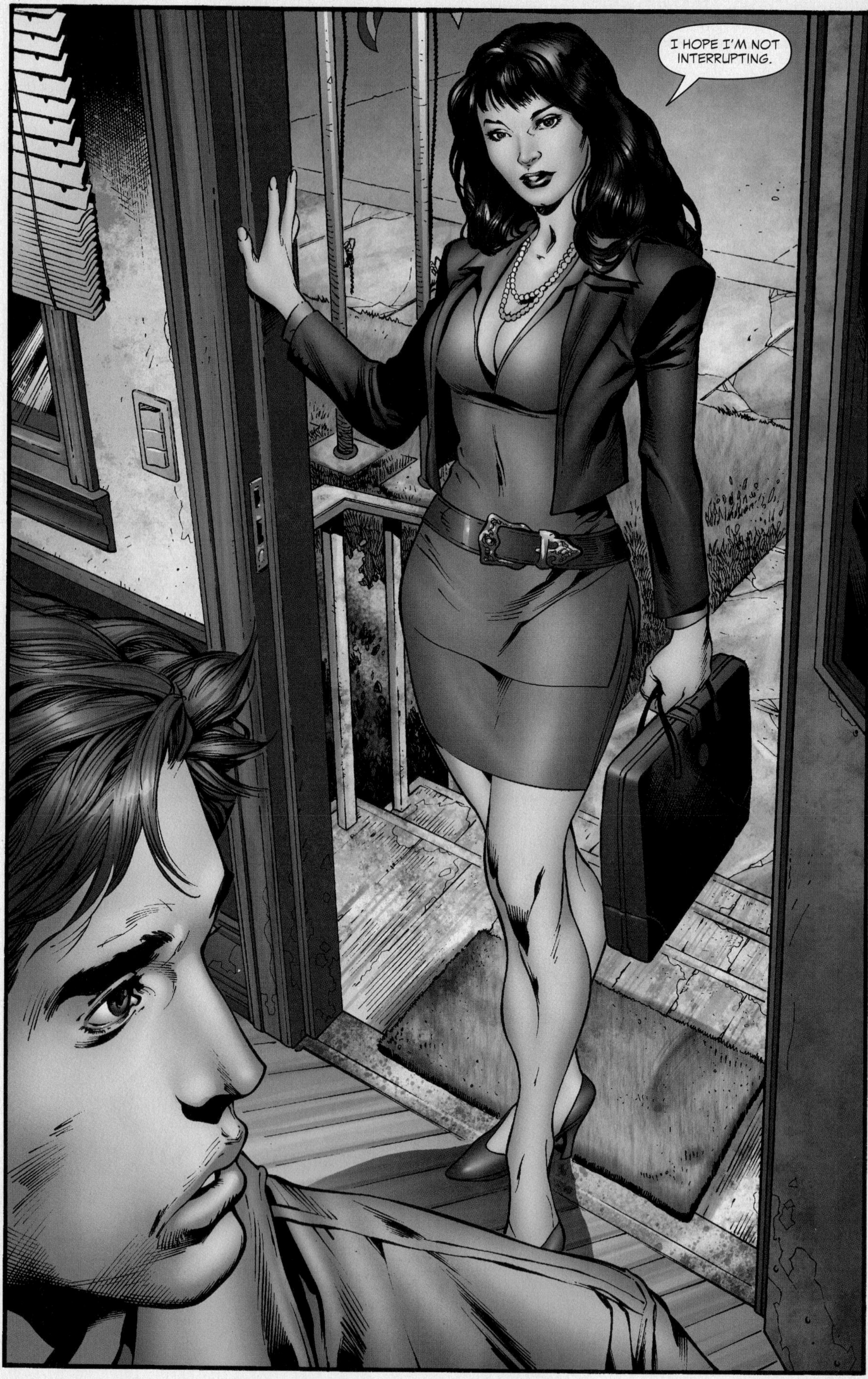
I HOPE I'M NOT INTERRUPTING.

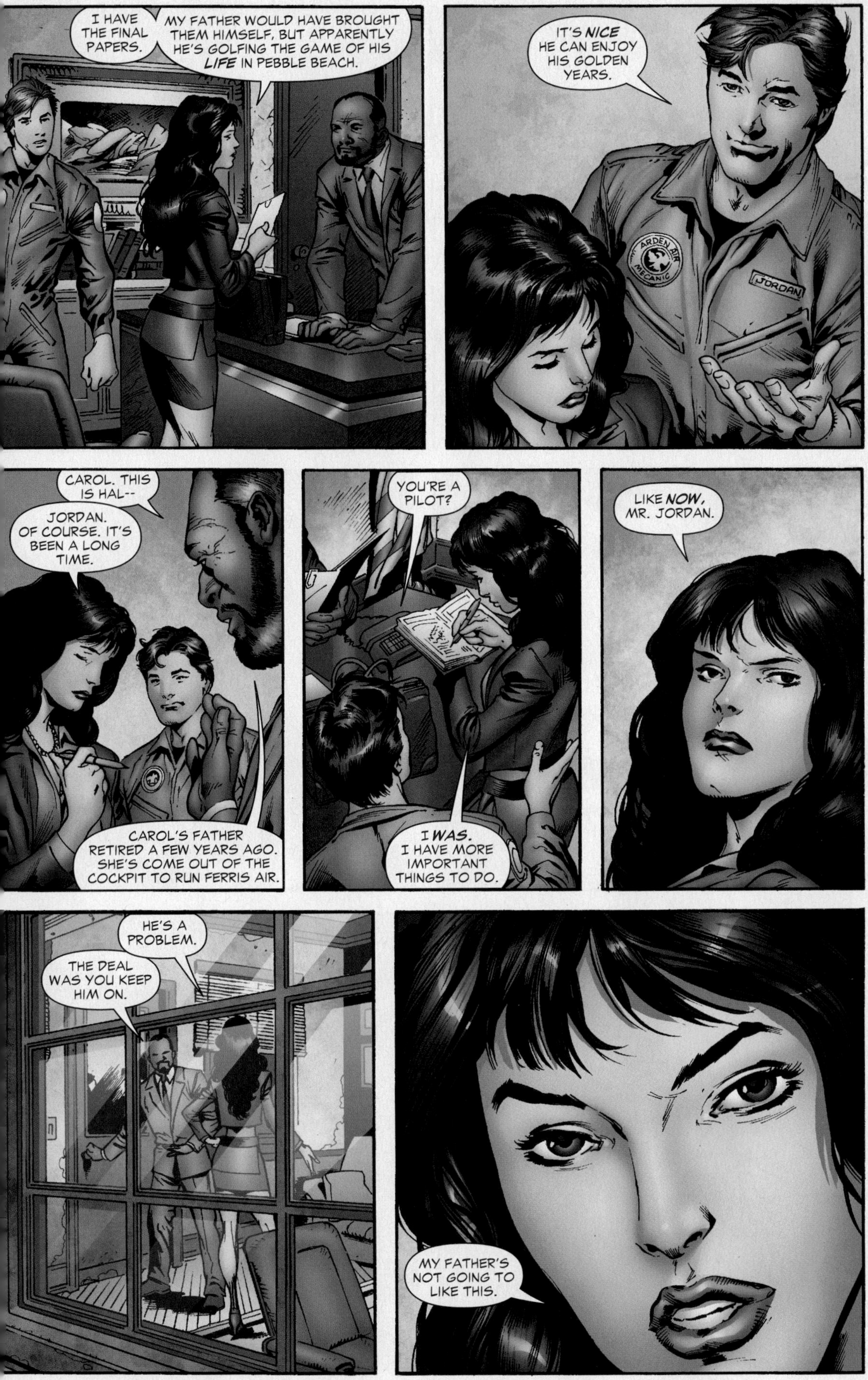
I HAVE THE FINAL PAPERS.
MY FATHER WOULD HAVE BROUGHT THEM HIMSELF, BUT APPARENTLY HE'S GOLFING THE GAME OF HIS LIFE IN PEBBLE BEACH.
IT'S NICE HE CAN ENJOY HIS GOLDEN YEARS.
ARDEN AIR MECANIC
JORDAN
CAROL. THIS IS HAL--
JORDAN. OF COURSE. IT'S BEEN A LONG TIME.
CAROL'S FATHER RETIRED A FEW YEARS AGO. SHE'S COME OUT OF THE COCKPIT TO RUN FERRIS AIR.
YOU'RE A PILOT?
I WAS. I HAVE MORE IMPORTANT THINGS TO DO.
LIKE NOW, MR. JORDAN.
HE'S A PROBLEM.
THE DEAL WAS YOU KEEP HIM ON.
MY FATHER'S NOT GOING TO LIKE THIS.

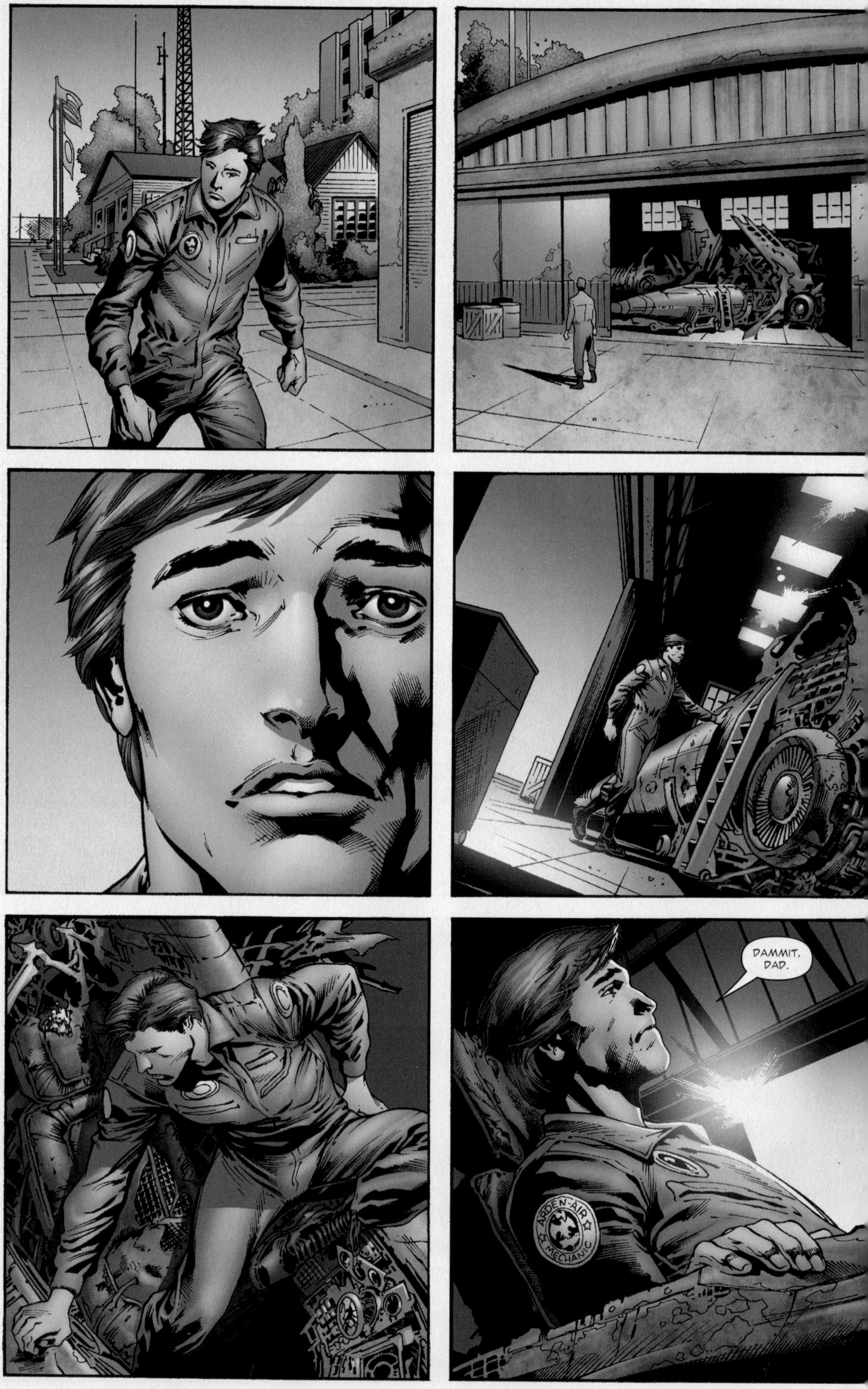
DAMMIT, DAD.
ARDEN-AIR
MECHANIC

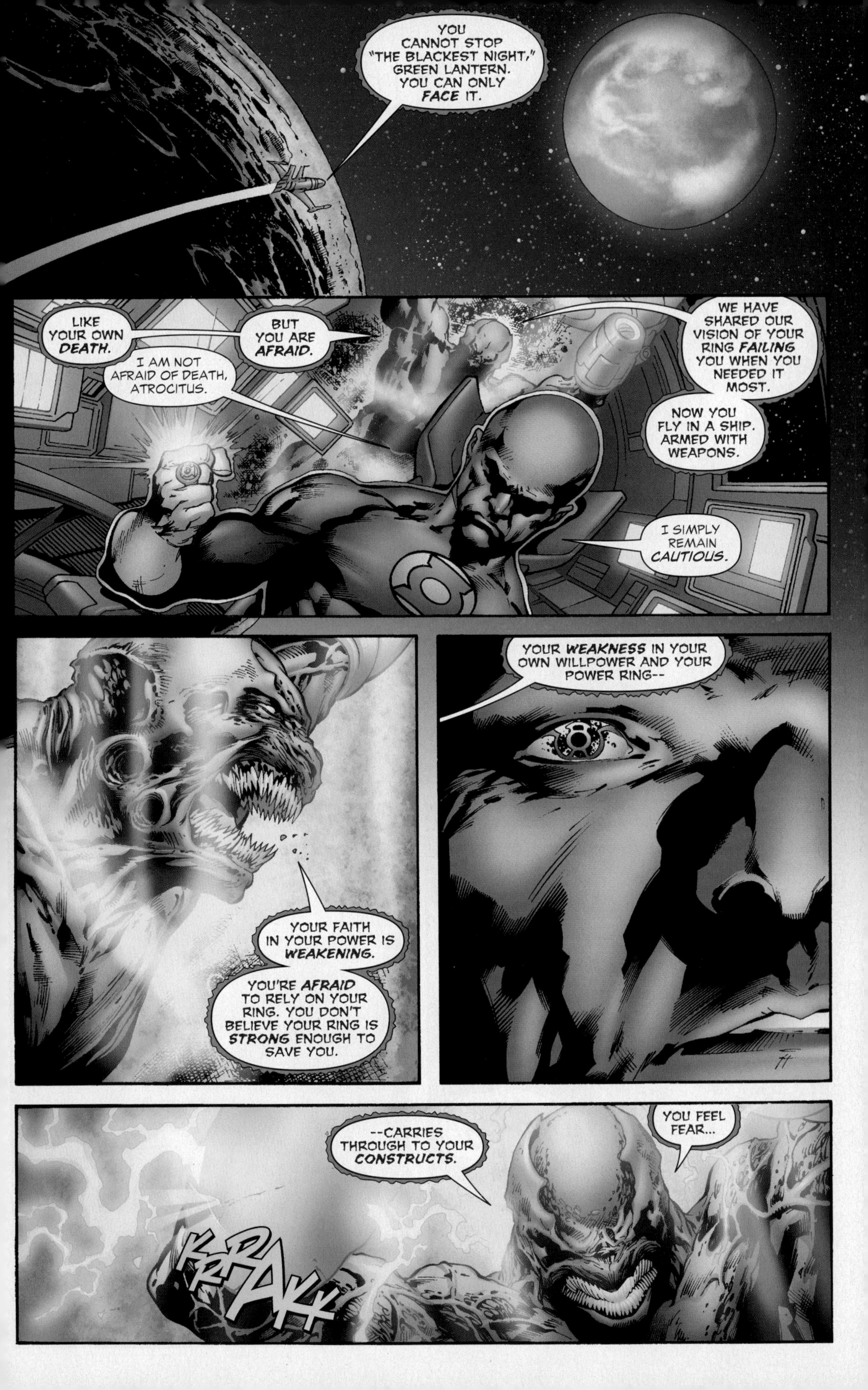
YOU CANNOT STOP "THE BLACKEST NIGHT," GREEN LANTERN. YOU CAN ONLY FACE IT.
LIKE YOUR OWN DEATH.
I AM NOT AFRAID OF DEATH, ATROCITUS.
BUT YOU ARE AFRAID.
WE HAVE SHARED OUR VISION OF YOUR RING FAILING YOU WHEN YOU NEEDED IT MOST.
NOW YOU FLY IN A SHIP. ARMED WITH WEAPONS.
I SIMPLY REMAIN CAUTIOUS.
YOUR FAITH IN YOUR POWER IS WEAKENING.
YOU'RE AFRAID TO RELY ON YOUR RING. YOU DON'T BELIEVE YOUR RING IS STRONG ENOUGH TO SAVE YOU.
YOUR WEAKNESS IN YOUR OWN WILLPOWER AND YOUR POWER RING--
--CARRIES THROUGH TO YOUR CONSTRUCTS.
YOU FEEL FEAR...
KRRAKK

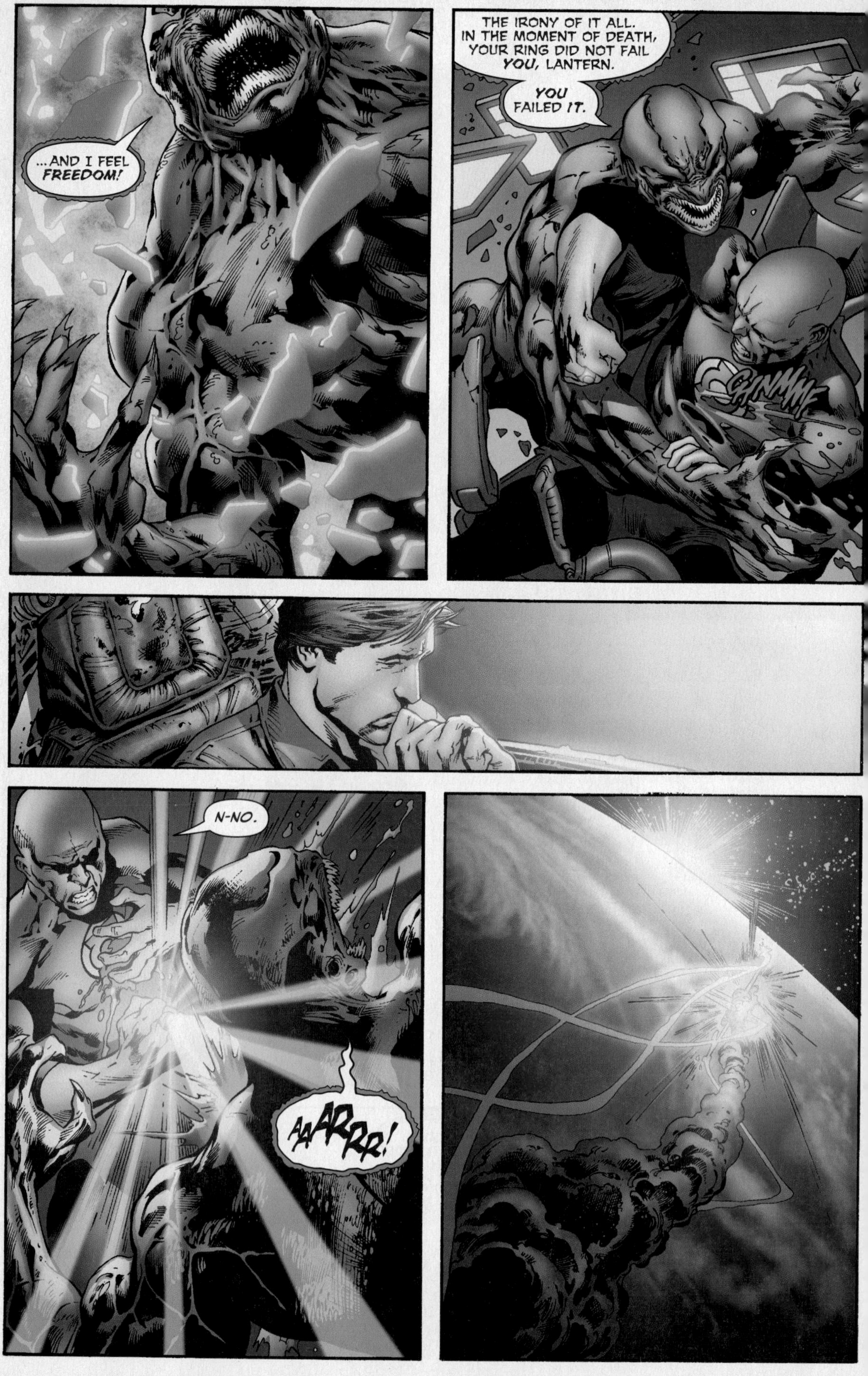
...AND I FEEL FREEDOM!
THE IRONY OF IT ALL. IN THE MOMENT OF DEATH, YOUR RING DID NOT FAIL YOU, LANTERN.
YOU FAILED IT.
N-NO.
AAARRR!

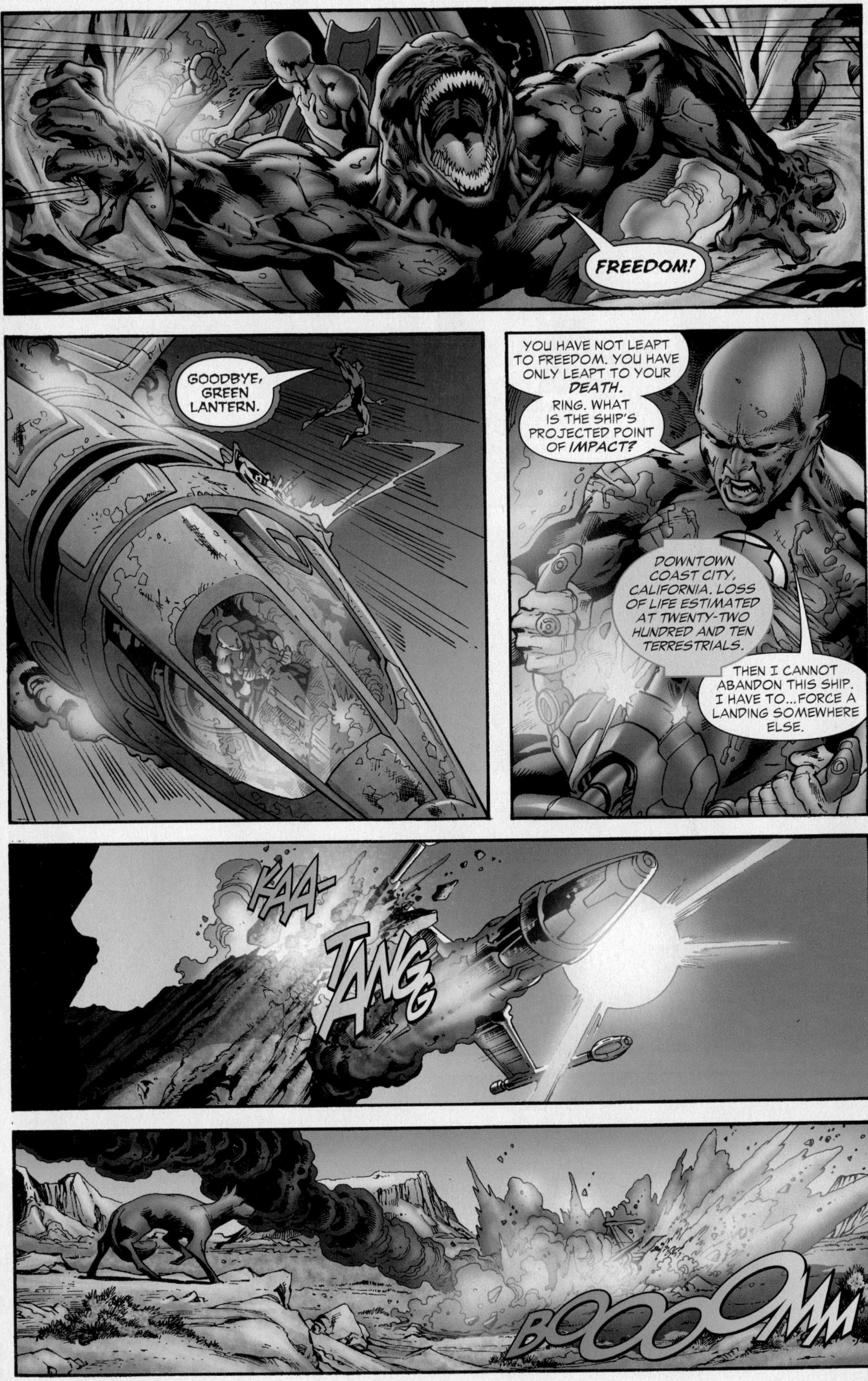
FREEDOM!
GOODBYE, GREEN LANTERN.
YOU HAVE NOT LEAPT TO FREEDOM. YOU HAVE ONLY LEAPT TO YOUR DEATH.
RING. WHAT IS THE SHIP'S PROJECTED POINT OF IMPACT?
DOWNTOWN COAST CITY, CALIFORNIA. LOSS OF LIFE ESTIMATED AT TWENTY-TWO HUNDRED AND TEN TERRESTRIALS.
THEN I CANNOT ABANDON THIS SHIP. I HAVE TO...FORCE A LANDING SOMEWHERE ELSE.
KAA-TANGG
BOOOOMM

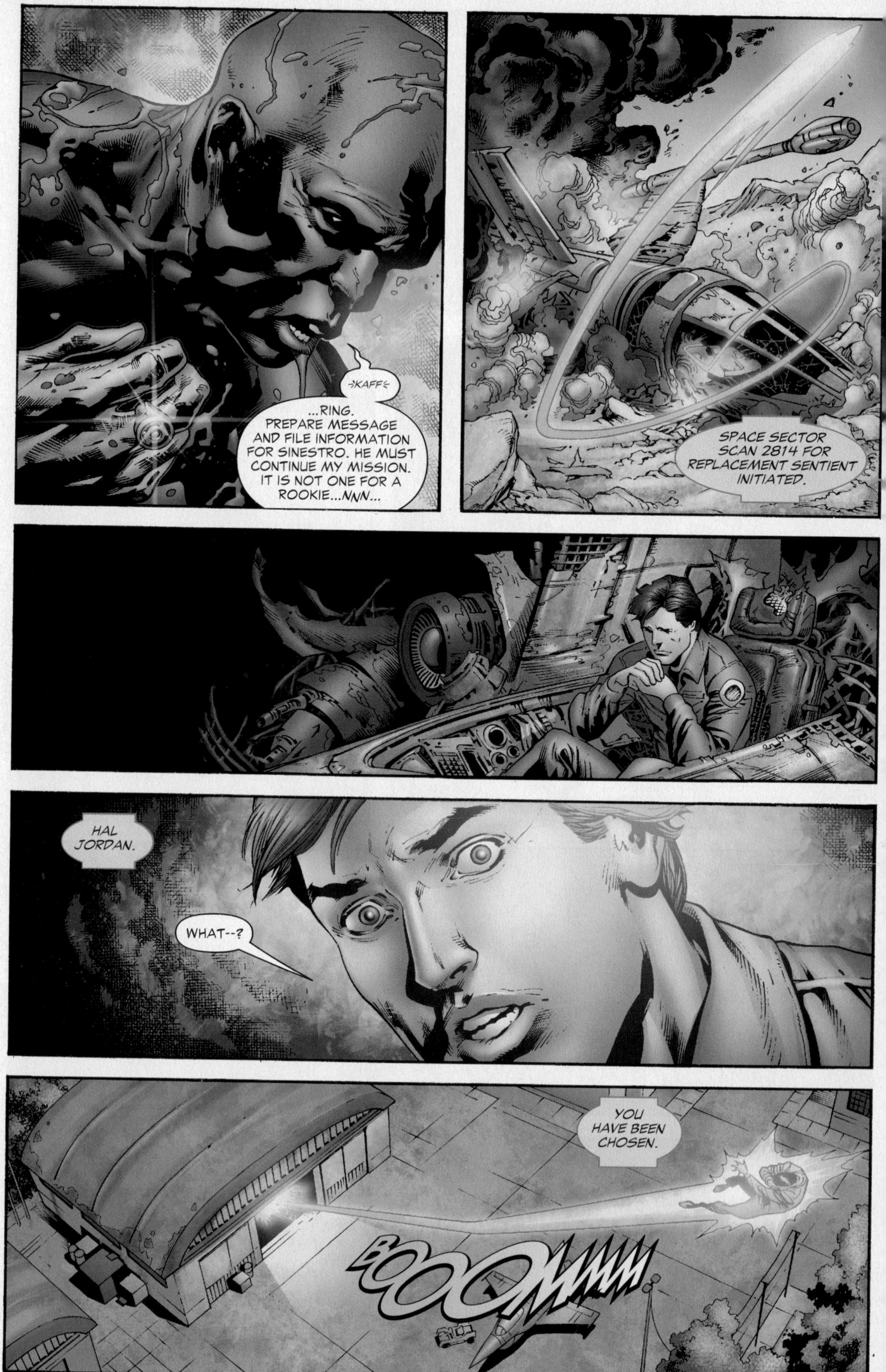

KAFF
...RING. PREPARE MESSAGE AND FILE INFORMATION FOR SINESTRO. HE MUST CONTINUE MY MISSION. IT IS NOT ONE FOR A ROOKIE...NNN...
SPACE SECTOR SCAN 2814 FOR REPLACEMENT SENTIENT INITIATED.
HAL JORDAN.
WHAT--?
YOU HAVE BEEN CHOSEN.
BOOOMMM

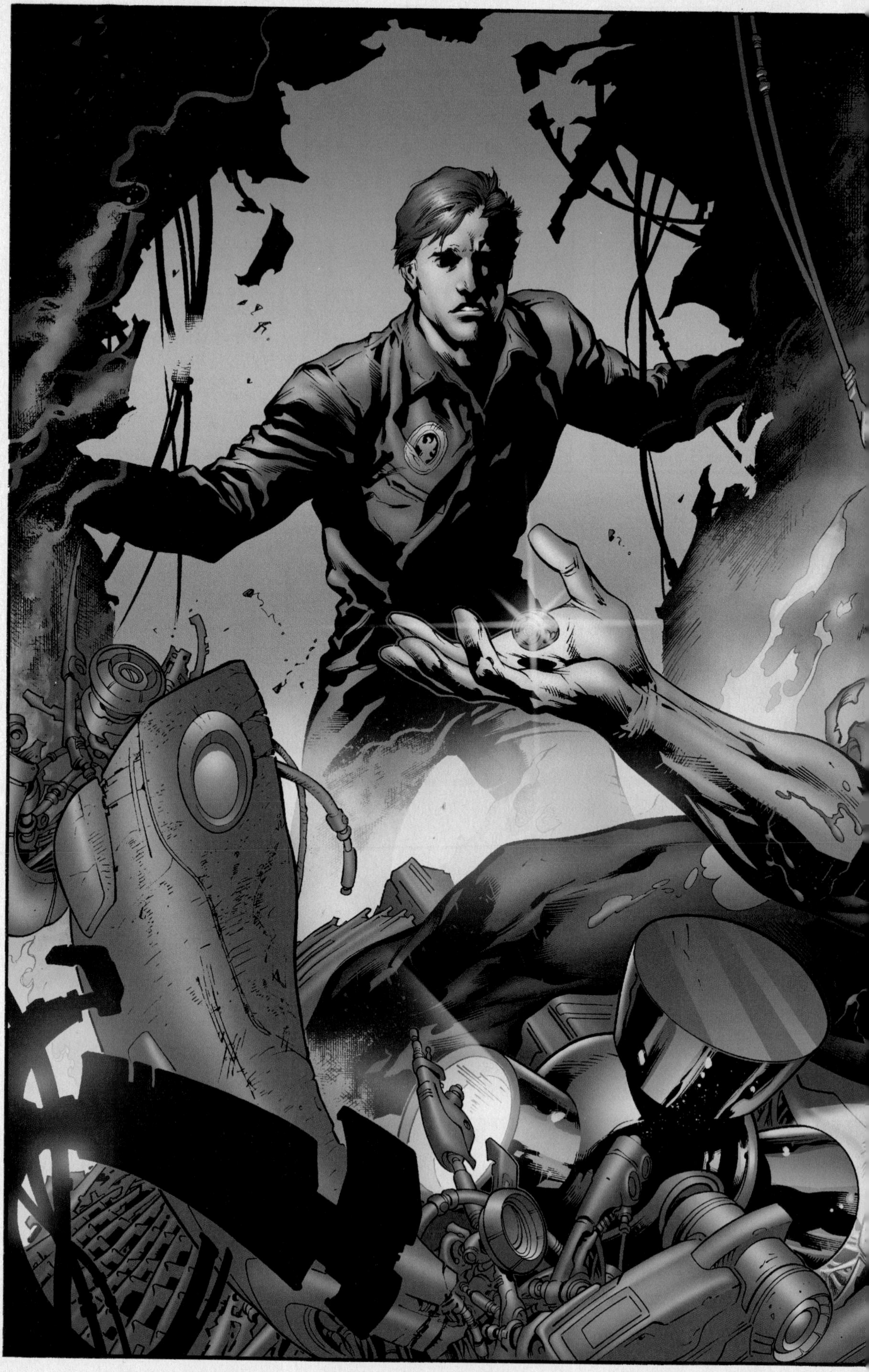

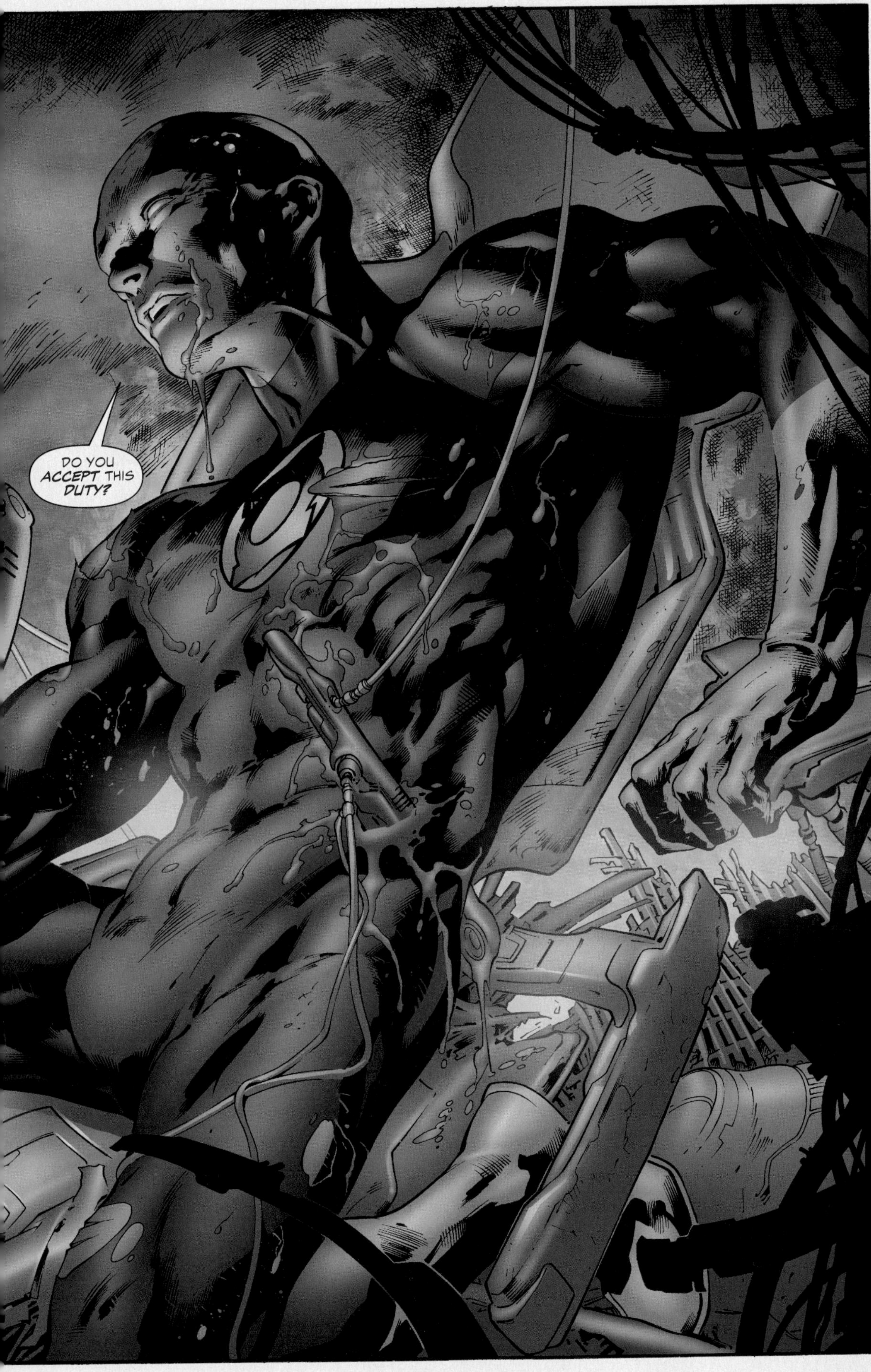
DO YOU ACCEPT THIS DUTY?

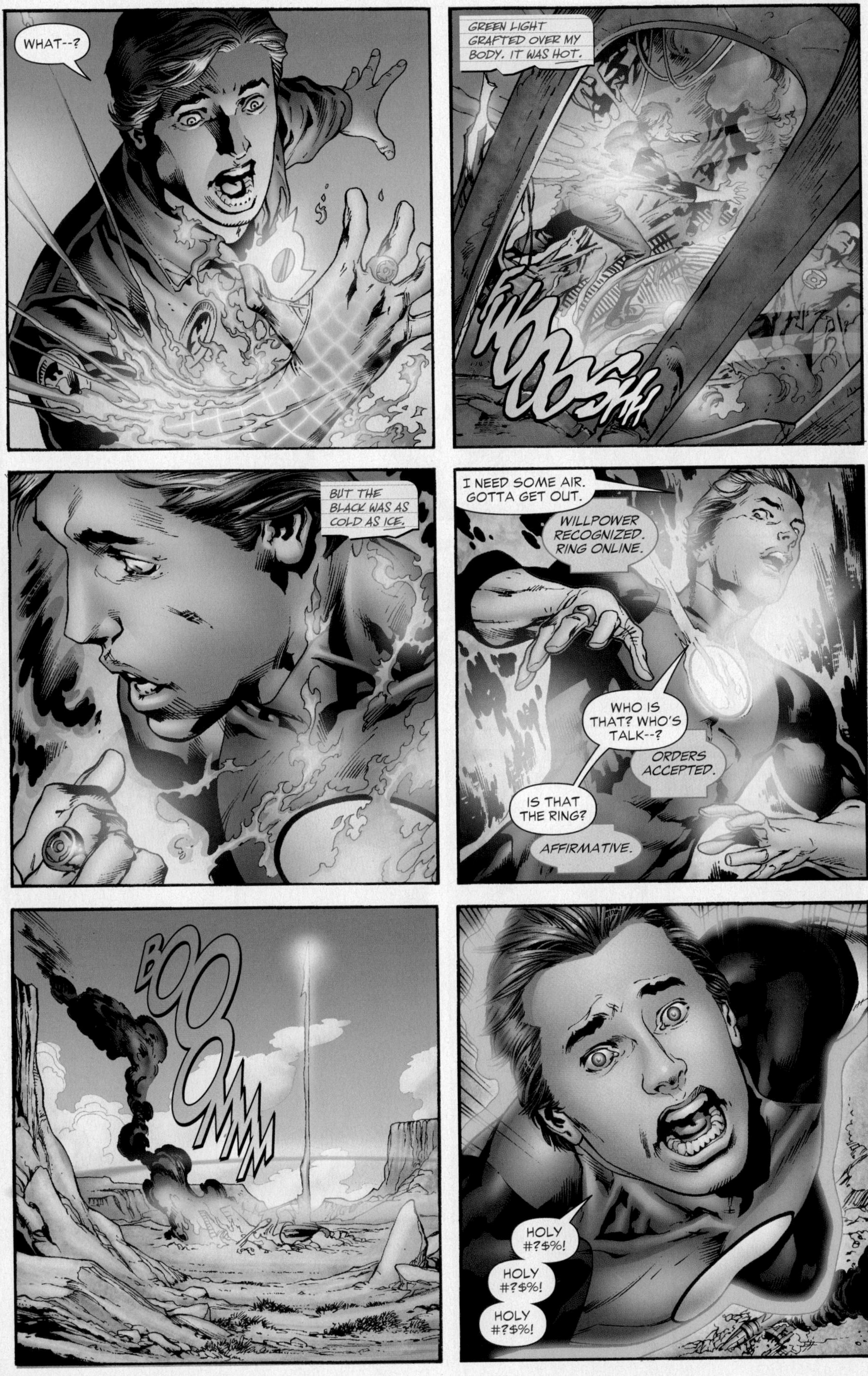
WHAT--?
GREEN LIGHT GRAFTED OVER MY BODY. IT WAS HOT.
FWOOOSHH
BUT THE BLACK WAS AS COLD AS ICE.
I NEED SOME AIR. GOTTA GET OUT.
WILLPOWER RECOGNIZED. RING ONLINE.
WHO IS THAT? WHO'S TALK--?
ORDERS ACCEPTED.
IS THAT THE RING?
AFFIRMATIVE.
BOOOMMM
HOLY #?$%!
HOLY #?$%!
HOLY #?$%!

THERE WAS NO RUMBLING OF ANY ENGINE.

IT WAS JUST ME.

NO STICK TO PULL ON.

NO TOWER TO GET PERMISSION FROM.

ME AND THE RING.

BOOOOMM

HAHAHA HAHAHA HAAA!

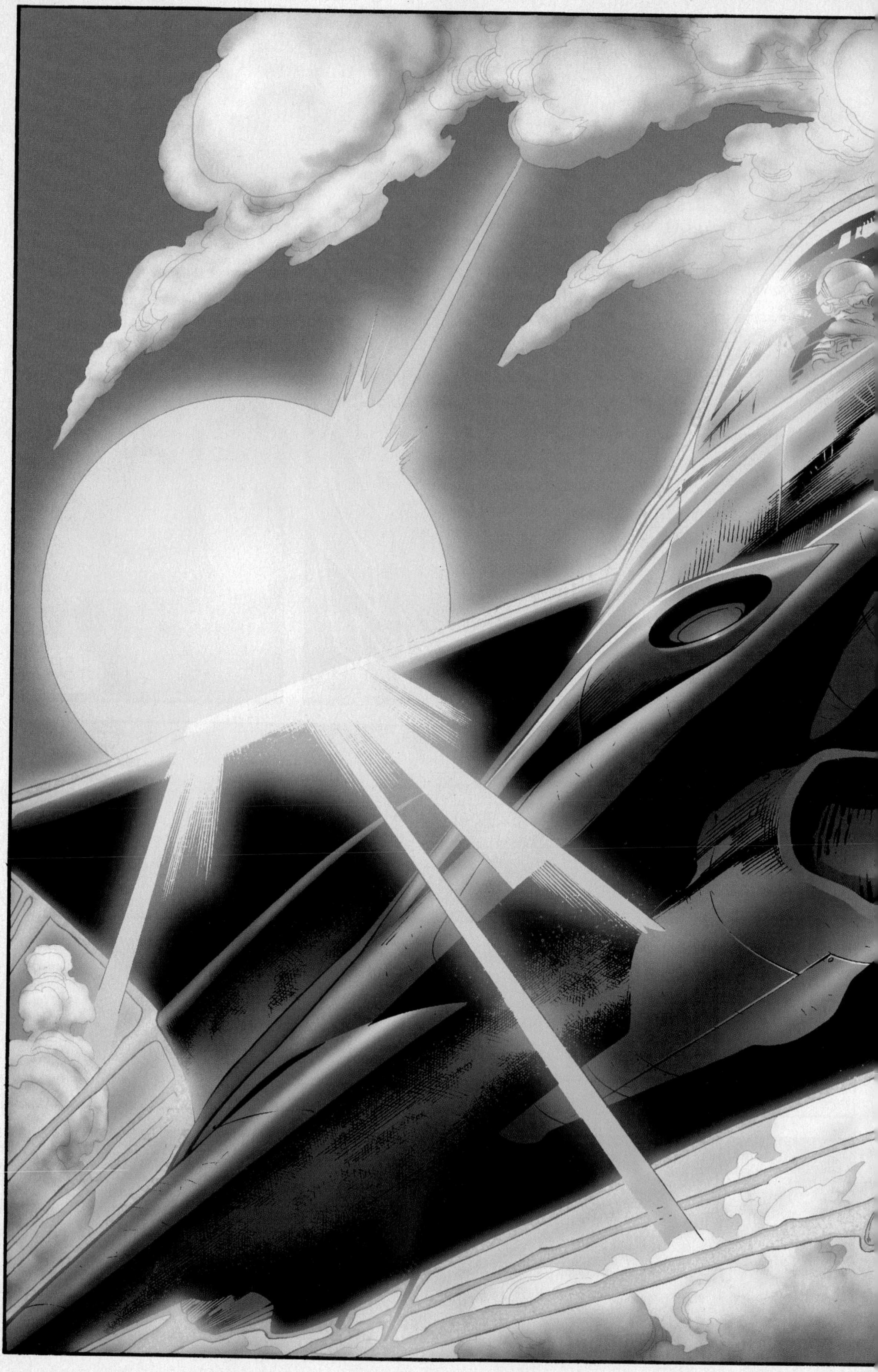

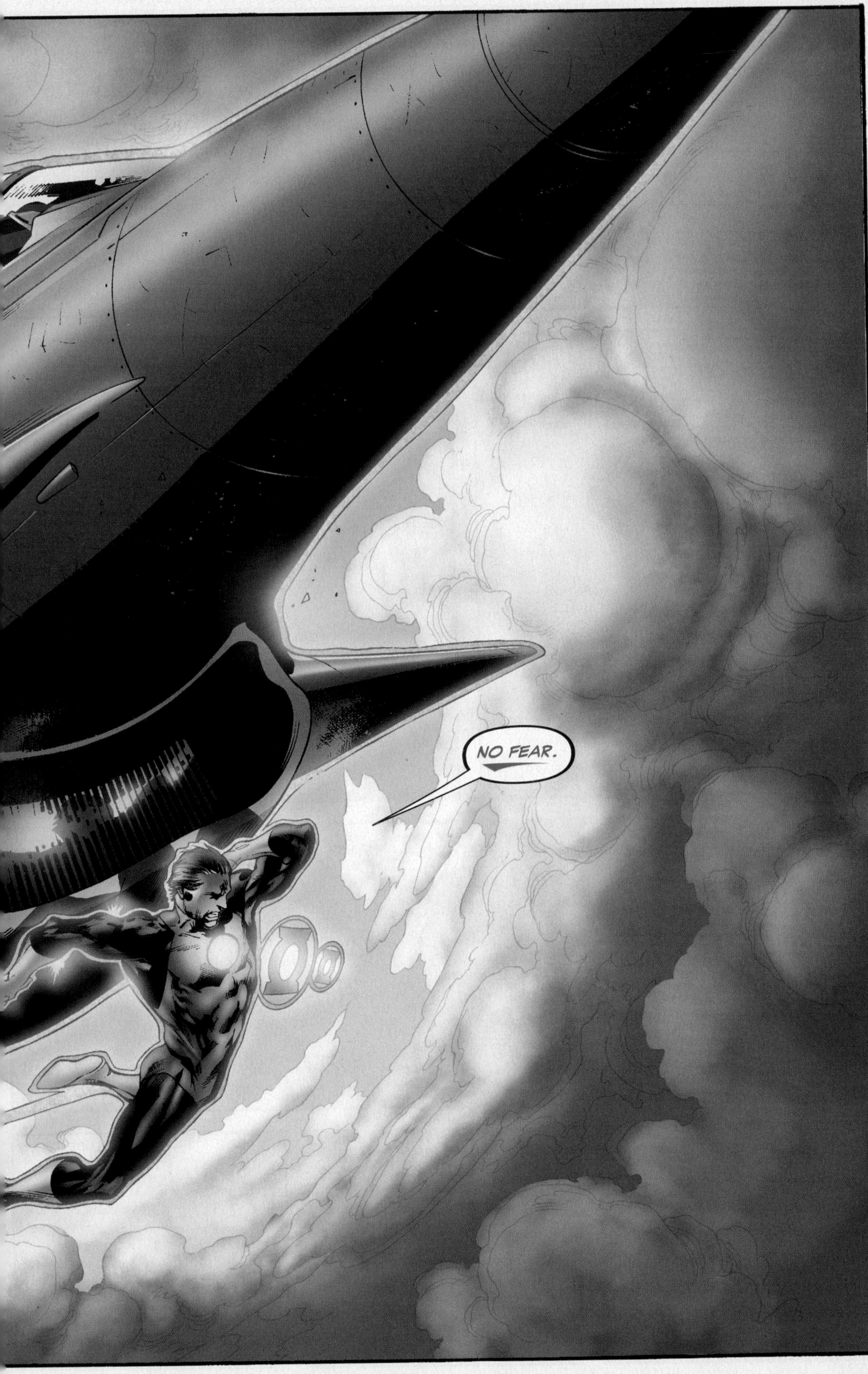
NO FEAR.

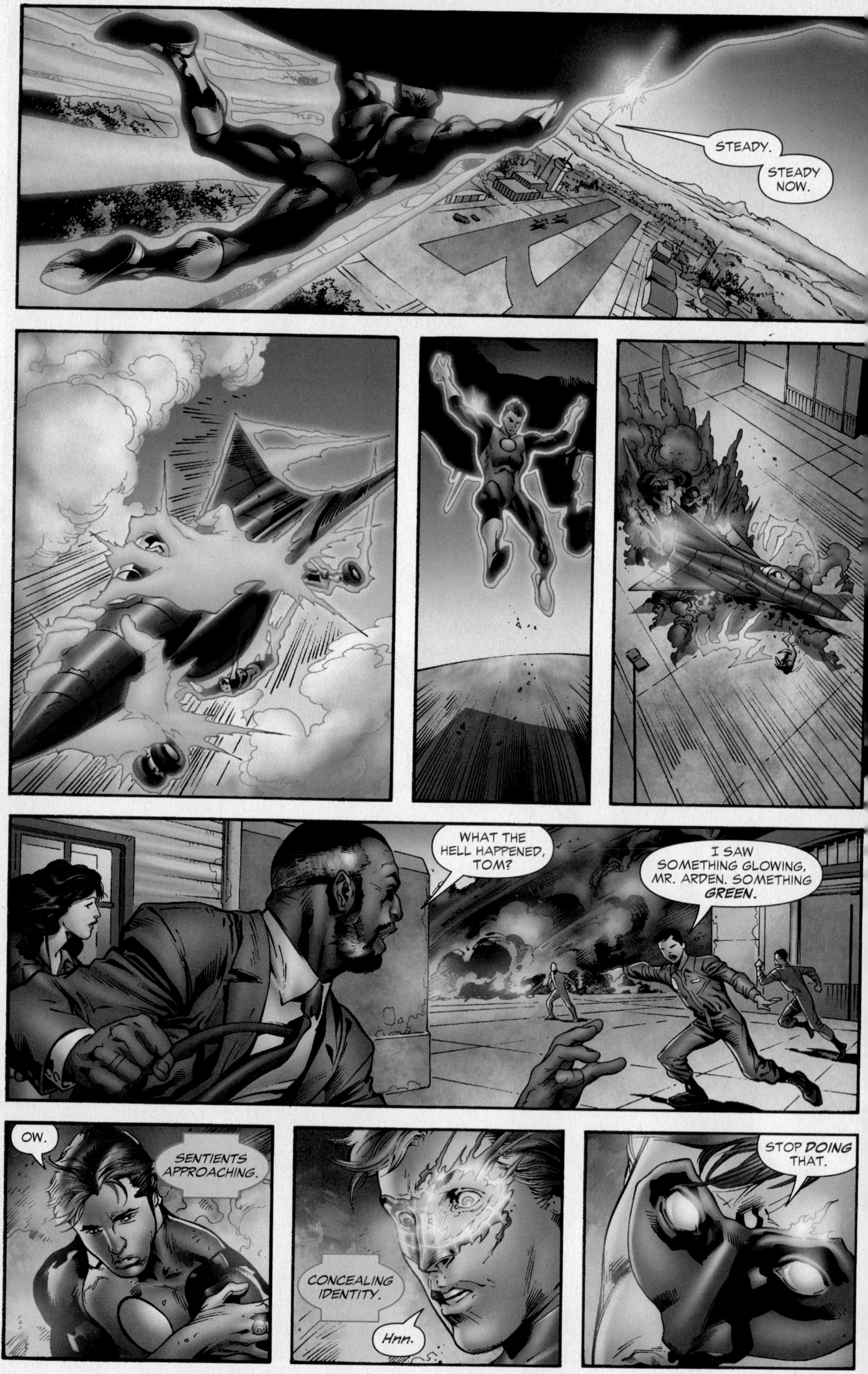
STEADY.
STEADY NOW.
WHAT THE HELL HAPPENED, TOM?
I SAW SOMETHING GLOWING, MR. ARDEN. SOMETHING **GREEN**.
OW.
SENTIENTS APPROACHING.
CONCEALING IDENTITY.
Hnn.
STOP ***DOING*** THAT.

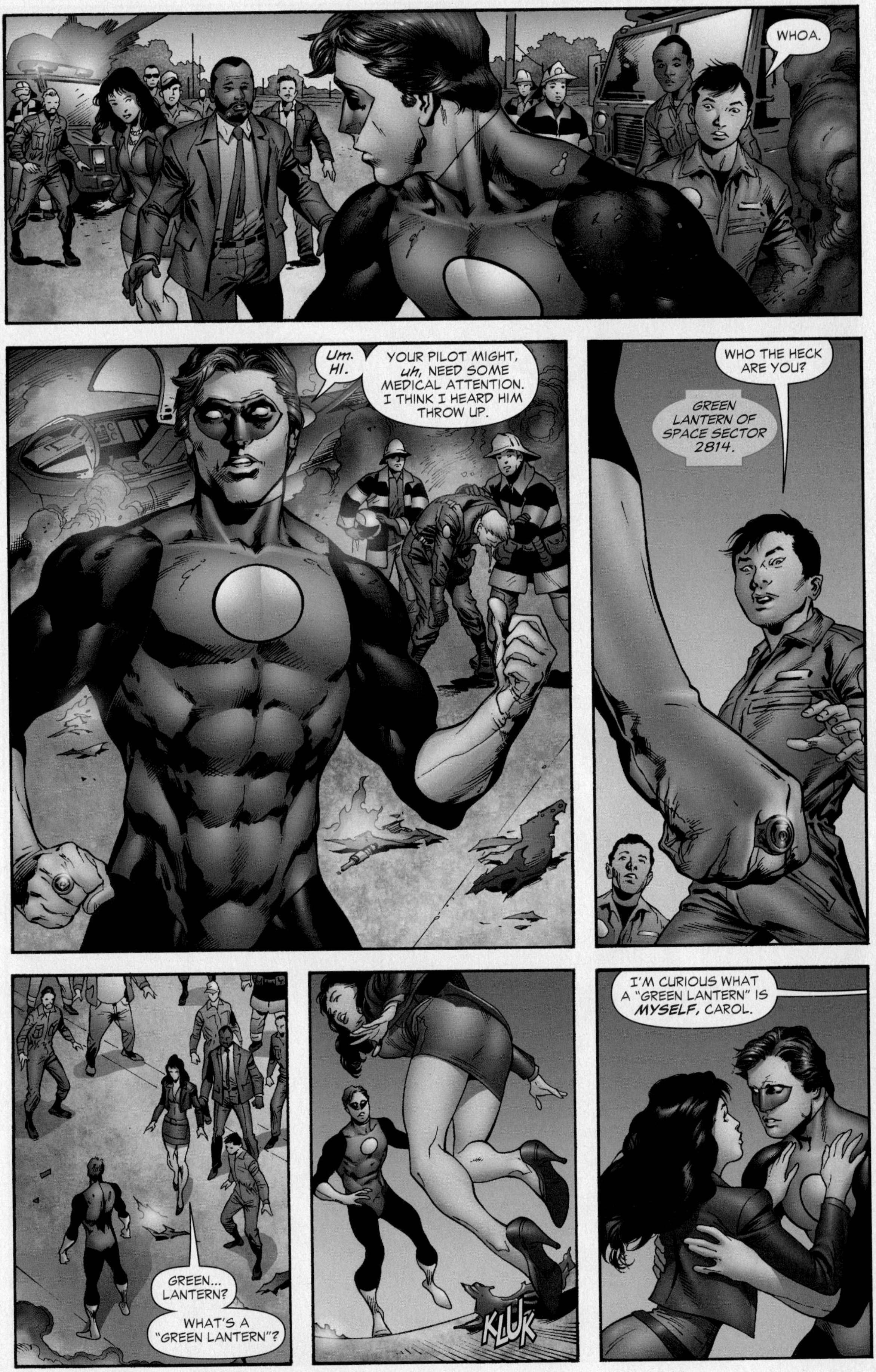
WHOA.
Um. Hi.
YOUR PILOT MIGHT, *uh*, NEED SOME MEDICAL ATTENTION. I THINK I HEARD HIM THROW UP.
WHO THE HECK ARE YOU?
GREEN LANTERN OF SPACE SECTOR 2814.
GREEN... LANTERN?
WHAT'S A "GREEN LANTERN"?
KLUK
I'M CURIOUS WHAT A "GREEN LANTERN" IS *MYSELF*, CAROL.

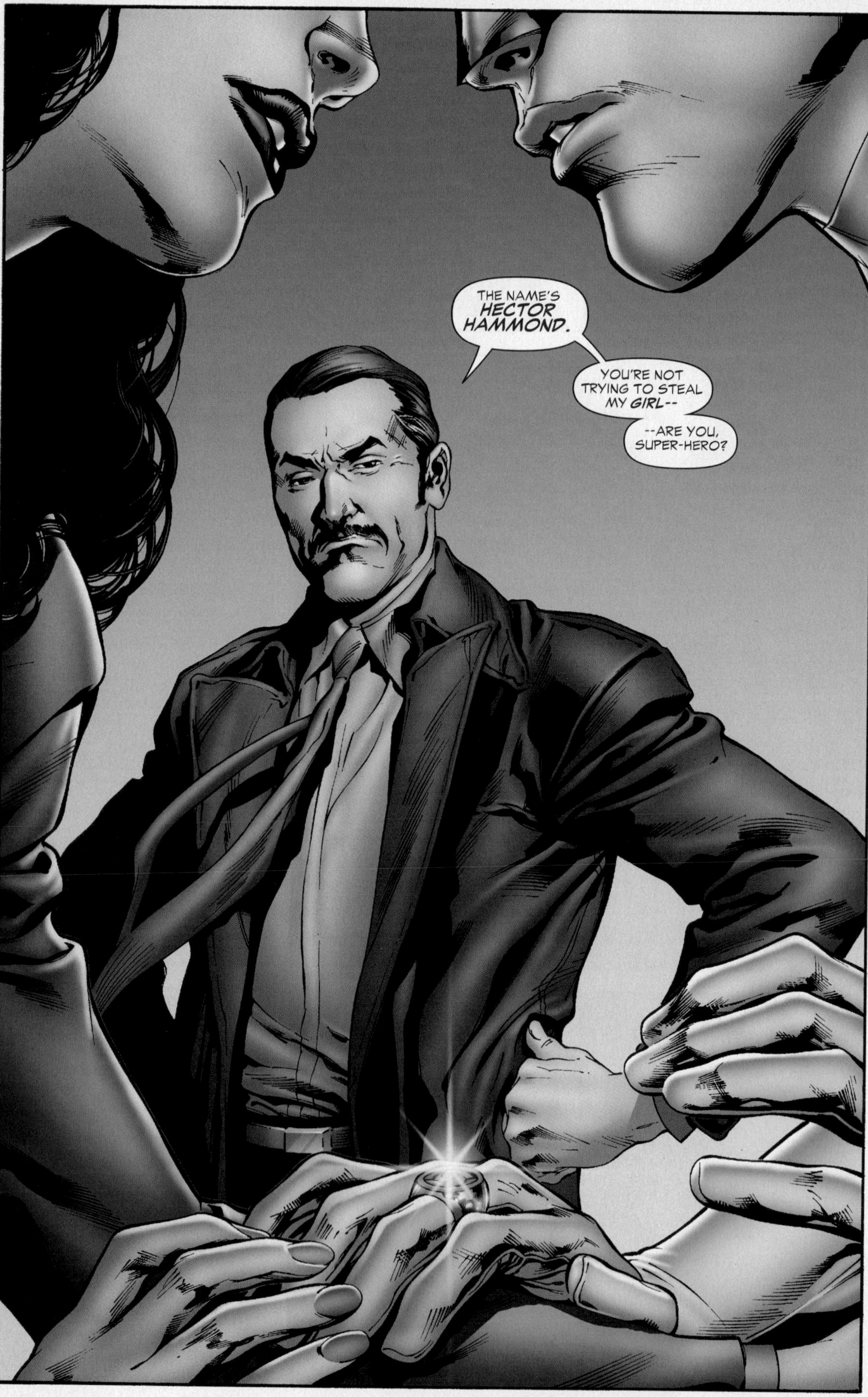
THE NAME'S HECTOR HAMMOND.
YOU'RE NOT TRYING TO STEAL MY GIRL--
--ARE YOU, SUPER-HERO?

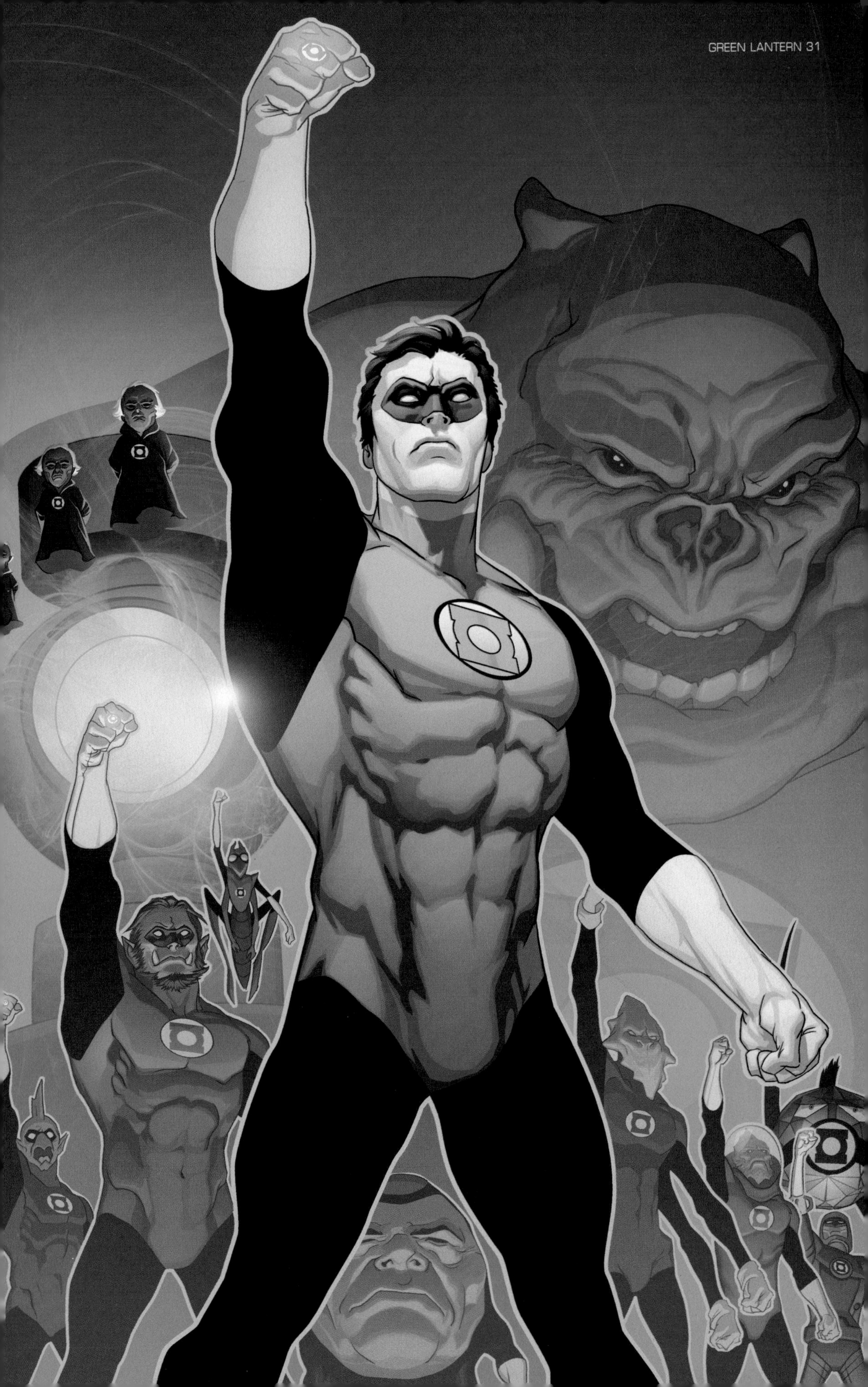

SECRET ORIGIN

BOOK THREE

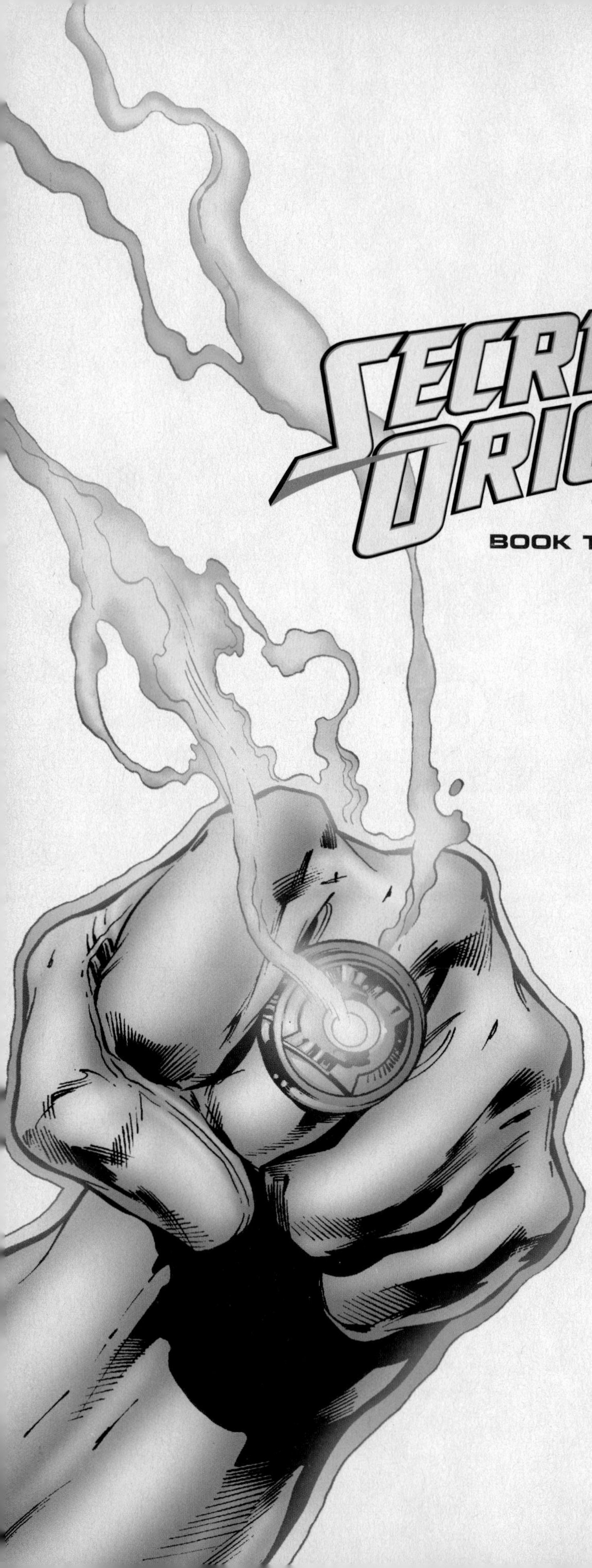

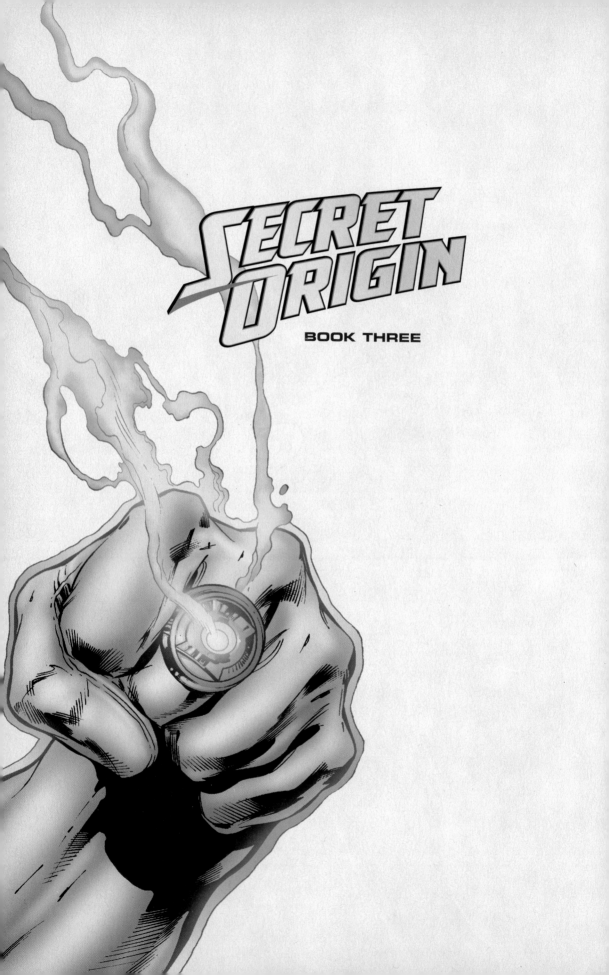

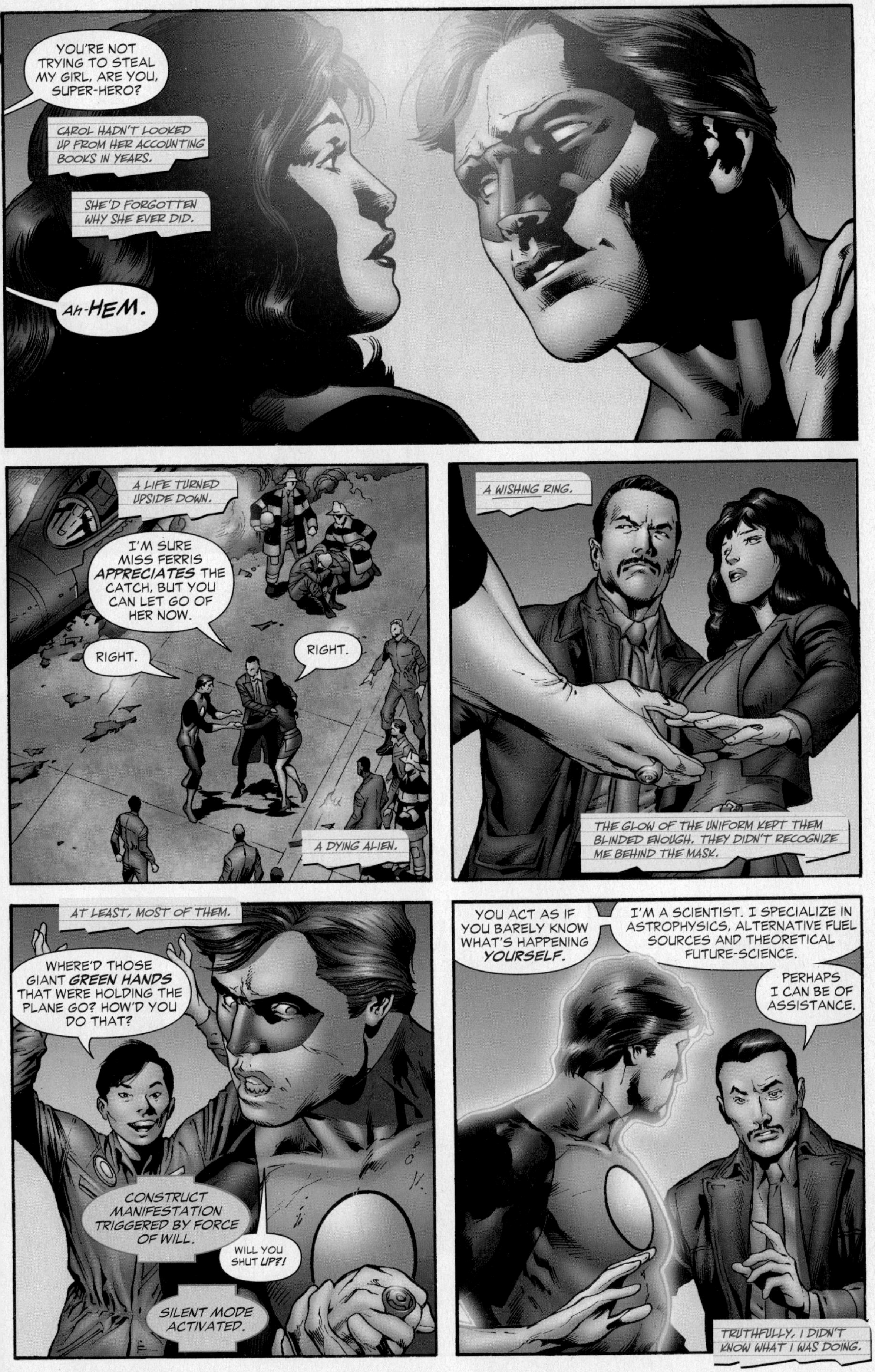
YOU'RE NOT TRYING TO STEAL MY GIRL, ARE YOU, SUPER-HERO?
CAROL HADN'T LOOKED UP FROM HER ACCOUNTING BOOKS IN YEARS.
SHE'D FORGOTTEN WHY SHE EVER DID.
Ah-HEM.
A LIFE TURNED UPSIDE DOWN.
I'M SURE MISS FERRIS APPRECIATES THE CATCH, BUT YOU CAN LET GO OF HER NOW.
RIGHT.
RIGHT.
A DYING ALIEN.
A WISHING RING.
THE GLOW OF THE UNIFORM KEPT THEM BLINDED ENOUGH. THEY DIDN'T RECOGNIZE ME BEHIND THE MASK.
AT LEAST, MOST OF THEM.
WHERE'D THOSE GIANT GREEN HANDS THAT WERE HOLDING THE PLANE GO? HOW'D YOU DO THAT?
CONSTRUCT MANIFESTATION TRIGGERED BY FORCE OF WILL.
WILL YOU SHUT UP?!
SILENT MODE ACTIVATED.
YOU ACT AS IF YOU BARELY KNOW WHAT'S HAPPENING YOURSELF.
I'M A SCIENTIST. I SPECIALIZE IN ASTROPHYSICS, ALTERNATIVE FUEL SOURCES AND THEORETICAL FUTURE-SCIENCE.
PERHAPS I CAN BE OF ASSISTANCE.
TRUTHFULLY, I DIDN'T KNOW WHAT I WAS DOING.

BUT I'D FIGURE IT OUT MYSELF.

NO, THANKS.

WHO IS HE?

WHERE'D HE COME FROM?

ARE YOU ALL RIGHT, CAROL?

CAROL.

I APPRECIATE YOUR CONCERN, DR. HAMMOND, BUT ONE DINNER DOES NOT MAKE ME "YOUR GIRL."

YOU'RE AN EMPLOYEE.

AND I'VE MADE IT CRYSTAL CLEAR. I DON'T DATE EMPLOYEES.

THAT'S WHAT I ALWAYS DID.

I'M NOT AN EMPLOYEE. I'M A CONSULTANT.

YOU CAN'T TREAT ME LIKE YOU DO EVERYONE ELSE. FERRIS AIR ISN'T THE ONLY COMPANY I WORK--

VEET VEET

TELL YOUR FATHER "HELLO."

WHO WAS HE?

THE GREEN LANTERN? IS THAT WHAT *THIS* IS?

RING? RING, YOU CAN *TALK* NOW.

THIS IS YOUR POWER BATTERY.

POWER BATTERY? WHAT'S A POWER BATTER--

HEY!

A GREEN LANTERN'S POWER BATTERY IS THEIR POWER RING'S CHARGING STATION. RECHARGING REQUIRED APPROXIMATELY EVERY TWENTY-FOUR TERRESTRIAL HOURS.

INCORRECT OATH.

LET GO, DAMMIT!

KLANK

POWER LEVELS 100%.

GREEN LANTERN OF SPACE SECTOR 2814.

YOU WILL REPORT TO OA FOR TRAINING IMMEDIATELY.

WHAT?

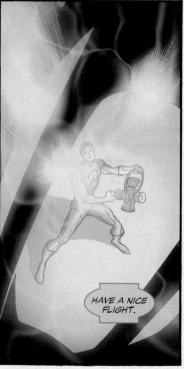

HAVE A NICE FLIGHT.

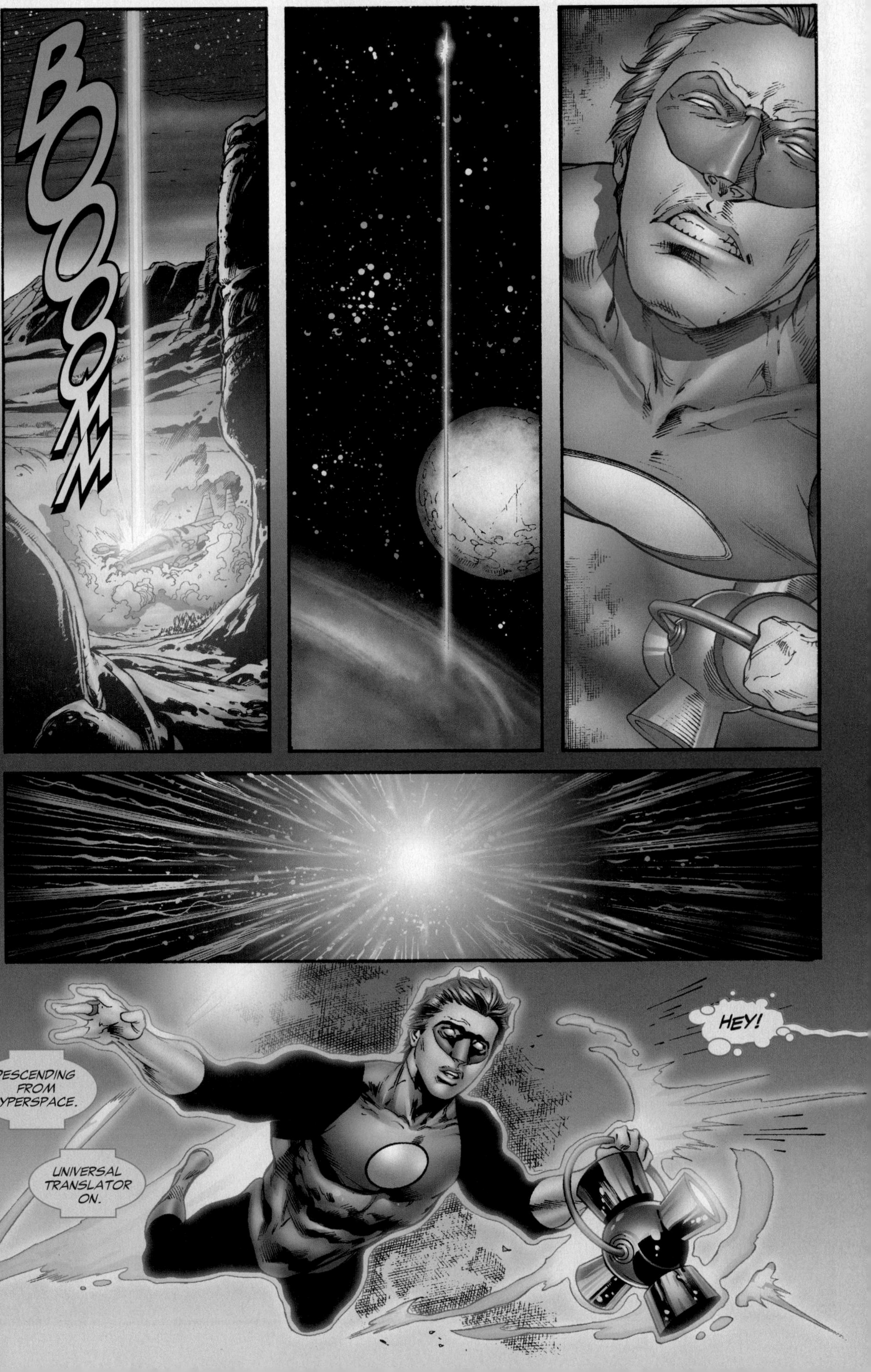
BOOOOOM
ESCENDING FROM YPERSPACE.
UNIVERSAL TRANSLATOR ON.
HEY!

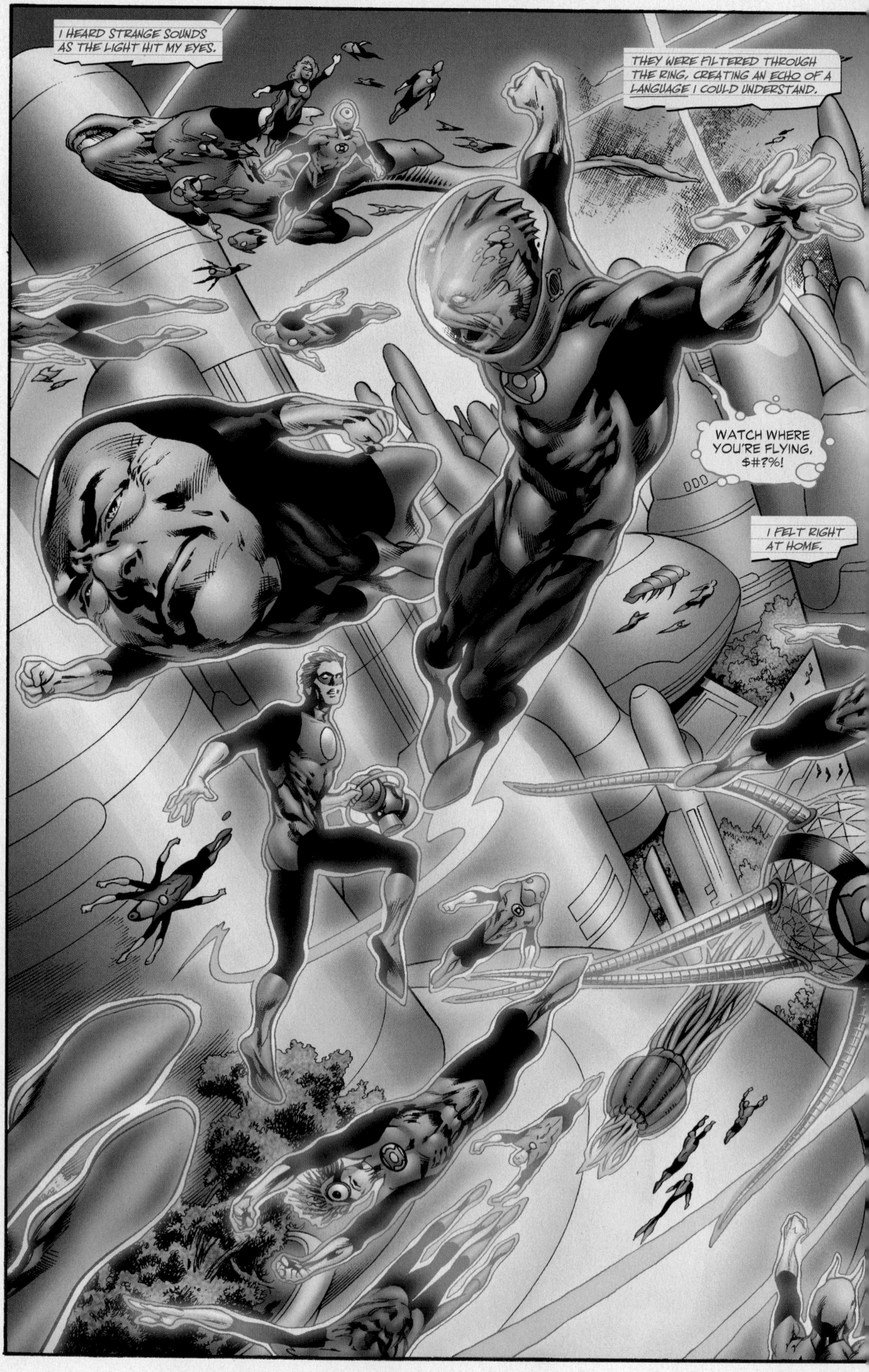
I HEARD STRANGE SOUNDS AS THE LIGHT HIT MY EYES.
THEY WERE FILTERED THROUGH THE RING, CREATING AN ECHO OF A LANGUAGE I COULD UNDERSTAND.
WATCH WHERE YOU'RE FLYING, $#?%!
I FELT RIGHT AT HOME.

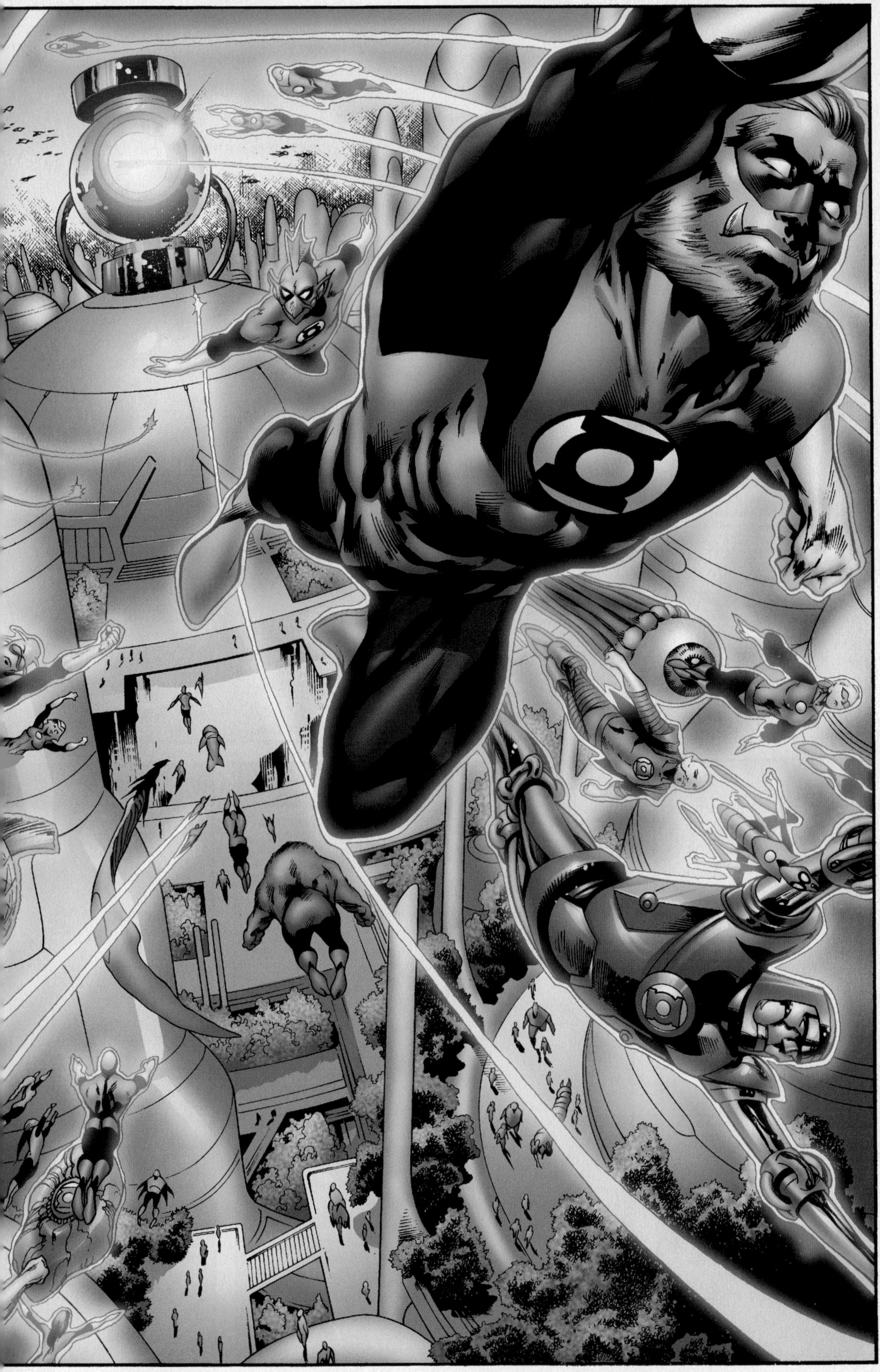

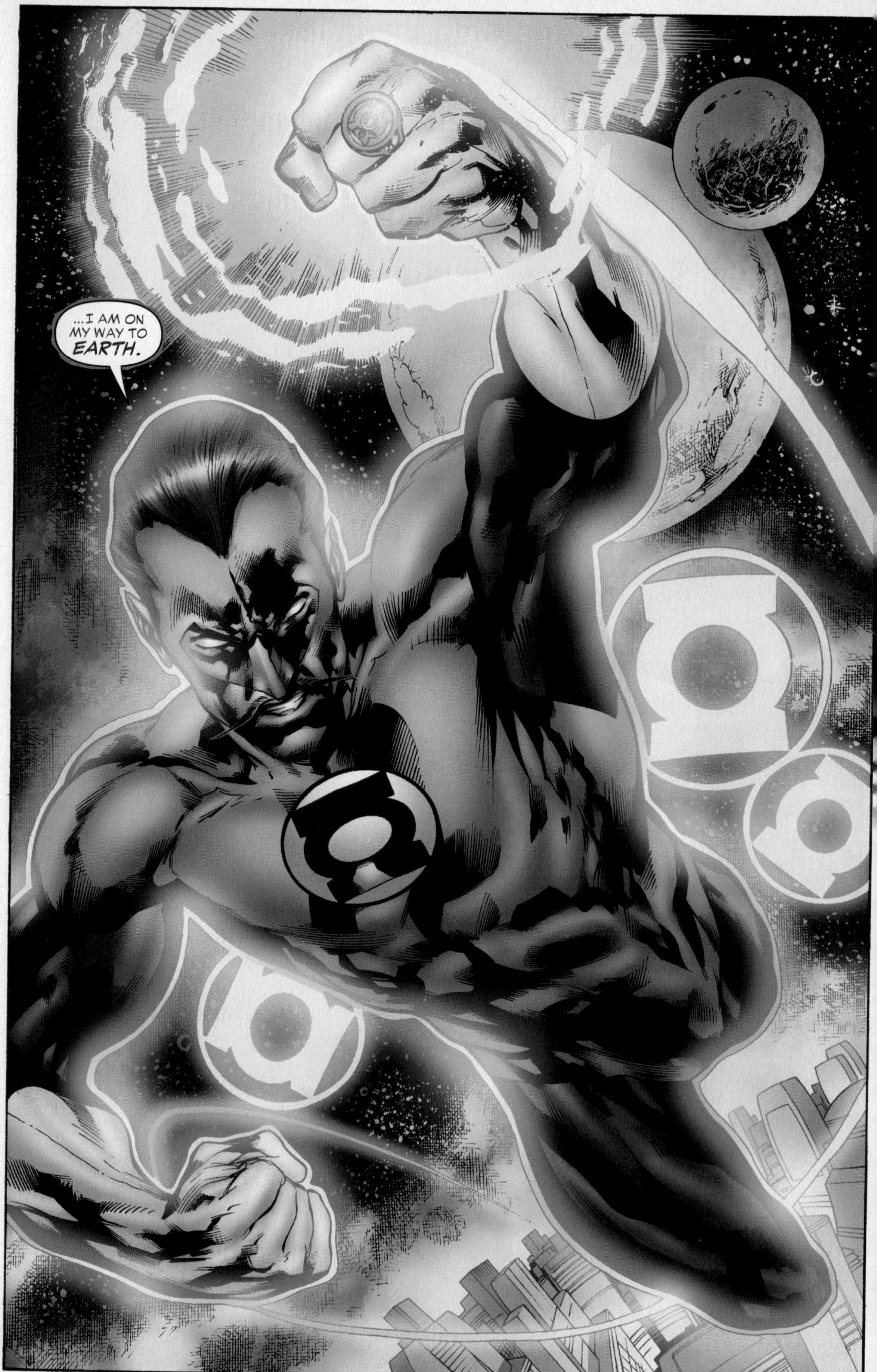
...I AM ON MY WAY TO EARTH.

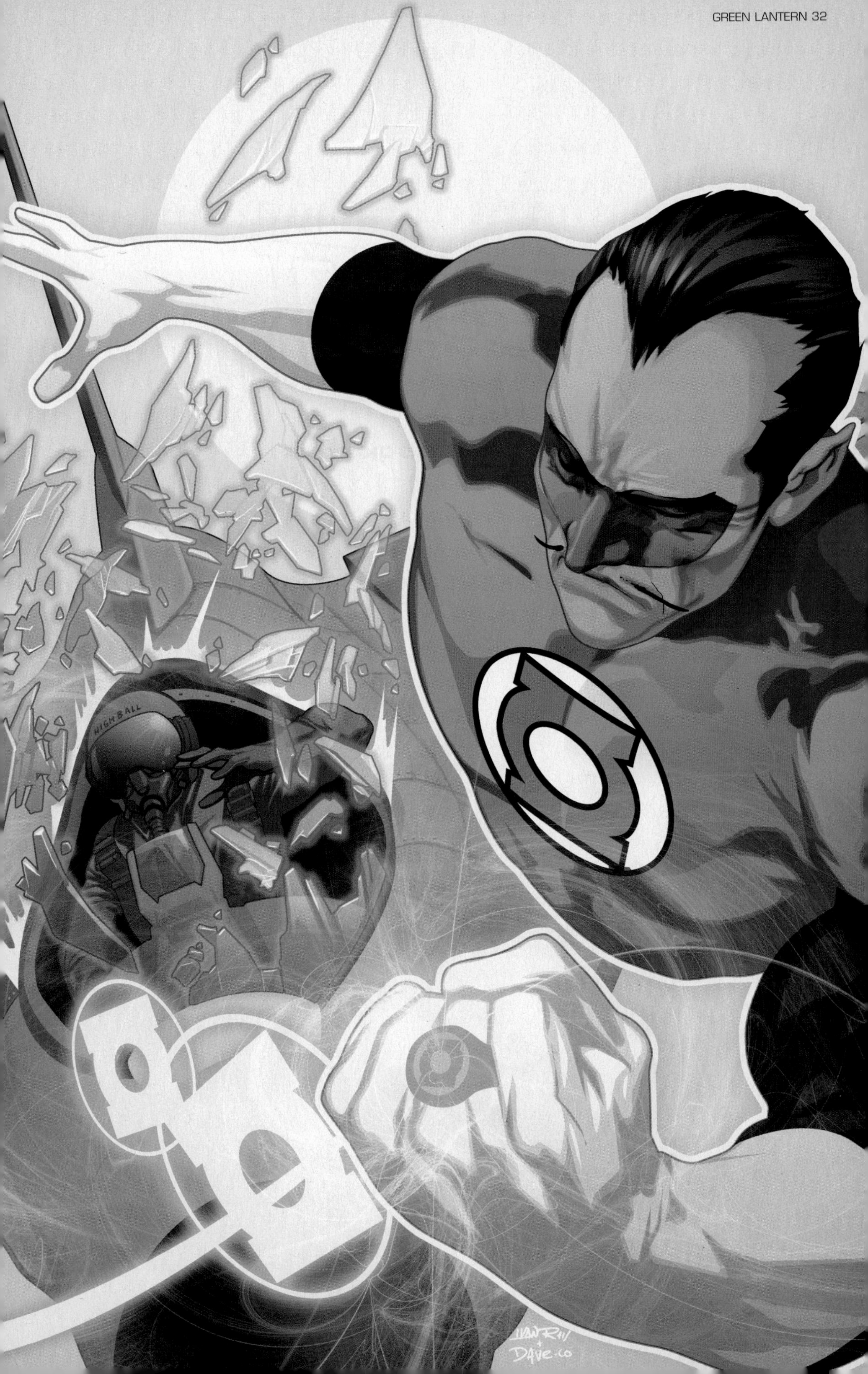
HIGHBALL

SECRET ORIGIN

BOOK FOUR

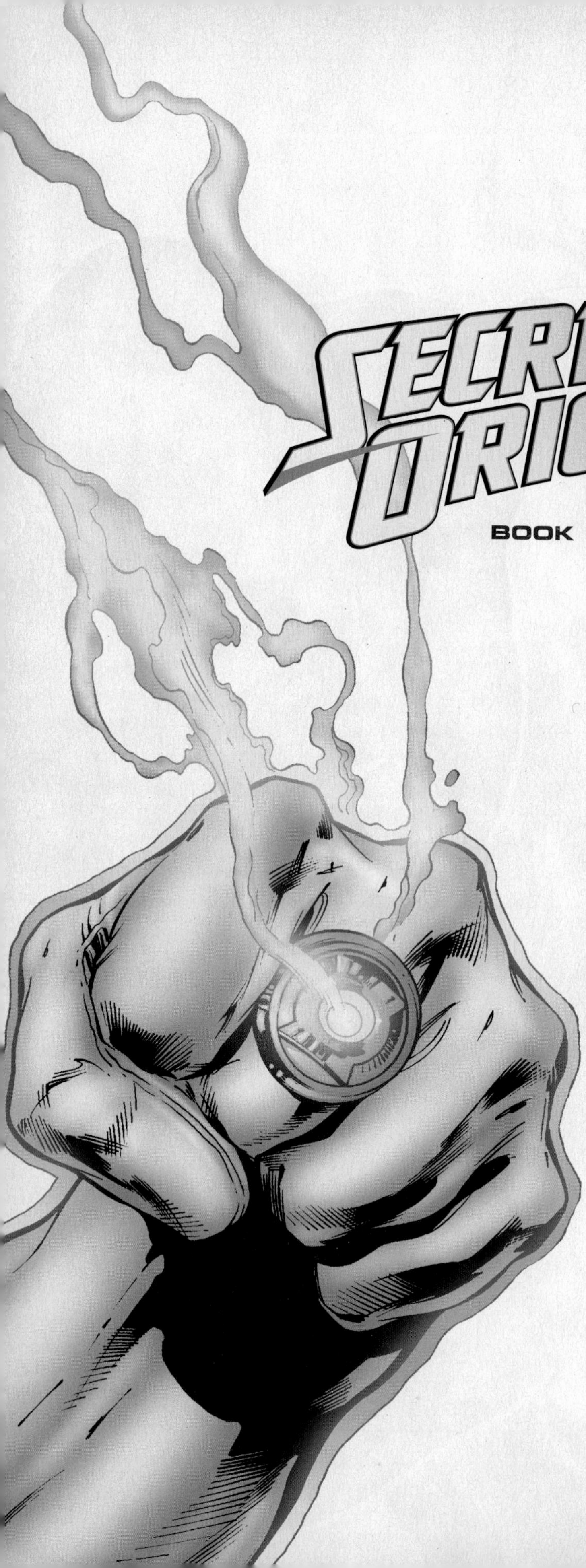

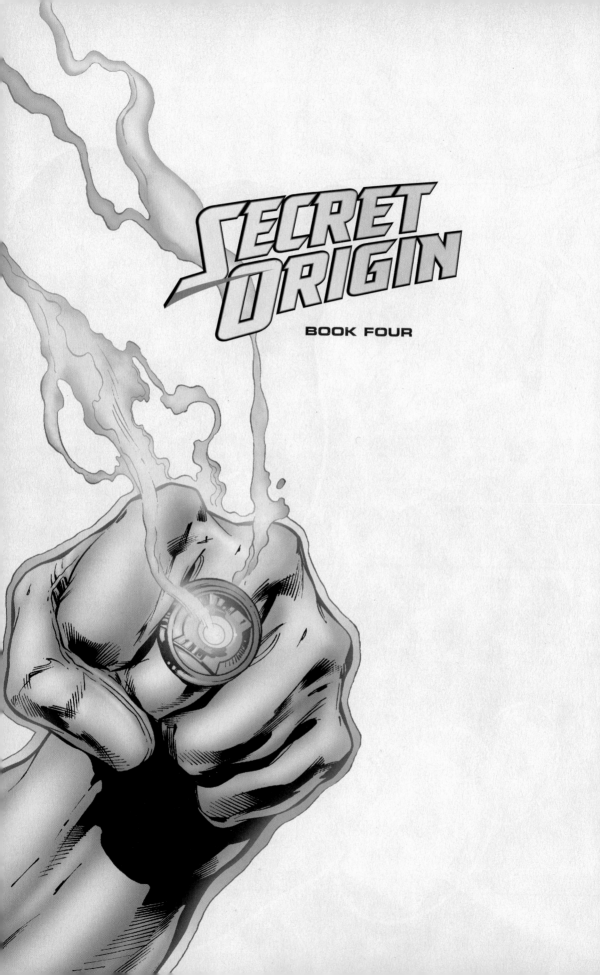

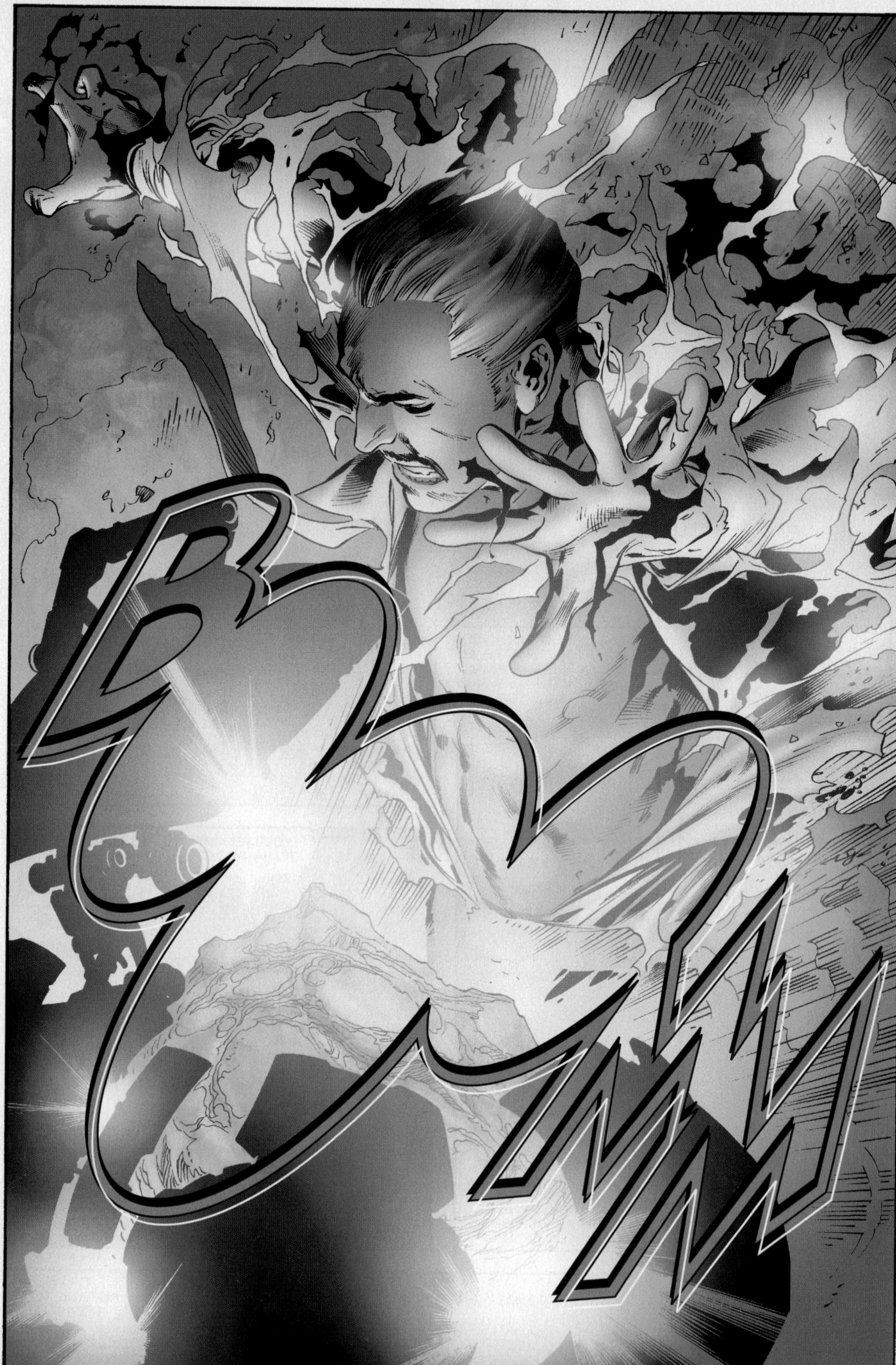

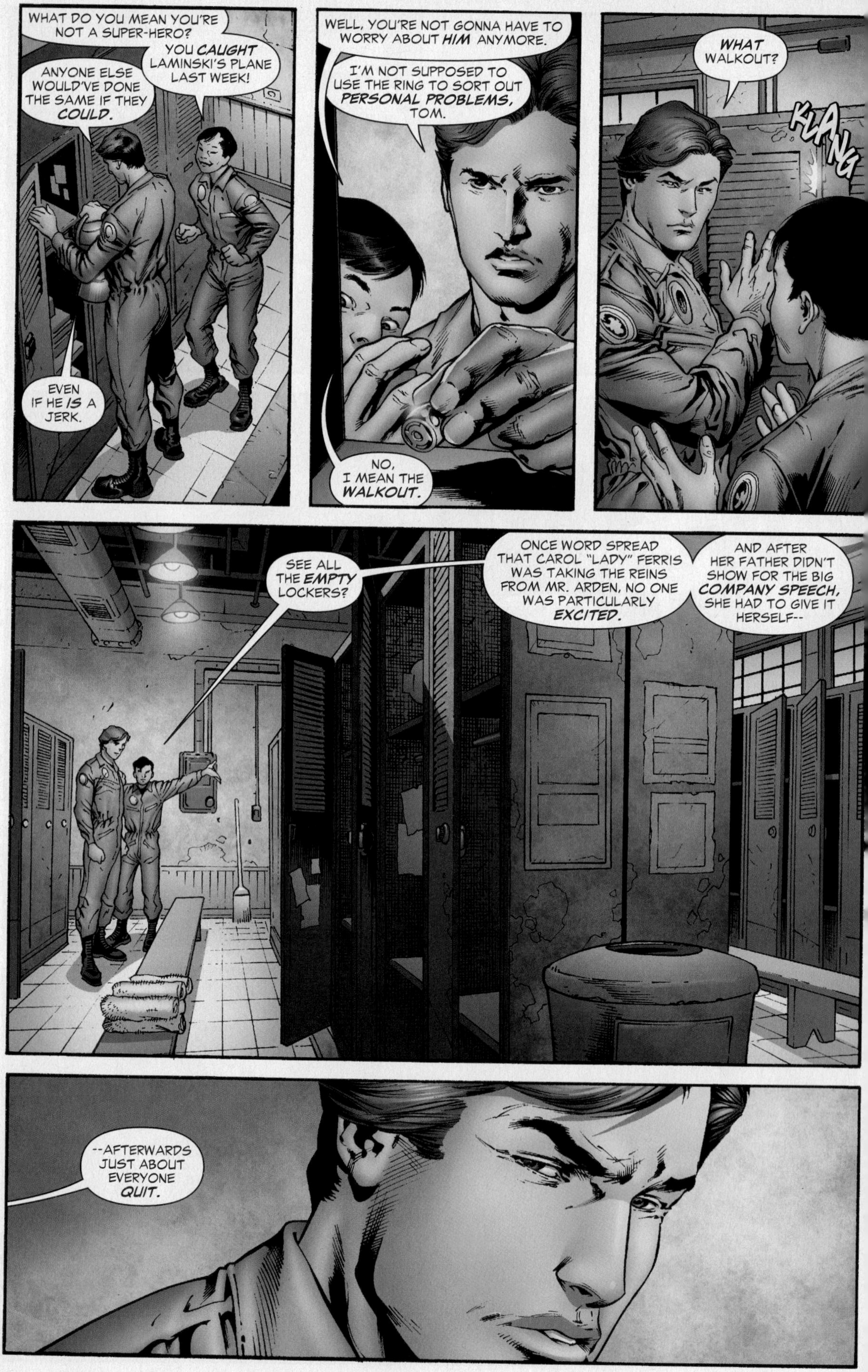

WHAT DO YOU MEAN YOU'RE NOT A SUPER-HERO?
YOU CAUGHT LAMINSKI'S PLANE LAST WEEK!
ANYONE ELSE WOULD'VE DONE THE SAME IF THEY COULD.
EVEN IF HE IS A JERK.
WELL, YOU'RE NOT GONNA HAVE TO WORRY ABOUT HIM ANYMORE.
I'M NOT SUPPOSED TO USE THE RING TO SORT OUT PERSONAL PROBLEMS, TOM.
NO, I MEAN THE WALKOUT.
WHAT WALKOUT?
KLANG
SEE ALL THE EMPTY LOCKERS?
ONCE WORD SPREAD THAT CAROL "LADY" FERRIS WAS TAKING THE REINS FROM MR. ARDEN, NO ONE WAS PARTICULARLY EXCITED.
AND AFTER HER FATHER DIDN'T SHOW FOR THE BIG COMPANY SPEECH, SHE HAD TO GIVE IT HERSELF--
--AFTERWARDS JUST ABOUT EVERYONE QUIT.

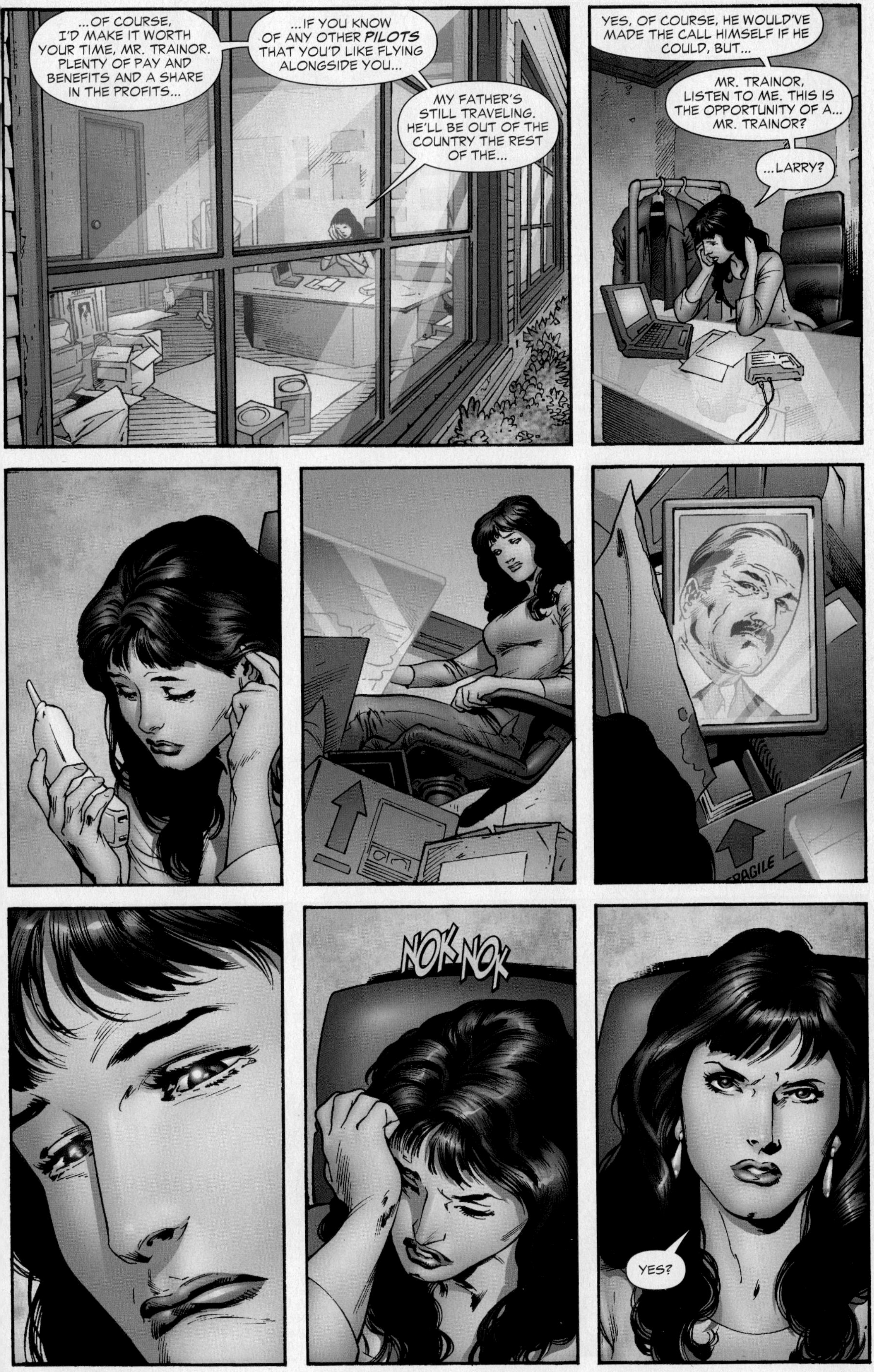
...OF COURSE, I'D MAKE IT WORTH YOUR TIME, MR. TRAINOR. PLENTY OF PAY AND BENEFITS AND A SHARE IN THE PROFITS...
...IF YOU KNOW OF ANY OTHER PILOTS THAT YOU'D LIKE FLYING ALONGSIDE YOU...
MY FATHER'S STILL TRAVELING. HE'LL BE OUT OF THE COUNTRY THE REST OF THE...
YES, OF COURSE, HE WOULD'VE MADE THE CALL HIMSELF IF HE COULD, BUT...
MR. TRAINOR, LISTEN TO ME. THIS IS THE OPPORTUNITY OF A... MR. TRAINOR?
...LARRY?
FRAGILE
NOK NOK
YES?

MR. JORDAN? WHAT ARE YOU DOING HERE?

MISS FERRIS.

I JUST WANTED TO THROW IN MY RESIGNATION ALONG WITH THE REST.

YOU HAVEN'T SHOWN YOUR FACE HERE ALL *WEEK.* I ASSUMED YOU ALREADY HAD.

YOU ASSUMED RIGHT. I GUESS I WANTED TO MAKE IT *OFFICIAL.*

AND IF YOUR *FATHER* WAS HERE--

WHAT? WHAT WOULD YOU *DO* IF MY FATHER *WAS* HERE?

I'D TELL HIM WHAT I'VE BEEN WANTING TO FOR *YEARS.*

I'D TELL HIM EVERYTHING MY MOTHER *BEGGED* ME *NOT* TO.

YOU KNOW WHAT, JORDAN? LET'S MAKE THIS DAY EVEN *BETTER* THAN IT *HAS* BEEN.

TELL *ME.*

YOUR FATHER PUT *MINE* IN A *DEATH TRAP!*

HE SAVED A FEW *BUCKS* AND HE SENT HIM OFF IN A PLANE THAT NEVER HAD A *CHANCE* AT *LANDING.*

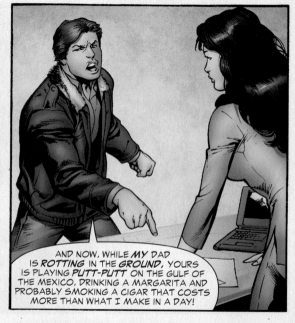

AND NOW, WHILE *MY* DAD IS *ROTTING* IN THE *GROUND,* YOURS IS PLAYING *PUTT-PUTT* ON THE GULF OF THE MEXICO, DRINKING A MARGARITA AND PROBABLY SMOKING A CIGAR THAT COSTS MORE THAN WHAT I MAKE IN A DAY!

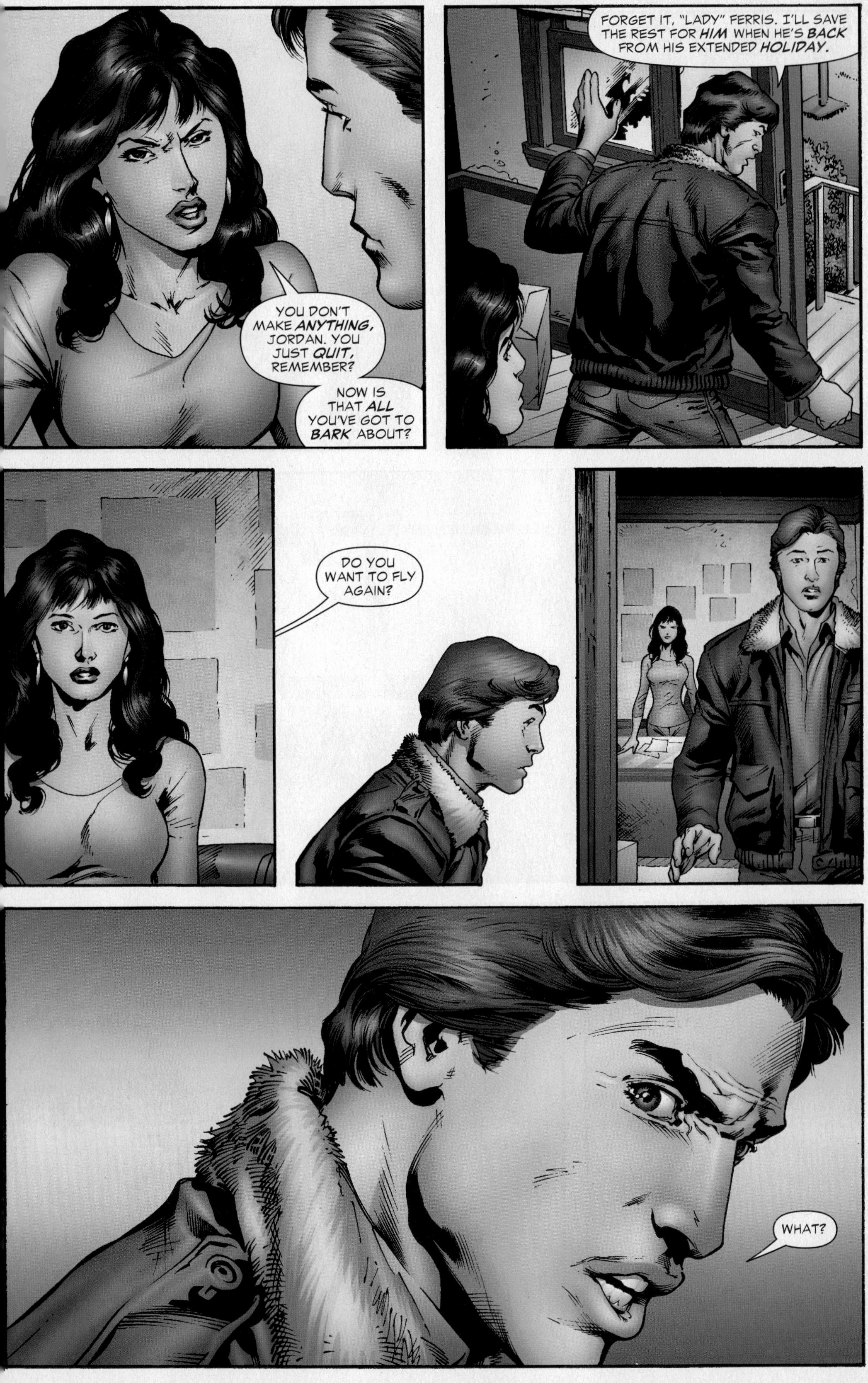
YOU DON'T MAKE ANYTHING, JORDAN. YOU JUST QUIT, REMEMBER?
NOW IS THAT ALL YOU'VE GOT TO BARK ABOUT?
FORGET IT, "LADY" FERRIS. I'LL SAVE THE REST FOR HIM WHEN HE'S BACK FROM HIS EXTENDED HOLIDAY.
DO YOU WANT TO FLY AGAIN?
WHAT?

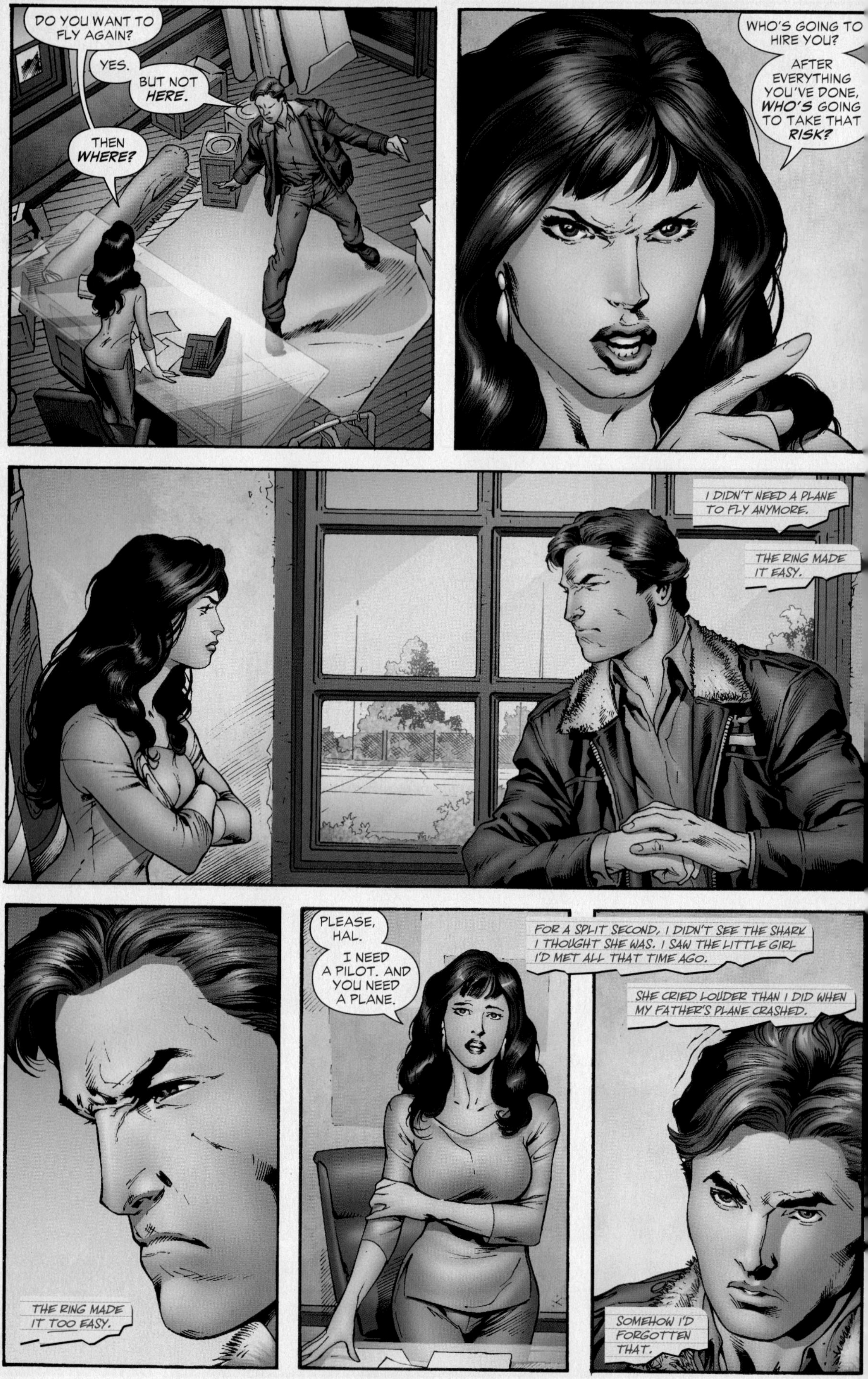
DO YOU WANT TO FLY AGAIN?
YES.
BUT NOT *HERE.*
THEN *WHERE?*
WHO'S GOING TO HIRE YOU?
AFTER EVERYTHING YOU'VE DONE, ***WHO'S*** GOING TO TAKE THAT ***RISK?***
I DIDN'T NEED A PLANE TO FLY ANYMORE.
THE RING MADE IT EASY.
THE RING MADE IT TOO EASY.
PLEASE, HAL.
I NEED A PILOT. AND YOU NEED A PLANE.
FOR A SPLIT SECOND, I DIDN'T SEE THE SHARK I THOUGHT SHE WAS. I SAW THE LITTLE GIRL I'D MET ALL THAT TIME AGO.
SHE CRIED LOUDER THAN I DID WHEN MY FATHER'S PLANE CRASHED.
SOMEHOW I'D FORGOTTEN THAT.

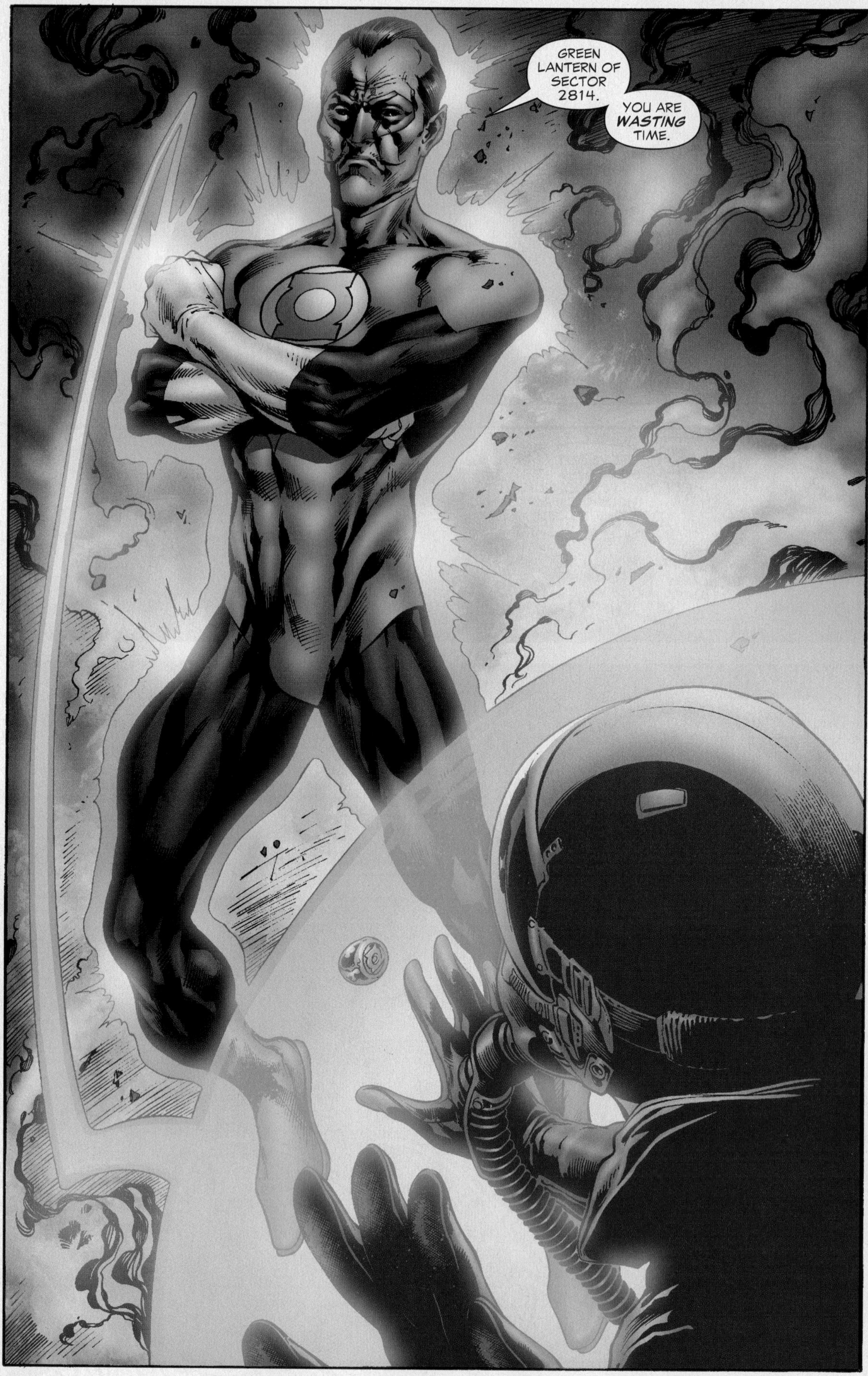
GREEN LANTERN OF SECTOR 2814.
YOU ARE *WASTING* TIME.

I DON'T BELIEVE IT.

WHAT?

LOOK.

EEERRRITT

OH, BOY.

WHAT THE HELL WAS *THAT?*

IT'S NOT WHAT IT LOOKS LIKE.

IT LOOKS LIKE YOU'RE PLAYING *GAMES,* MR. JORDAN.

PURPOSELY FLYING BELOW RADAR, REFUSING TO COMMUNICATE.

CAROL--

I MUST'VE BEEN *CRAZY* TO THINK THIS WAS A GOOD IDEA.

YOU'RE NOT *INSANE,* CAROL.

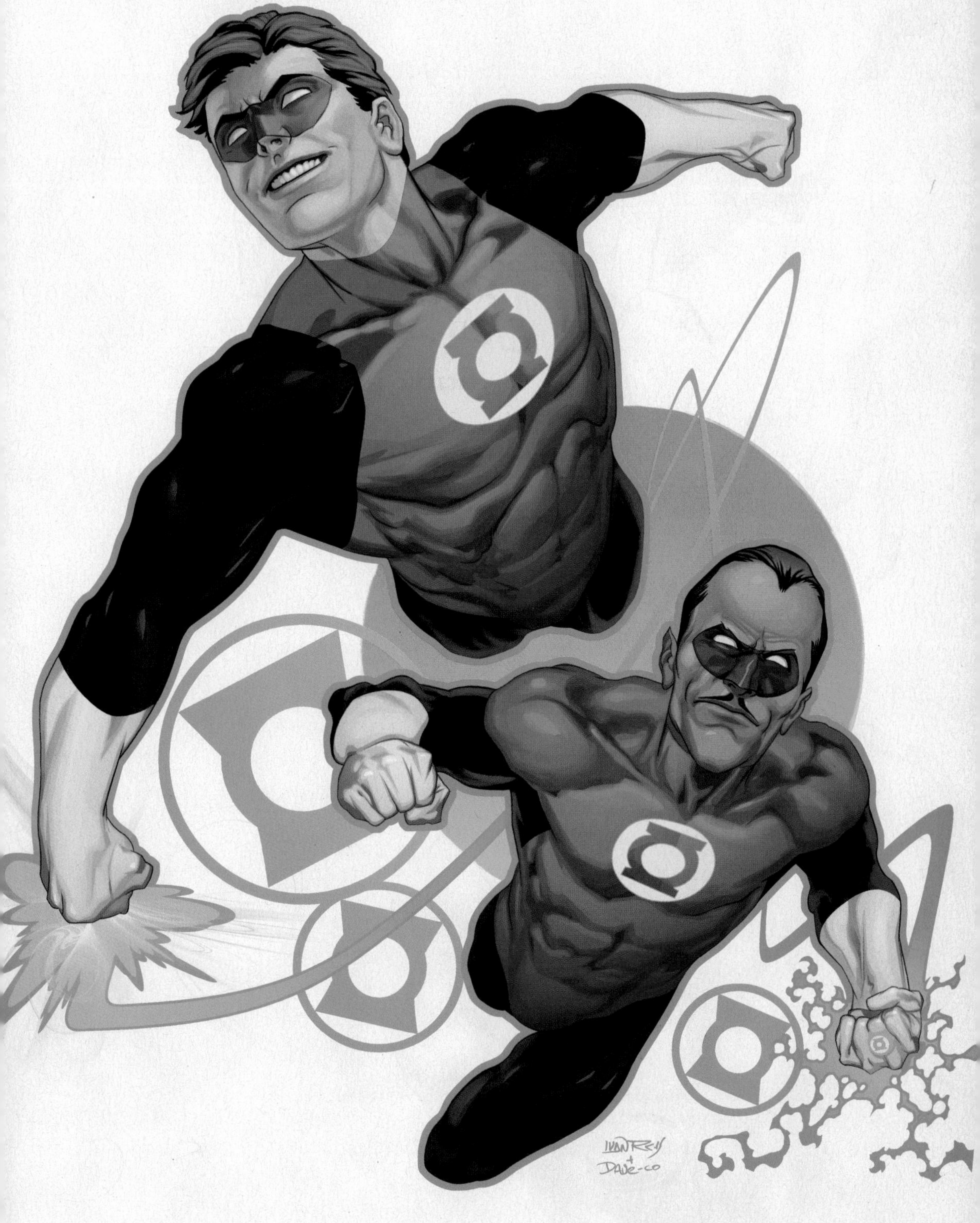

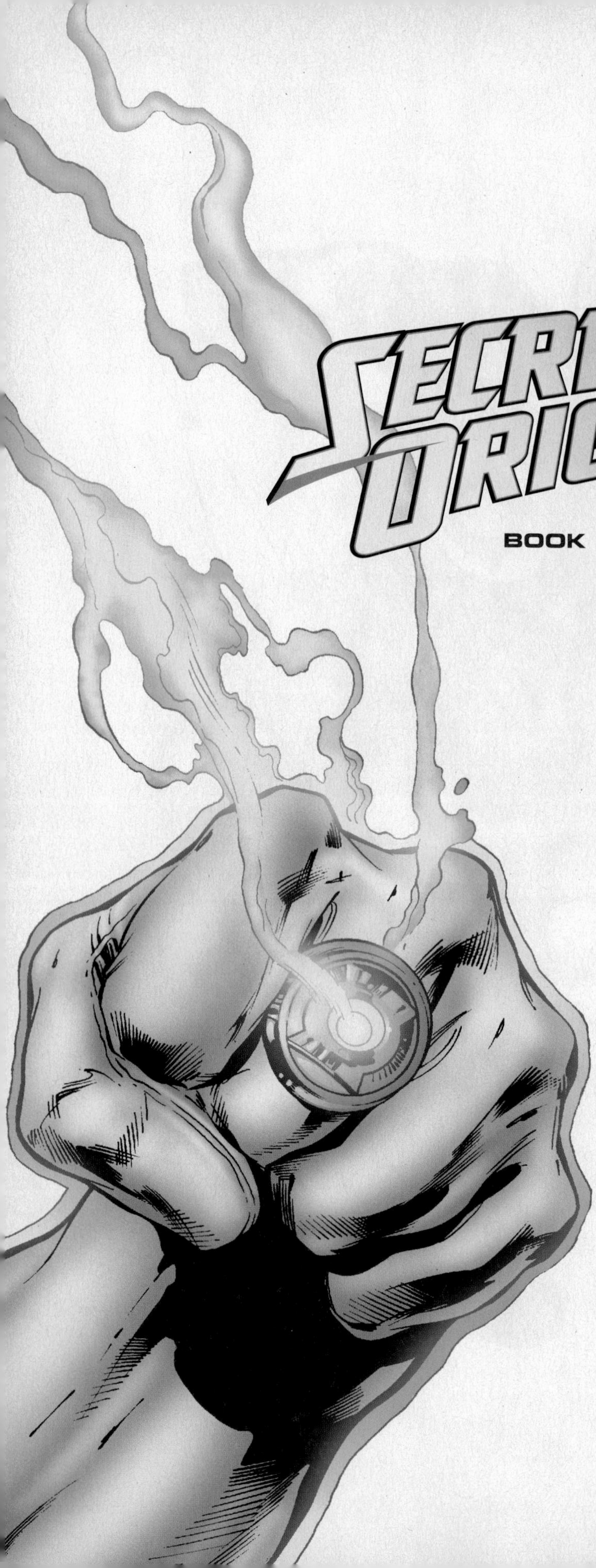

SECRET ORIGIN

BOOK FIVE

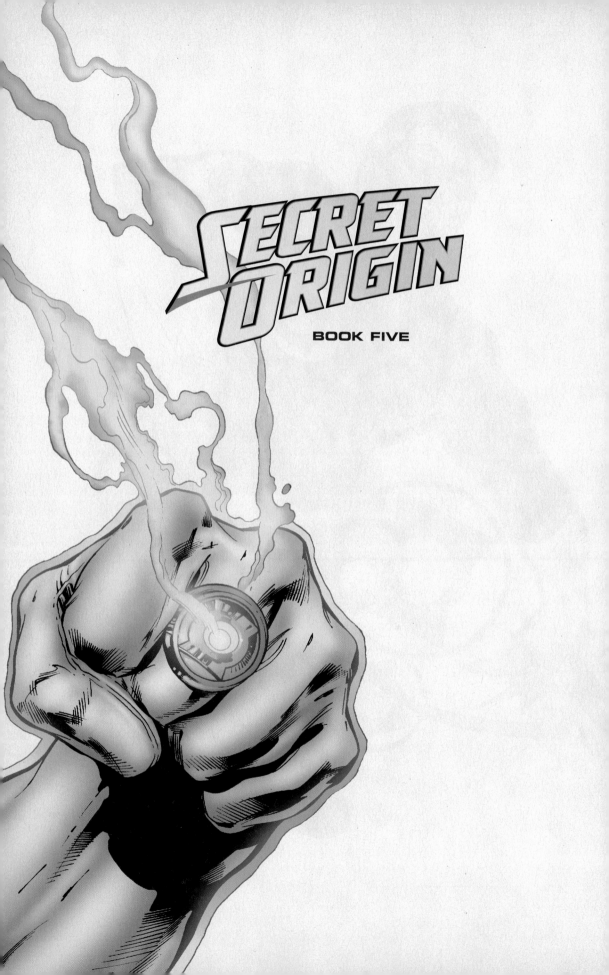

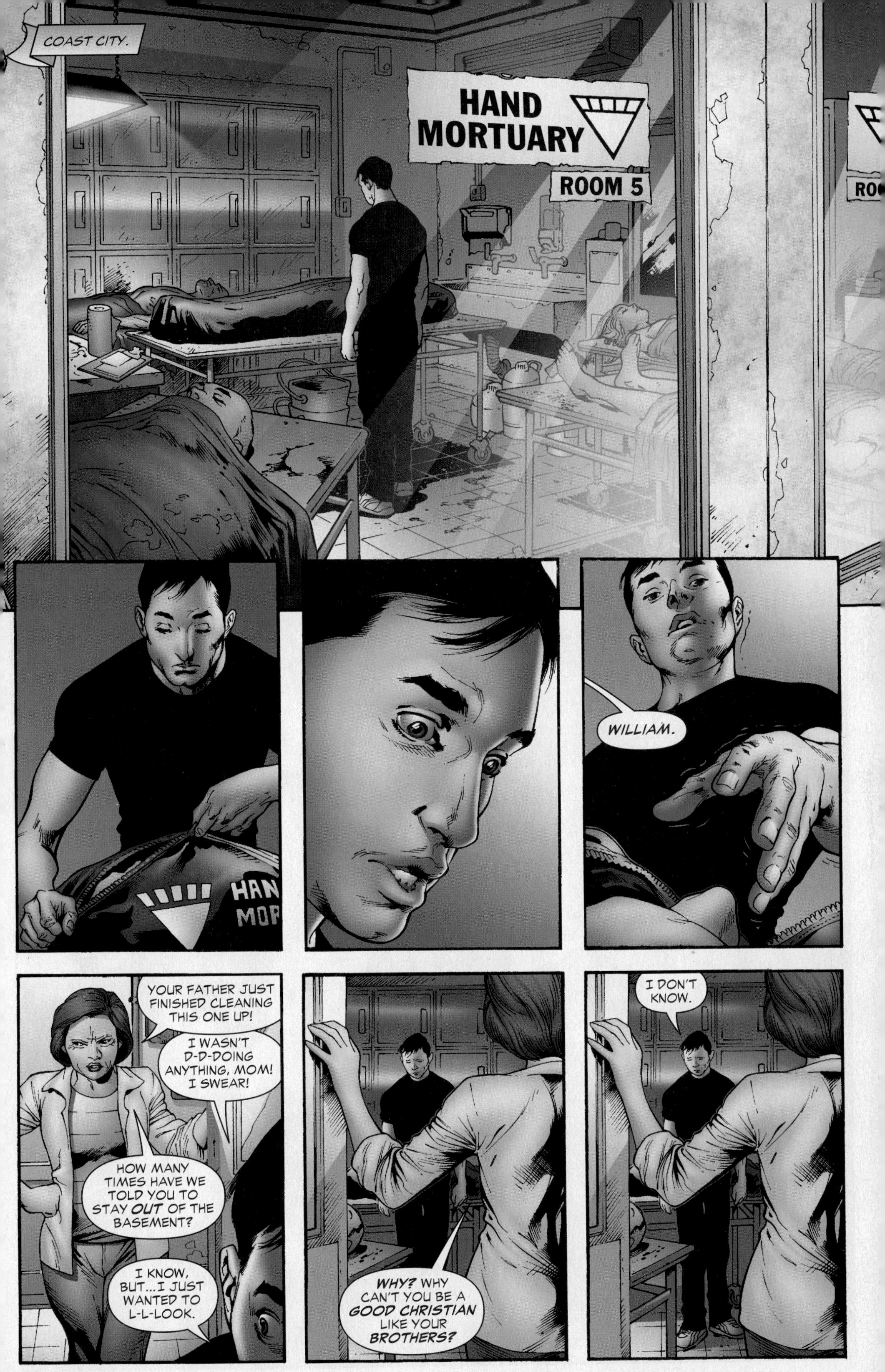
COAST CITY.
HAND MORTUARY
ROOM 5
HAND MOR
WILLIAM.
YOUR FATHER JUST FINISHED CLEANING THIS ONE UP!
I WASN'T D-D-DOING ANYTHING, MOM! I SWEAR!
HOW MANY TIMES HAVE WE TOLD YOU TO STAY OUT OF THE BASEMENT?
I KNOW, BUT...I JUST WANTED TO L-L-LOOK.
WHY? WHY CAN'T YOU BE A GOOD CHRISTIAN LIKE YOUR BROTHERS?
I DON'T KNOW.

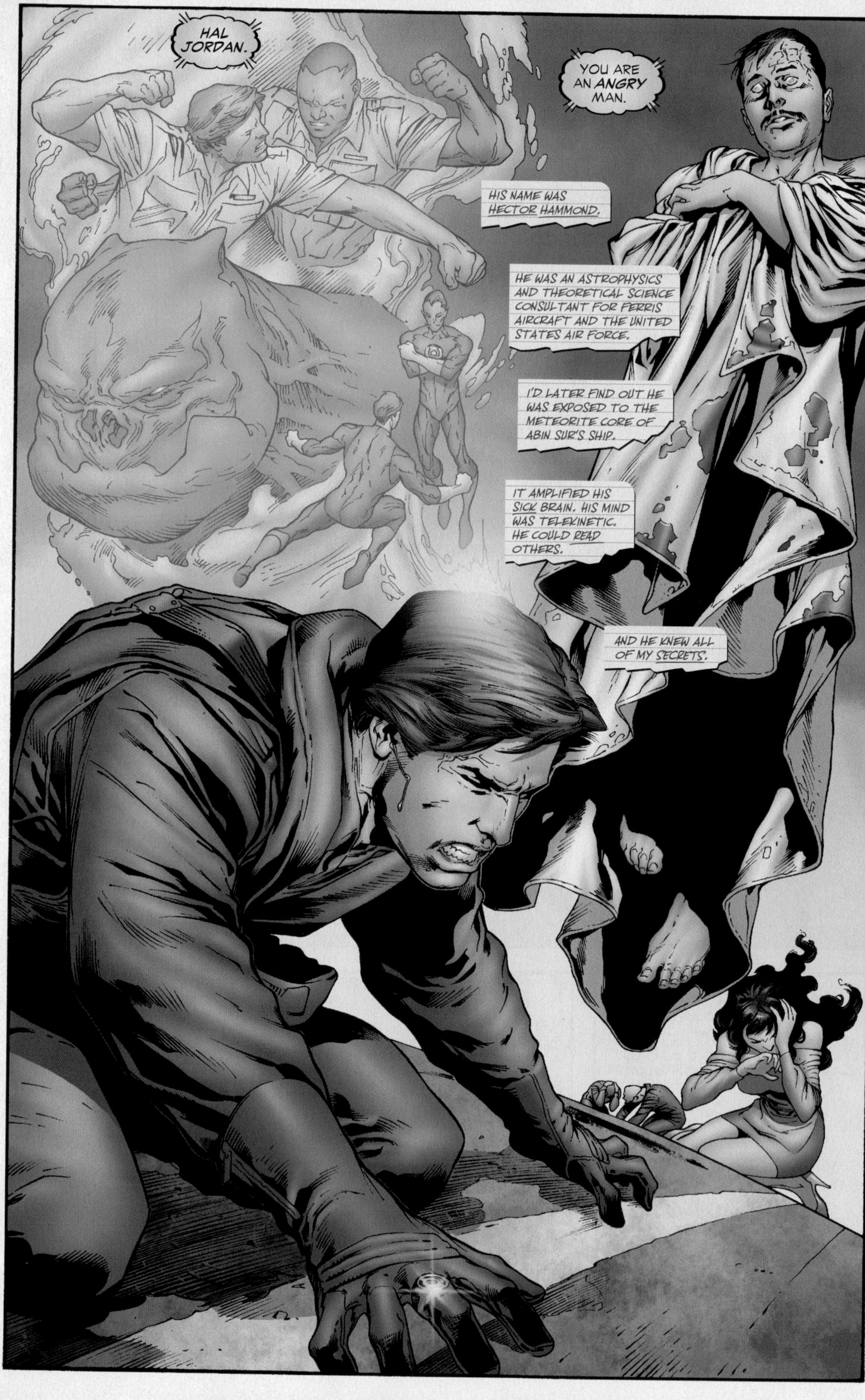
HAL JORDAN.
YOU ARE AN ANGRY MAN.
HIS NAME WAS HECTOR HAMMOND.
HE WAS AN ASTROPHYSICS AND THEORETICAL SCIENCE CONSULTANT FOR FERRIS AIRCRAFT AND THE UNITED STATES AIR FORCE.
I'D LATER FIND OUT HE WAS EXPOSED TO THE METEORITE CORE OF ABIN SUR'S SHIP.
IT AMPLIFIED HIS SICK BRAIN. HIS MIND WAS TELEKINETIC. HE COULD READ OTHERS.
AND HE KNEW ALL OF MY SECRETS.

YOU HAVE MET EXTRA-TERRESTRIALS.

LIFE FAR BEYOND OURS.

THEY GAVE YOU A POWER RING. A BAND OF ENERGY AND WILL.

THEY CALLED IT THE GREATEST WEAPON IN THE UNIVERSE.

THE GREATEST TECHNOLOGY.

HA HA HA HA HA!

GIVE ME THIS EMERALD MIRACLE, HAL JORDAN. GIVE...

...NO.

NO, YOU CAN'T HAVE HER.

NO, CAROL FERRIS IS MINE.

SHE'S MINE!

I DON'T... WANT HER, HAMMOND.

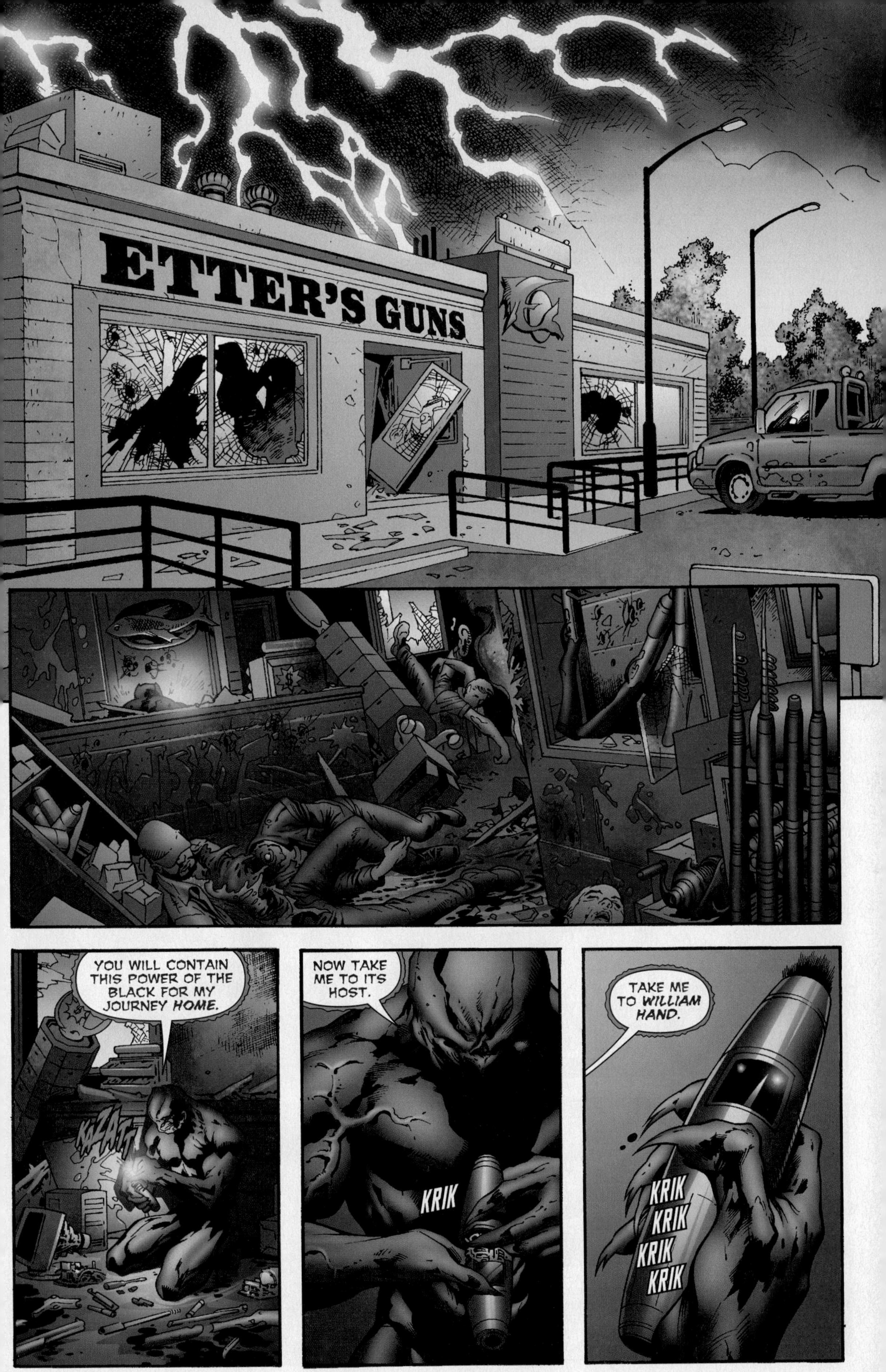
ETTER'S GUNS
YOU WILL CONTAIN THIS POWER OF THE BLACK FOR MY JOURNEY *HOME*.
NOW TAKE ME TO ITS HOST.
KRIK
TAKE ME TO *WILLIAM HAND*.
KRIK
KRIK
KRIK
KRIK

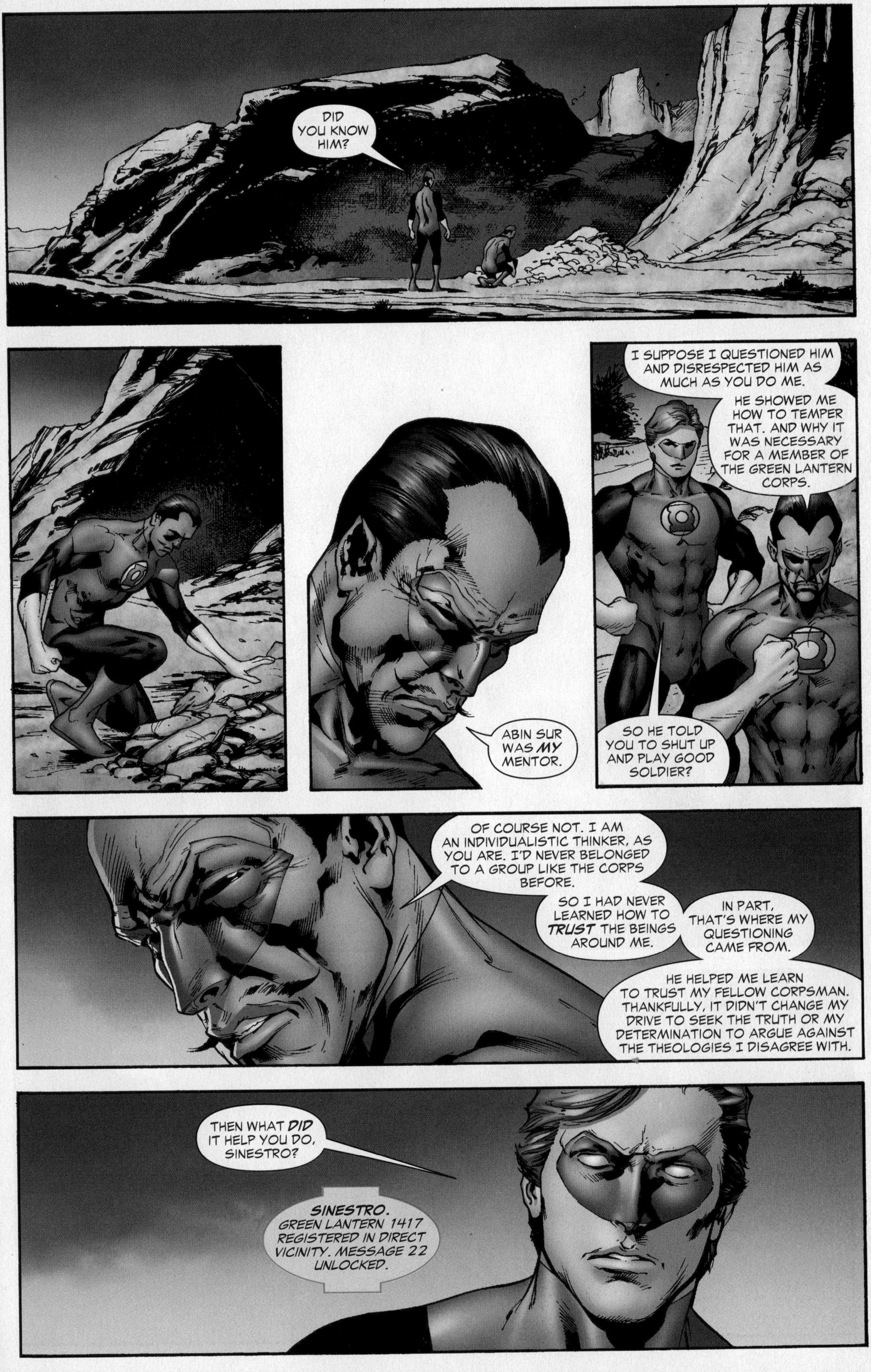
DID YOU KNOW HIM?
ABIN SUR WAS MY MENTOR.
I SUPPOSE I QUESTIONED HIM AND DISRESPECTED HIM AS MUCH AS YOU DO ME.
HE SHOWED ME HOW TO TEMPER THAT. AND WHY IT WAS NECESSARY FOR A MEMBER OF THE GREEN LANTERN CORPS.
SO HE TOLD YOU TO SHUT UP AND PLAY GOOD SOLDIER?
OF COURSE NOT. I AM AN INDIVIDUALISTIC THINKER, AS YOU ARE. I'D NEVER BELONGED TO A GROUP LIKE THE CORPS BEFORE.
SO I HAD NEVER LEARNED HOW TO TRUST THE BEINGS AROUND ME.
IN PART, THAT'S WHERE MY QUESTIONING CAME FROM.
HE HELPED ME LEARN TO TRUST MY FELLOW CORPSMAN. THANKFULLY, IT DIDN'T CHANGE MY DRIVE TO SEEK THE TRUTH OR MY DETERMINATION TO ARGUE AGAINST THE THEOLOGIES I DISAGREE WITH.
THEN WHAT DID IT HELP YOU DO, SINESTRO?
SINESTRO. GREEN LANTERN 1417 REGISTERED IN DIRECT VICINITY. MESSAGE 22 UNLOCKED.

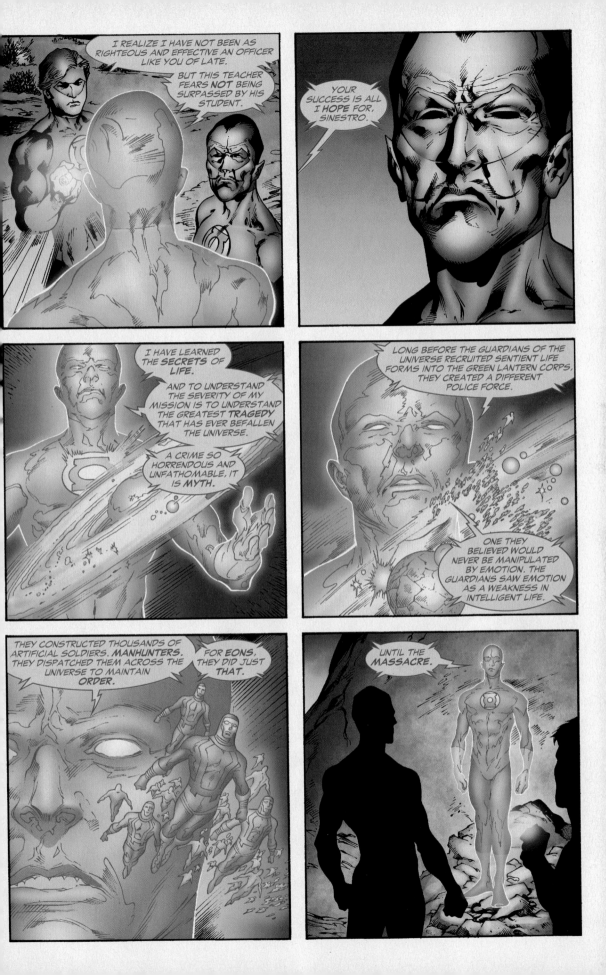

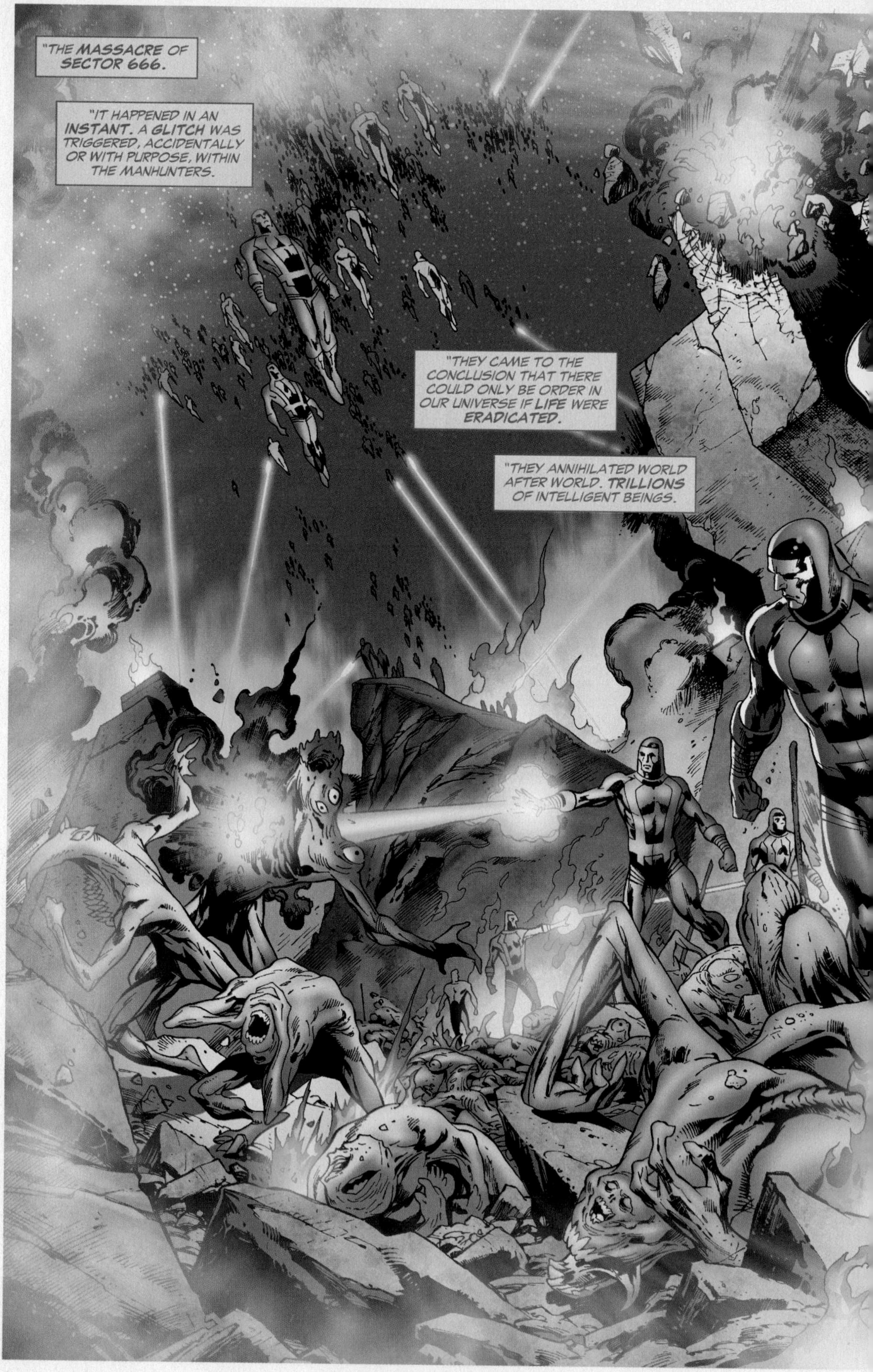
"THE MASSACRE OF SECTOR 666.
"IT HAPPENED IN AN INSTANT. A GLITCH WAS TRIGGERED, ACCIDENTALLY OR WITH PURPOSE, WITHIN THE MANHUNTERS.
"THEY CAME TO THE CONCLUSION THAT THERE COULD ONLY BE ORDER IN OUR UNIVERSE IF LIFE WERE ERADICATED.
"THEY ANNIHILATED WORLD AFTER WORLD. TRILLIONS OF INTELLIGENT BEINGS.

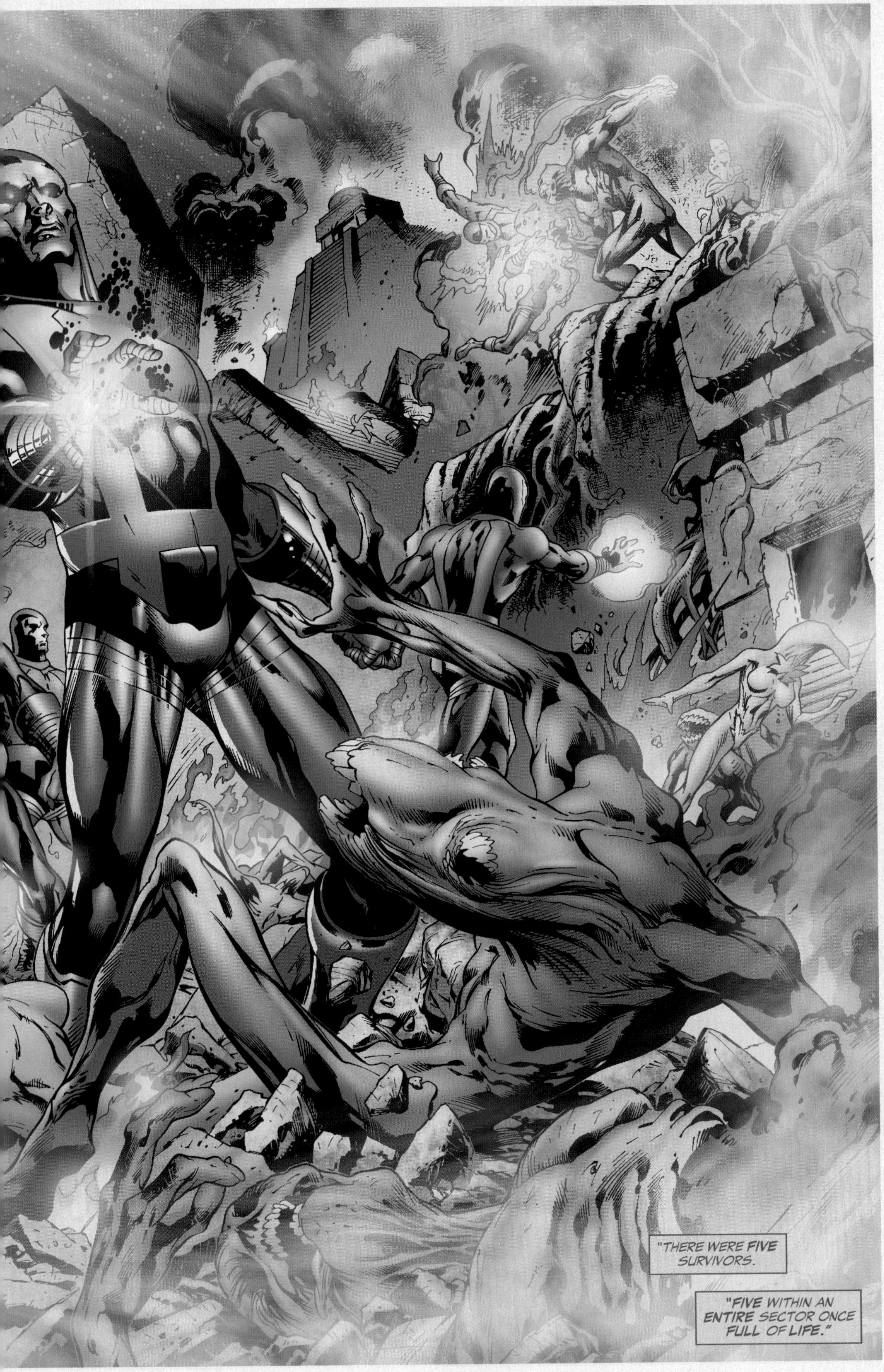
"THERE WERE FIVE SURVIVORS.
"FIVE WITHIN AN ENTIRE SECTOR ONCE FULL OF LIFE."

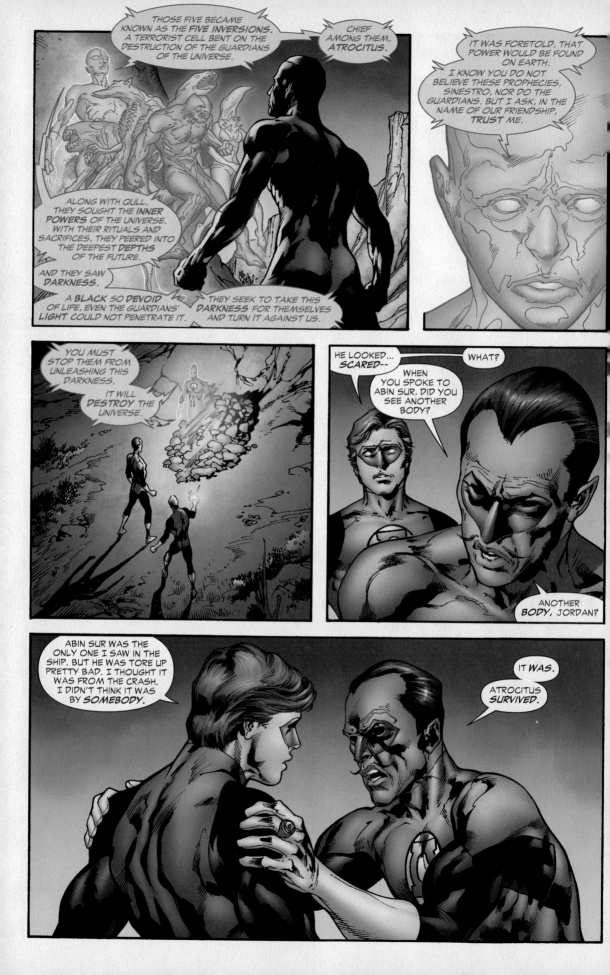

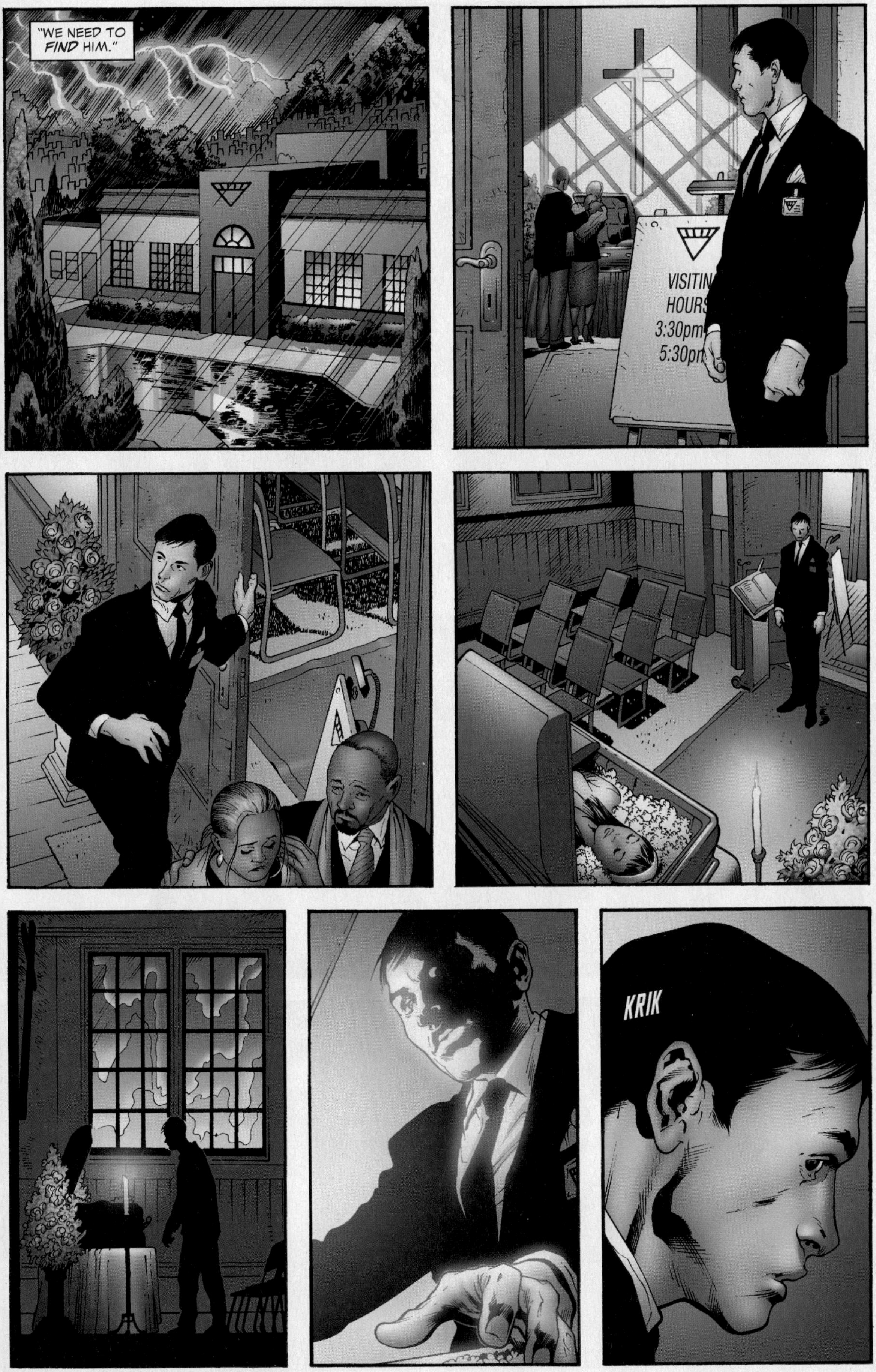
"WE NEED TO FIND HIM."
VISITIN HOURS 3:30pm 5:30pm
KRIK

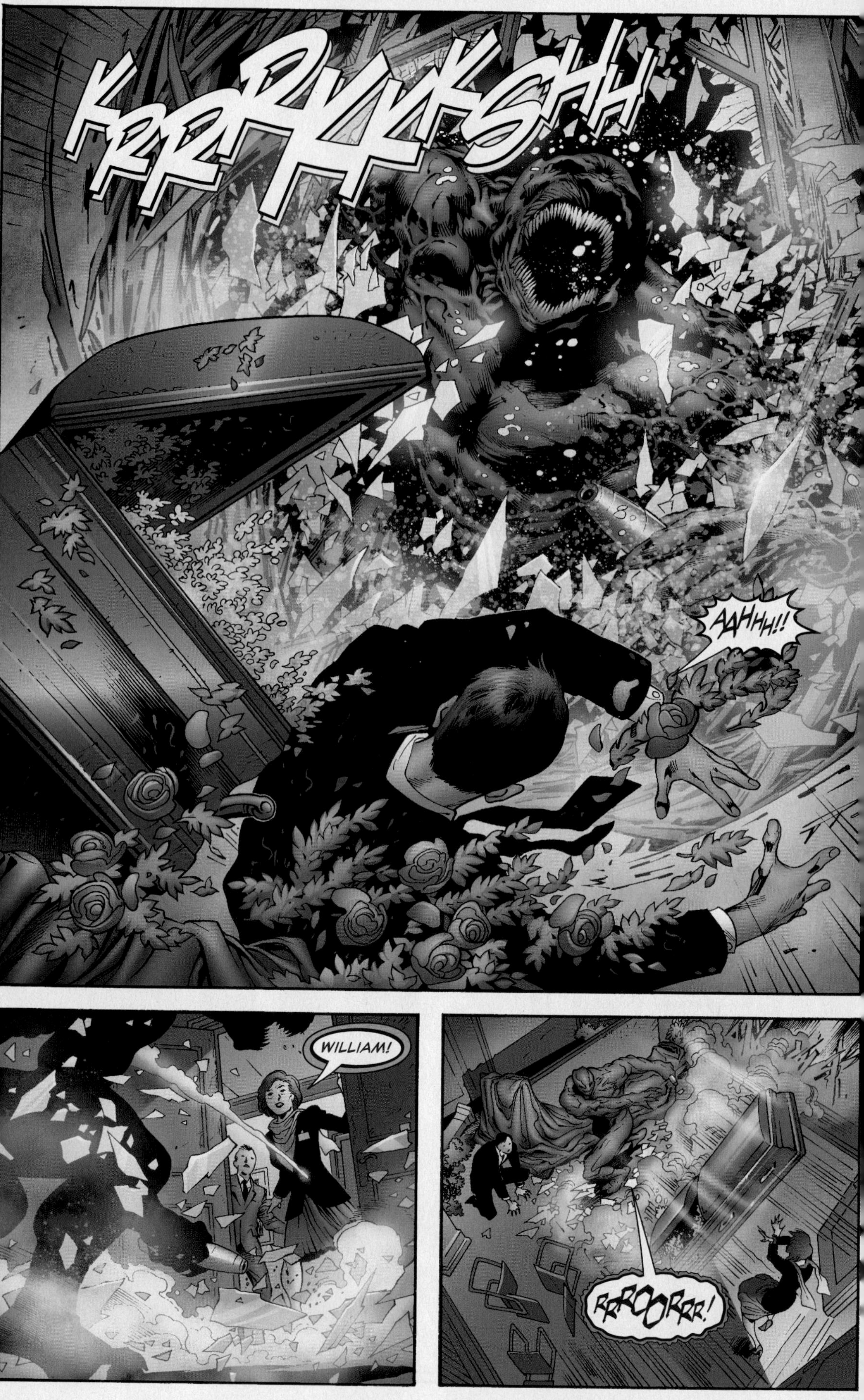
KRRRKKSHH
AAHHH!!
WILLIAM!
RRROORRR!

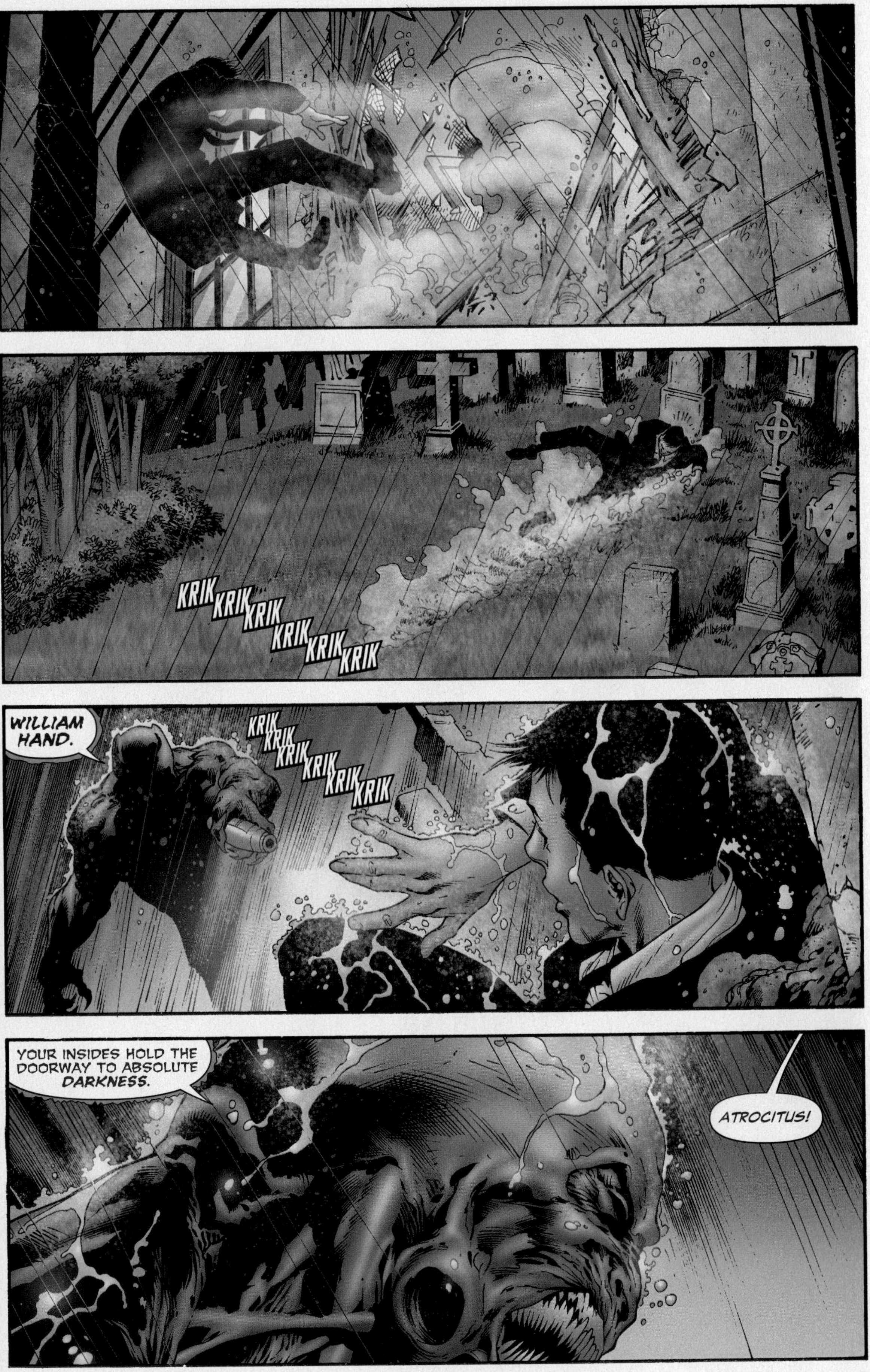
KRIK KRIK KRIK KRIK KRIK KRIK
WILLIAM HAND.
KRIK KRIK KRIK KRIK KRIK KRIK
YOUR INSIDES HOLD THE DOORWAY TO ABSOLUTE DARKNESS.
ATROCITUS!

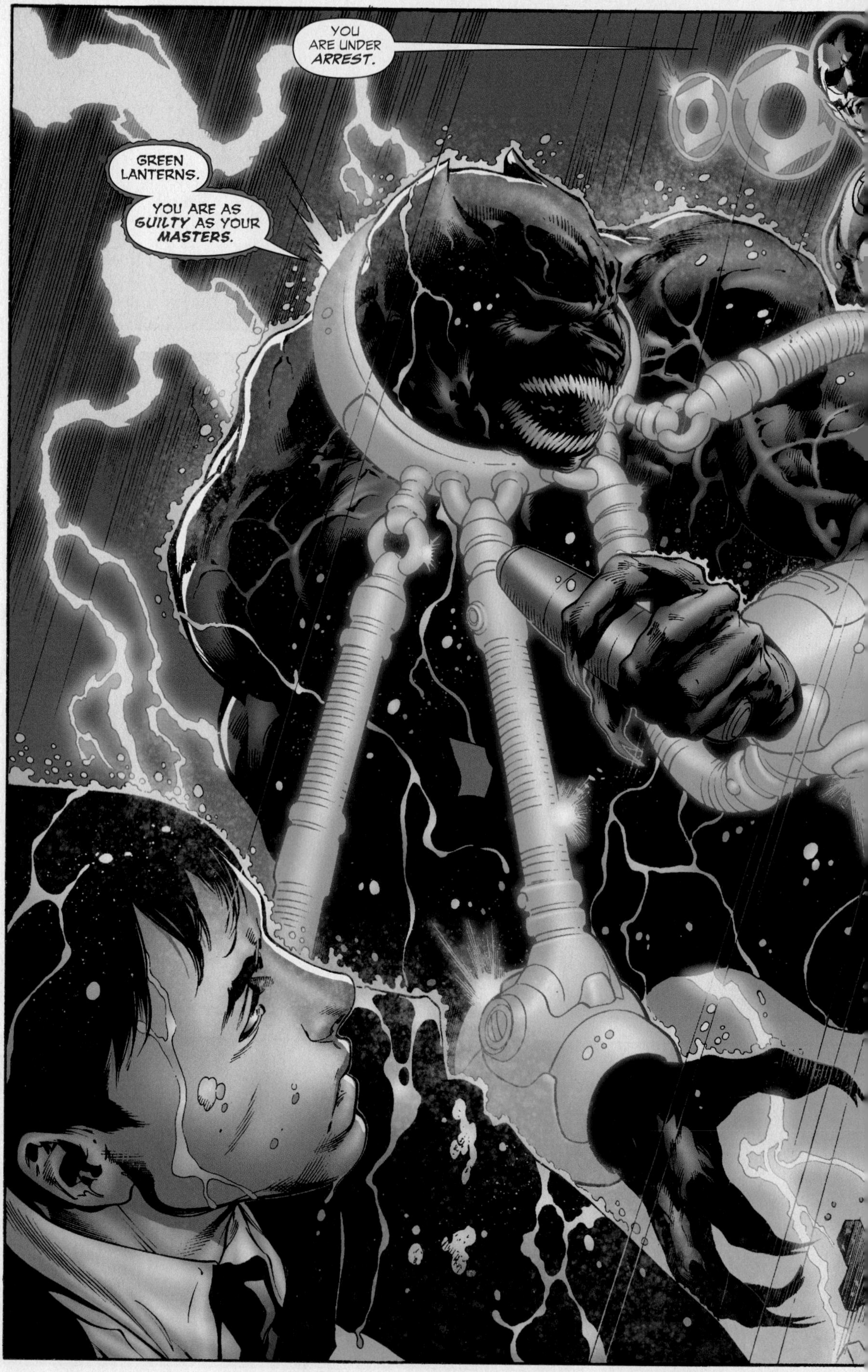
YOU ARE UNDER ARREST.
GREEN LANTERNS.
YOU ARE AS GUILTY AS YOUR MASTERS.

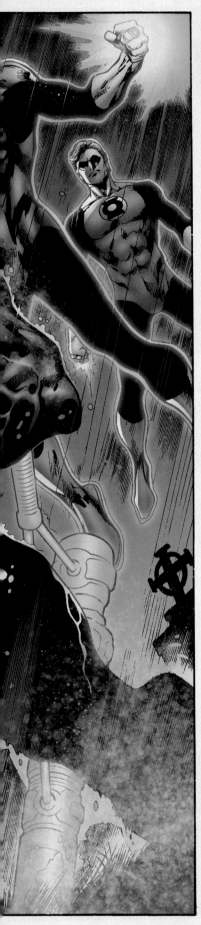

FEEL MY **RAGE.**

KID! GET OUT OF HERE!

RUN, DAMMIT!

NNGGFF!

WARNING. POWER LEVELS DEPLETING.

POWER LEVELS AT 38.7%

SINESTRO? WHAT'S... HAPPENING?

HE'S BUILT A COSMIC **DIVINING ROD.**

IT CAN **LOCATE** POWER--

--AND IT CAN **TAKE** IT.

WARNING. POWER LEVELS APPROACHING 0.0%

GET ON YOUR **FEET,** JORDAN.

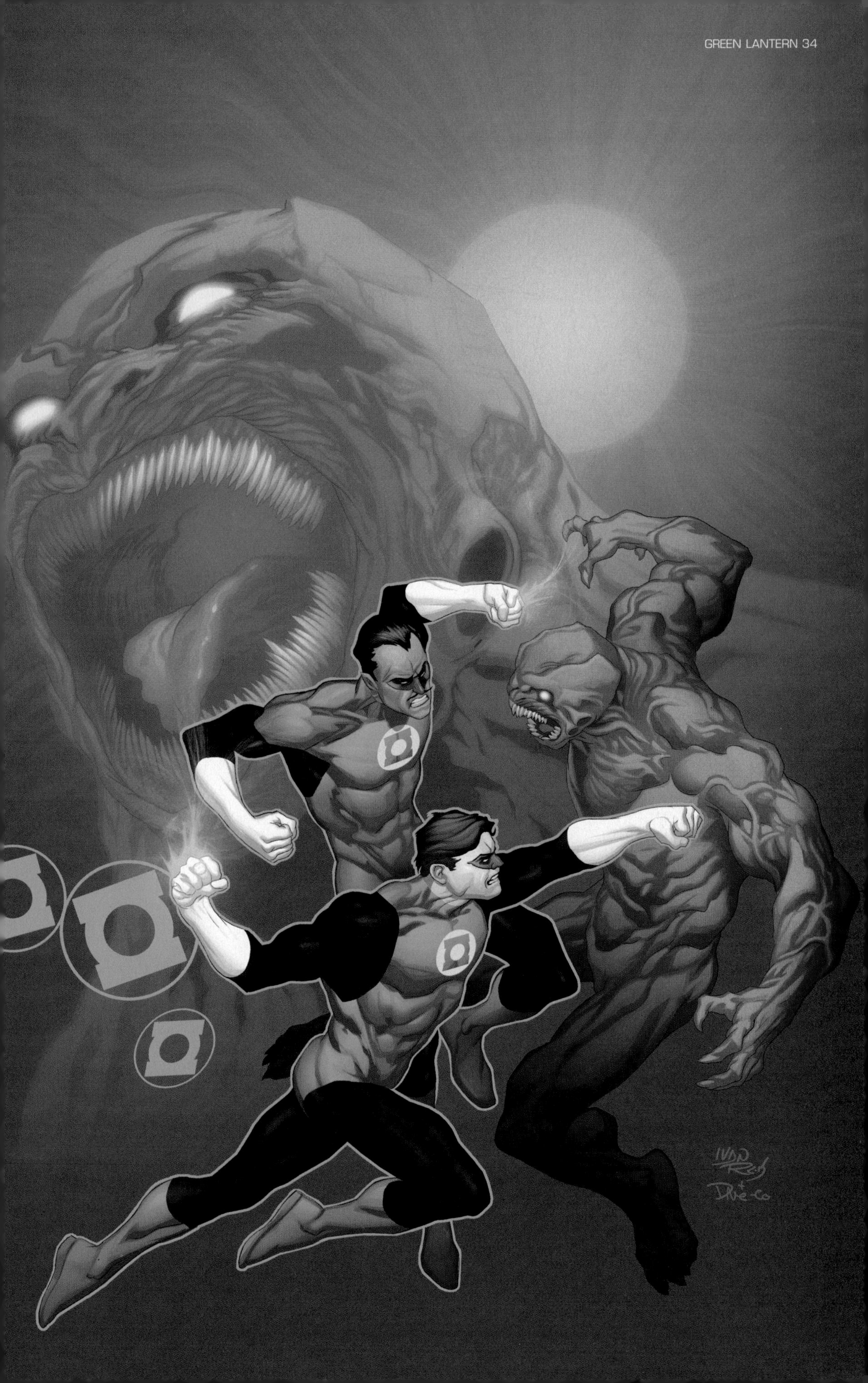

SECRET ORIGIN

BOOK SIX

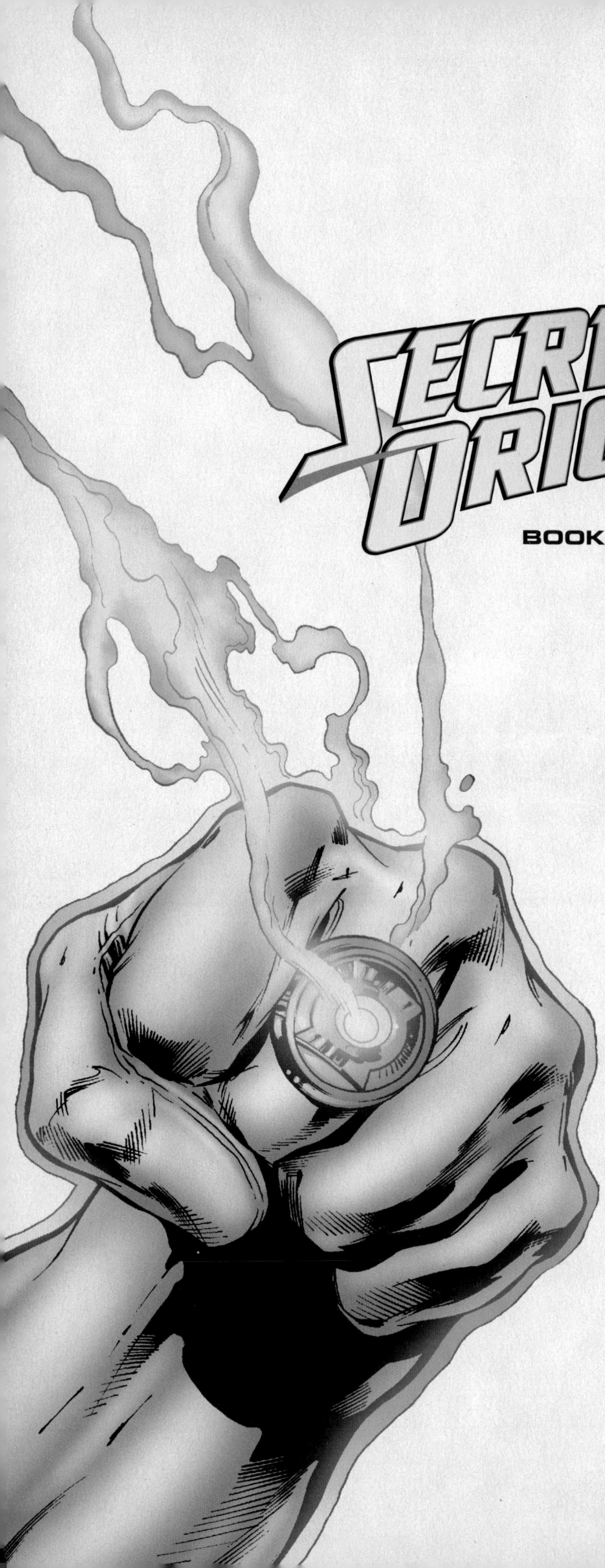

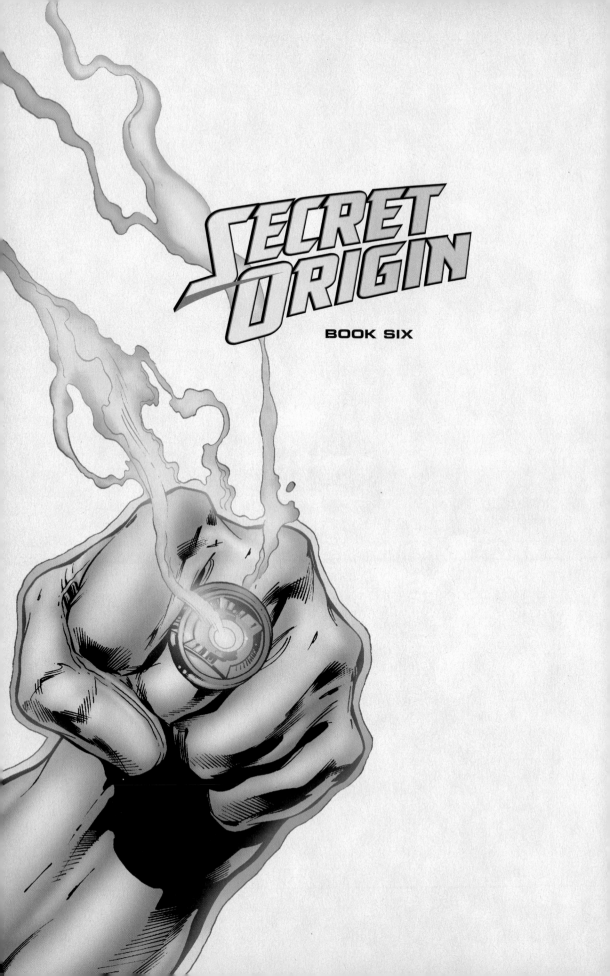

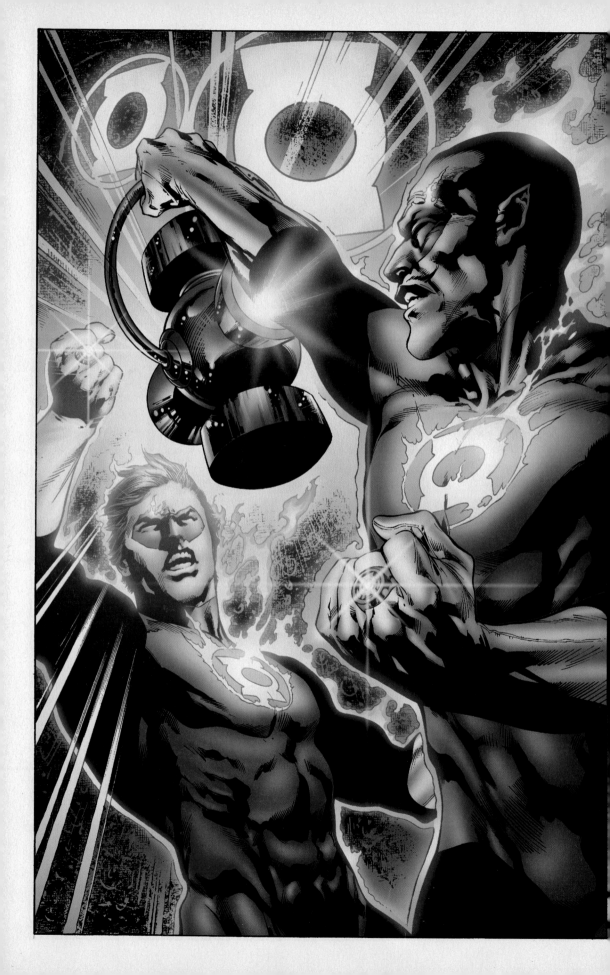

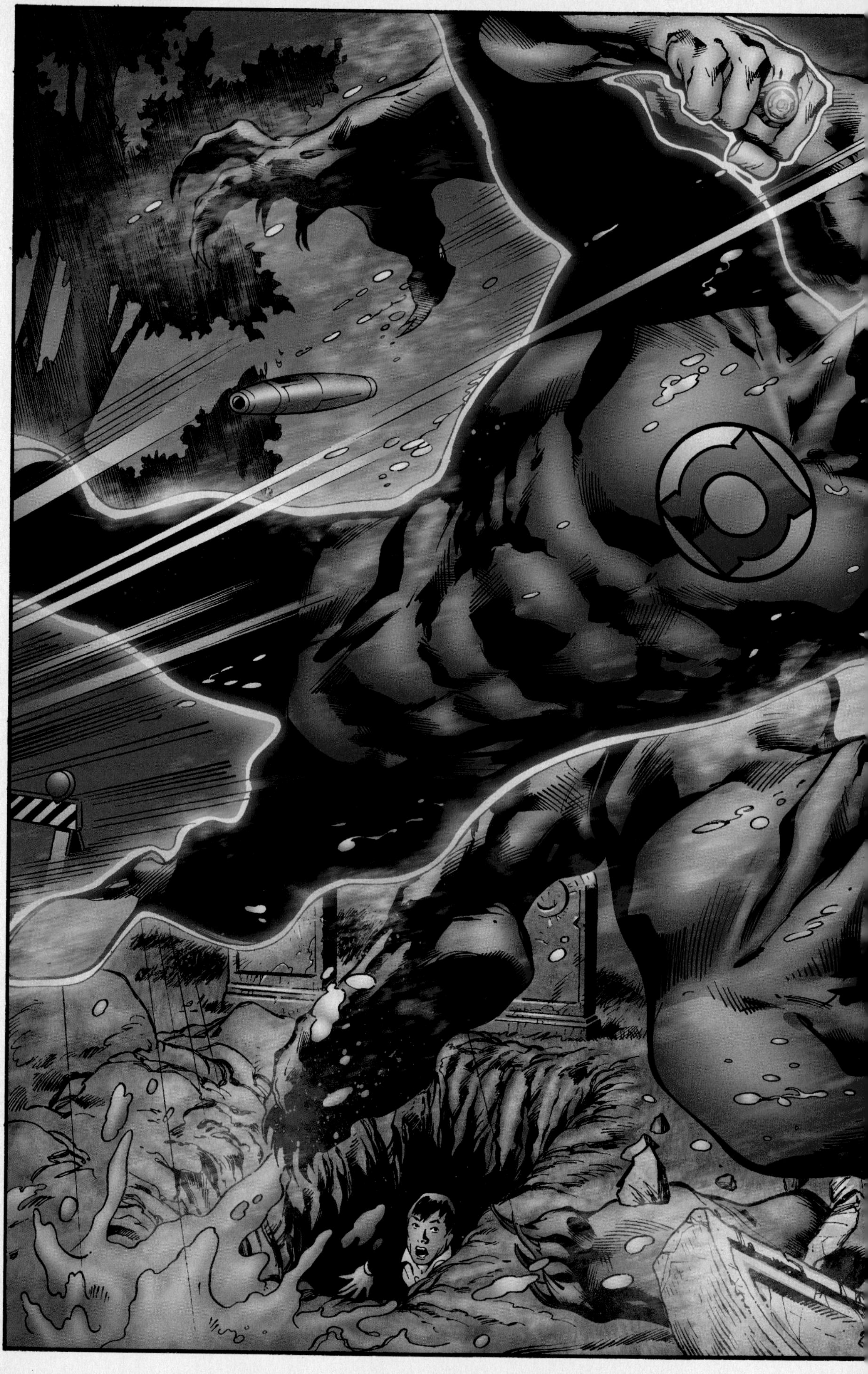

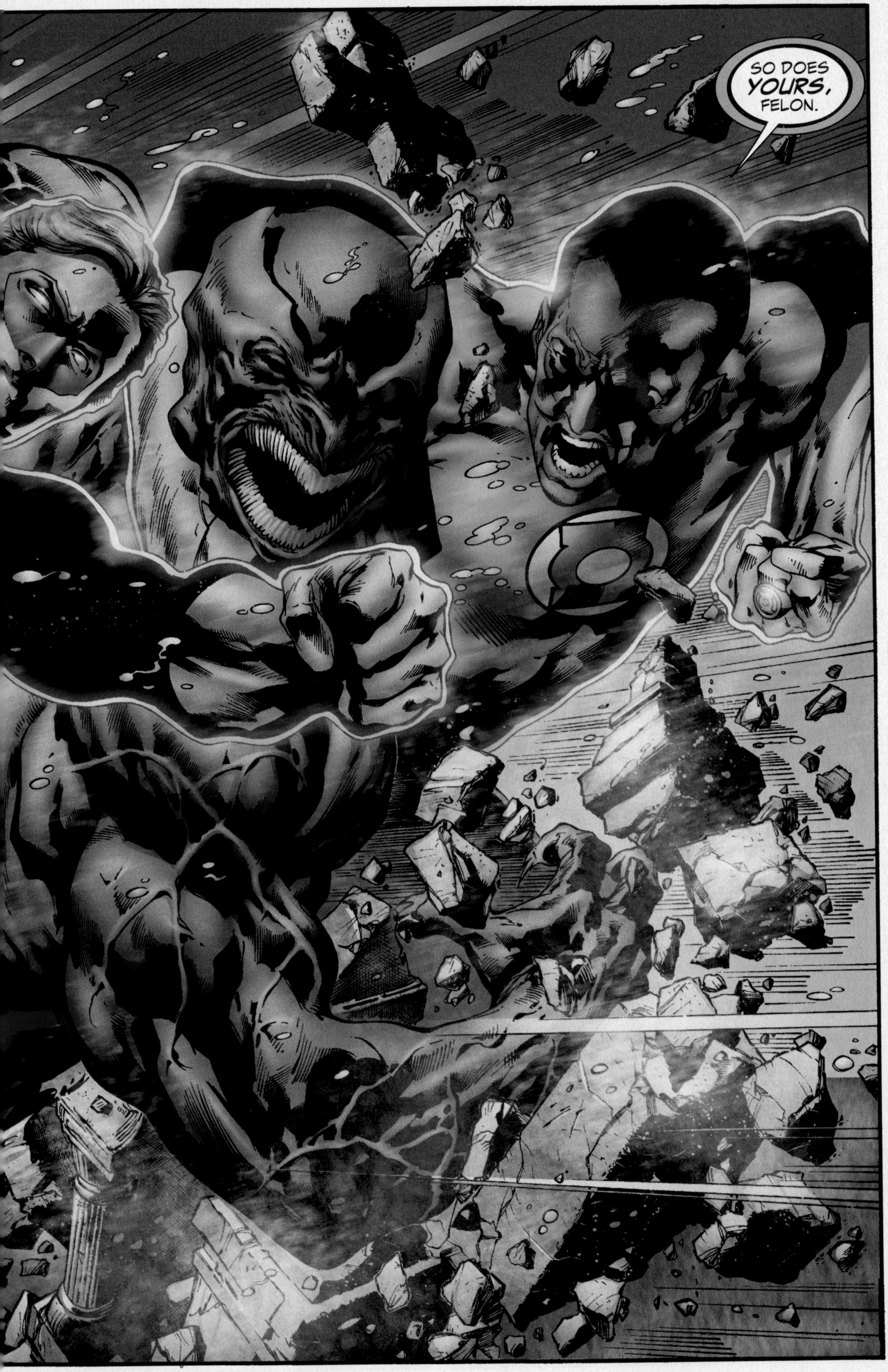
SO DOES YOURS, FELON.

OUR PROPHECIES SAY YOU ARE THE *GREATEST* OF THEM ALL.

THEY SAY IF *ANYONE* IS TO OPPOSE OUR *REVENGE*, IT IS *YOU*.

NN...

BUT THEY ALSO SAY YOU HAVE A *WEAKNESS*.

LIKE *ALL* OF THE GUARDIANS' TERRORISTS.

I WILL BATHE IN YOUR BLOOD, *"GREAT ONE."*

NO!

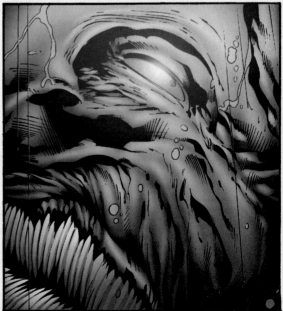

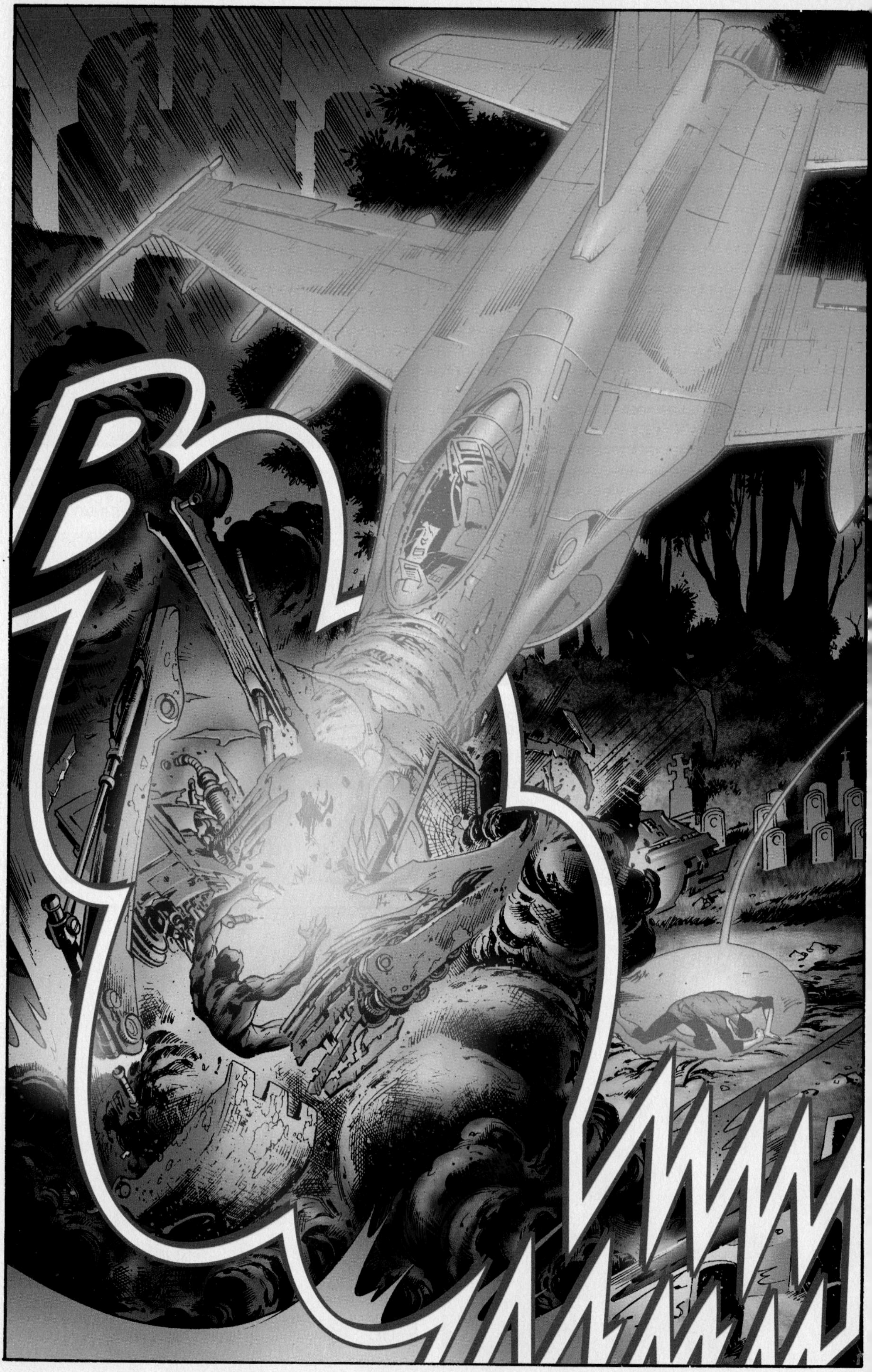

YELLOW...?

...THAT WAS...NOT POSSIBLE...

YOU KNOW MY NAME, ATROCITUS?

GOOD.

TELL THE OTHER *FOUR* OF THE *INVERSIONS* WHO THEY HAVE TO *FEAR*.

GHOOOOMMM

SINESTRO. THE *GREATEST* GREEN LANTERN OF THEM *ALL*.

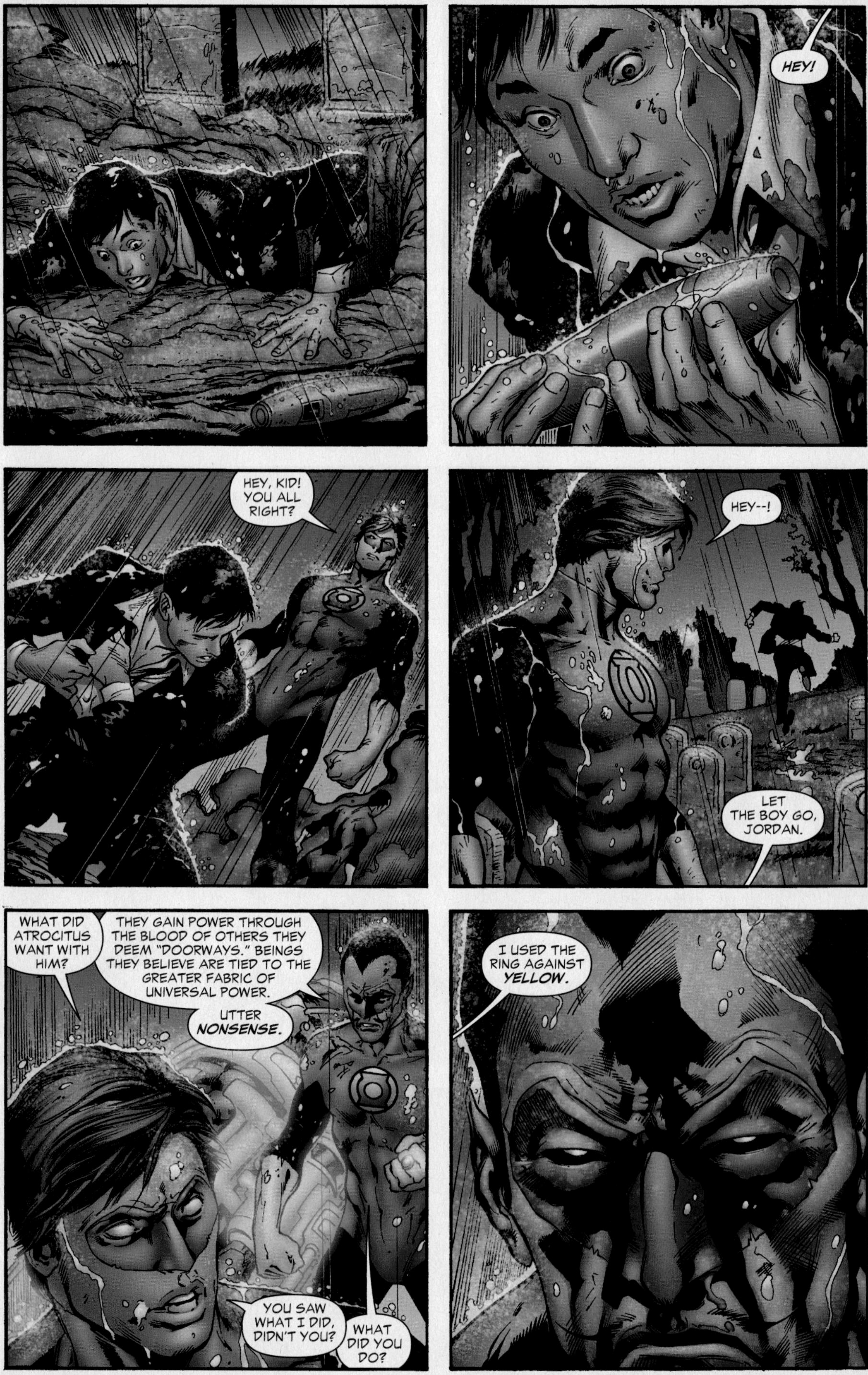
HEY!
HEY, KID! YOU ALL RIGHT?
HEY--!
LET THE BOY GO, JORDAN.
WHAT DID ATROCITUS WANT WITH HIM?
THEY GAIN POWER THROUGH THE BLOOD OF OTHERS THEY DEEM "DOORWAYS." BEINGS THEY BELIEVE ARE TIED TO THE GREATER FABRIC OF UNIVERSAL POWER.
UTTER NONSENSE.
YOU SAW WHAT I DID, DIDN'T YOU?
WHAT DID YOU DO?
I USED THE RING AGAINST YELLOW.

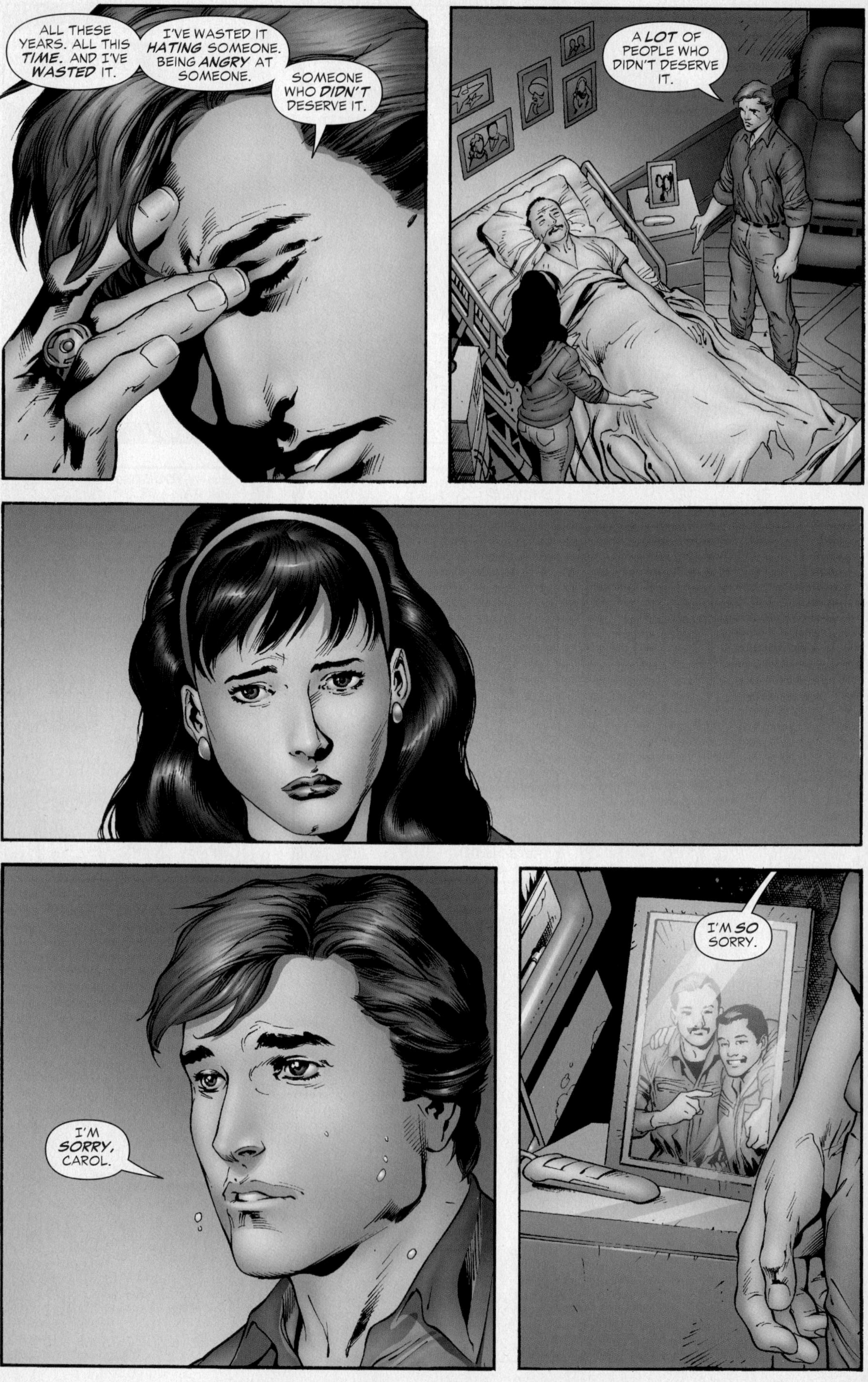
ALL THESE YEARS. ALL THIS TIME. AND I'VE WASTED IT.
I'VE WASTED IT HATING SOMEONE. BEING ANGRY AT SOMEONE.
SOMEONE WHO DIDN'T DESERVE IT.
A LOT OF PEOPLE WHO DIDN'T DESERVE IT.
I'M SORRY, CAROL.
I'M SO SORRY.

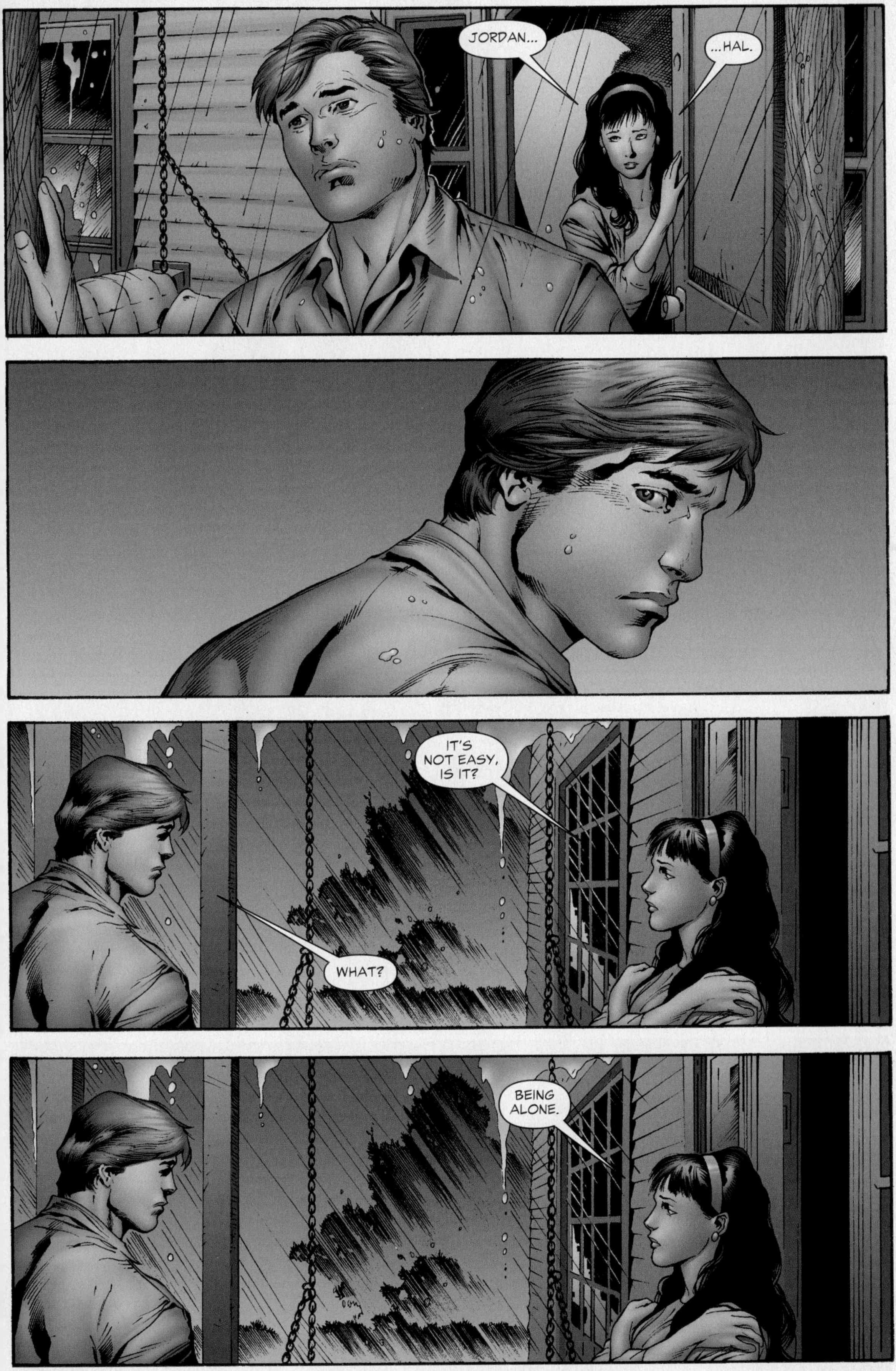
JORDAN...
...HAL.
IT'S NOT EASY, IS IT?
WHAT?
BEING ALONE.

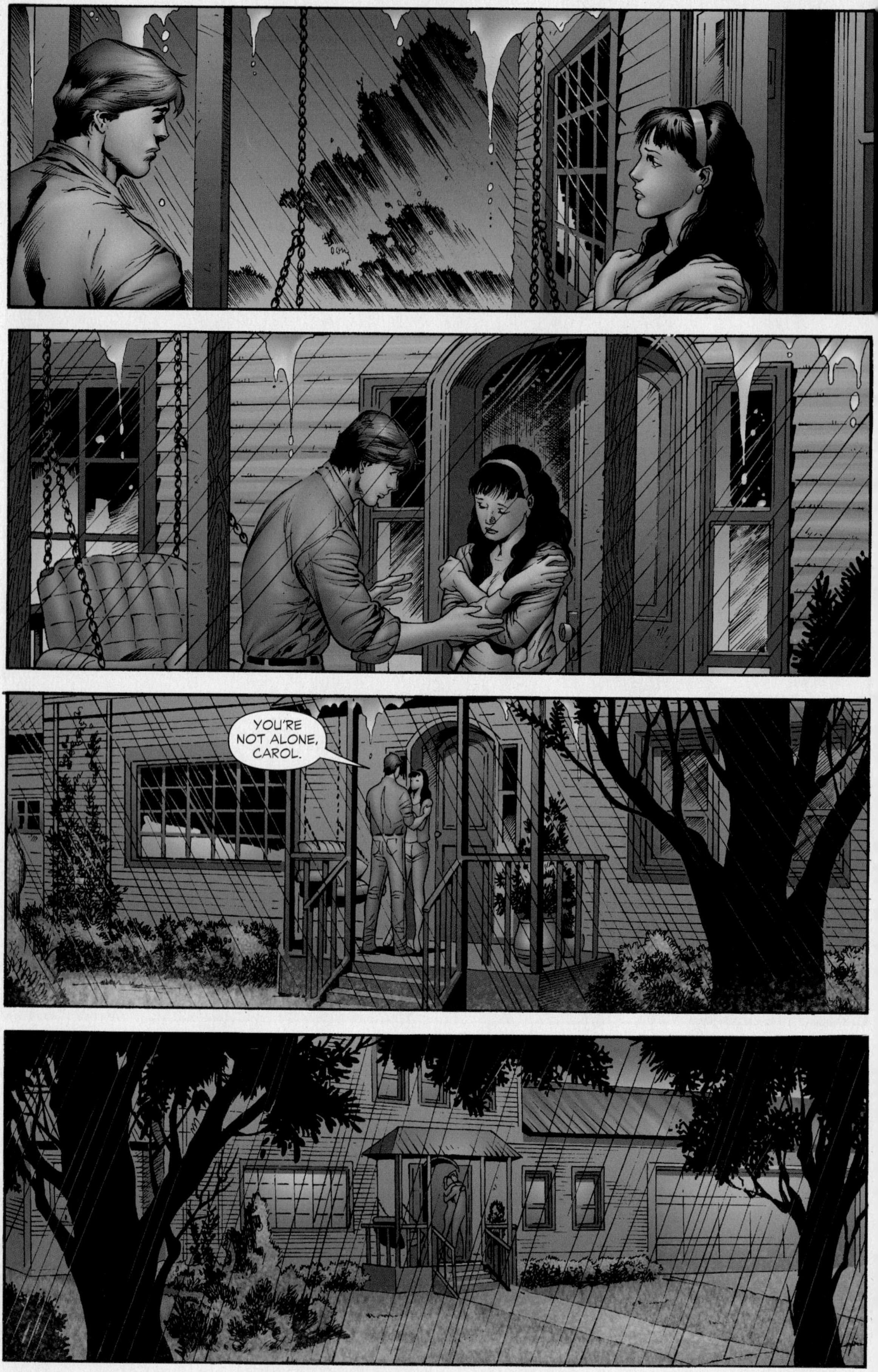
YOU'RE NOT ALONE, CAROL.

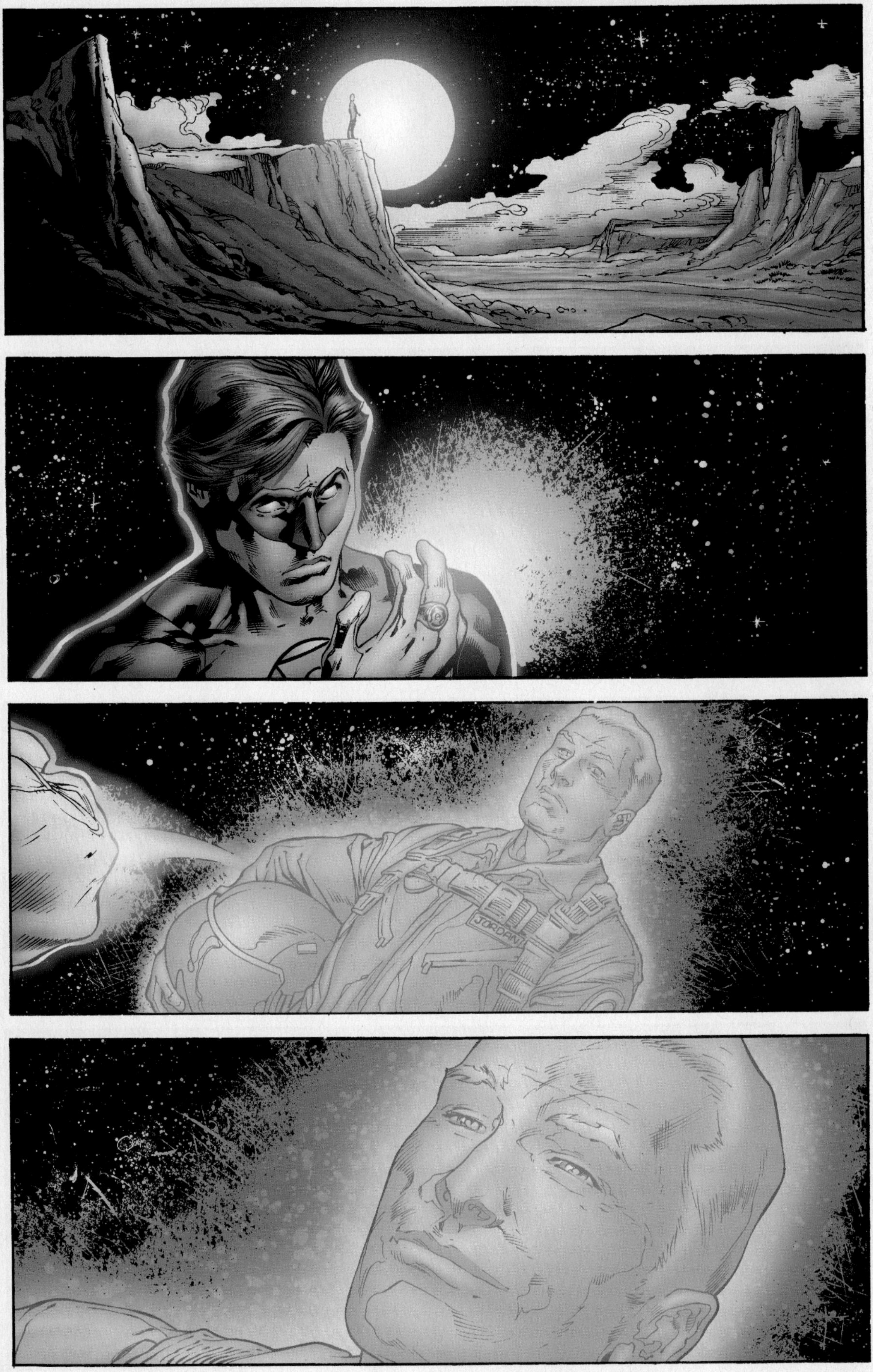
JORDAN

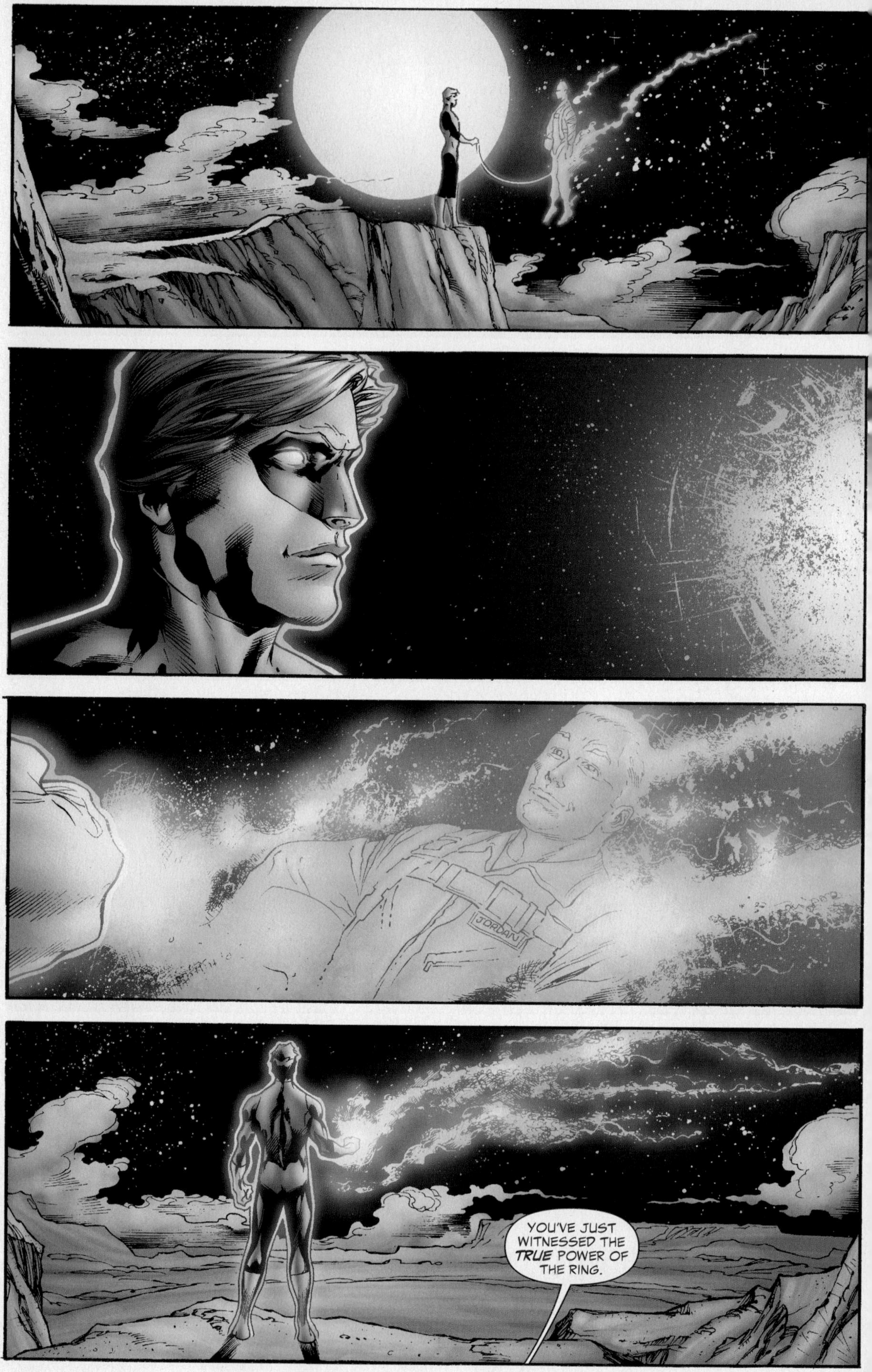
YOU'VE JUST WITNESSED THE *TRUE* POWER OF THE RING.

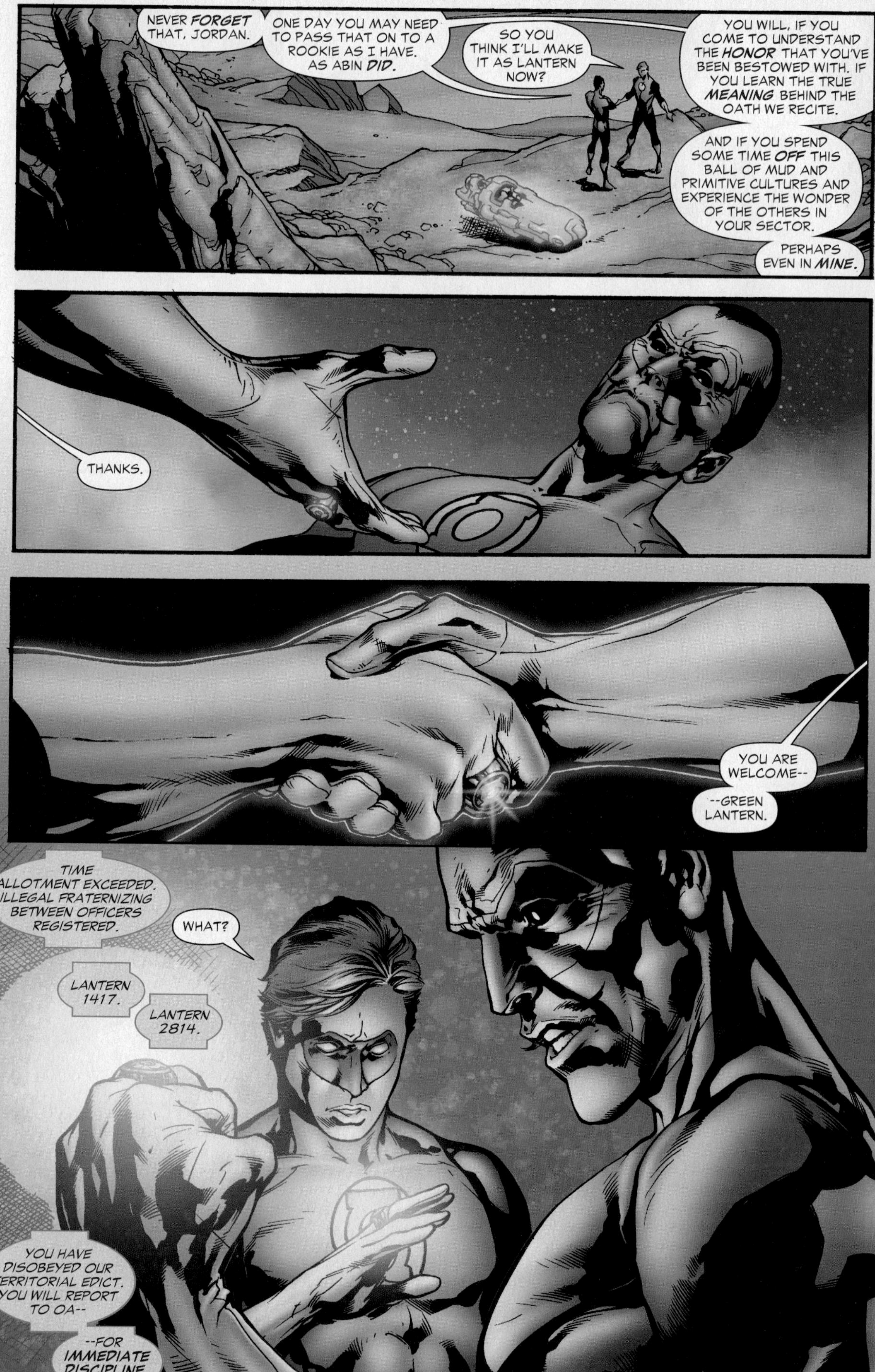
NEVER FORGET THAT, JORDAN.
ONE DAY YOU MAY NEED TO PASS THAT ON TO A ROOKIE AS I HAVE. AS ABIN DID.
SO YOU THINK I'LL MAKE IT AS LANTERN NOW?
YOU WILL, IF YOU COME TO UNDERSTAND THE HONOR THAT YOU'VE BEEN BESTOWED WITH. IF YOU LEARN THE TRUE MEANING BEHIND THE OATH WE RECITE.
AND IF YOU SPEND SOME TIME OFF THIS BALL OF MUD AND PRIMITIVE CULTURES AND EXPERIENCE THE WONDER OF THE OTHERS IN YOUR SECTOR.
PERHAPS EVEN IN MINE.
THANKS.
YOU ARE WELCOME--
--GREEN LANTERN.
TIME ALLOTMENT EXCEEDED. ILLEGAL FRATERNIZING BETWEEN OFFICERS REGISTERED.
WHAT?
LANTERN 1417.
LANTERN 2814.
YOU HAVE DISOBEYED OUR TERRITORIAL EDICT. YOU WILL REPORT TO OA--
--FOR IMMEDIATE DISCIPLINE.

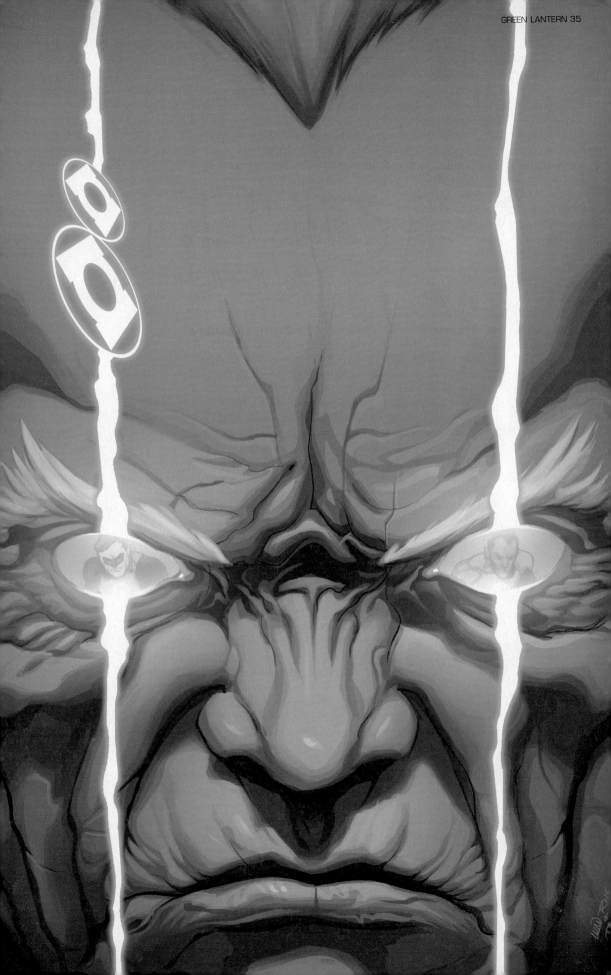

SECRET ORIGIN

BOOK SEVEN

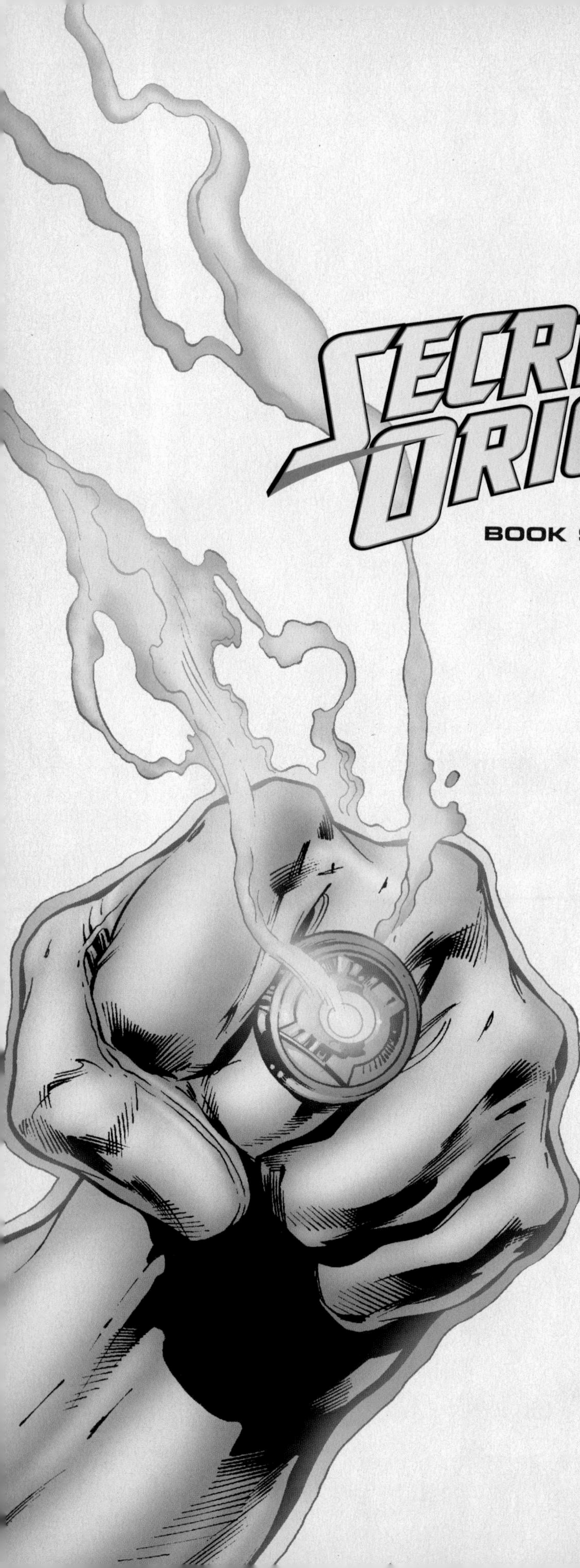

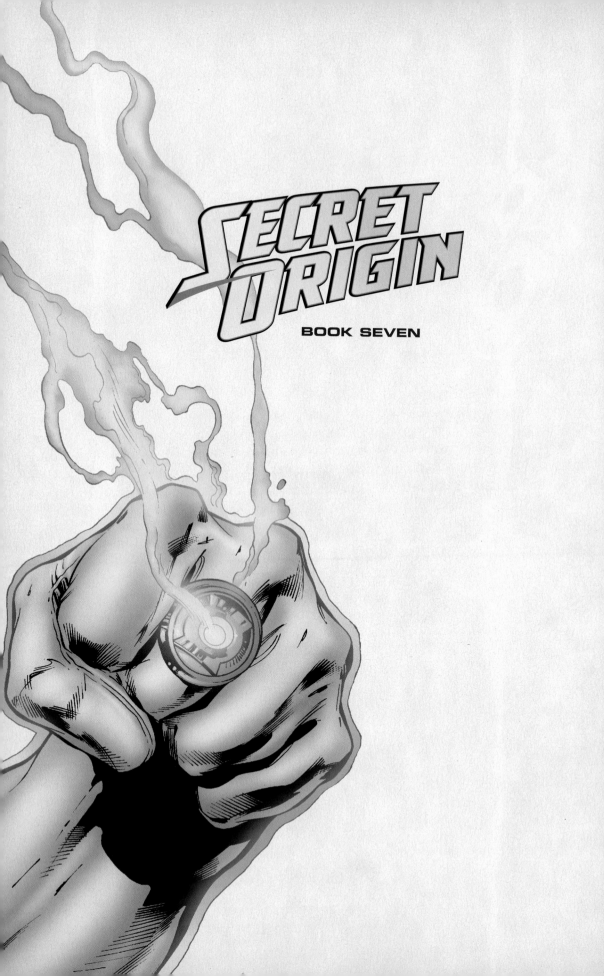

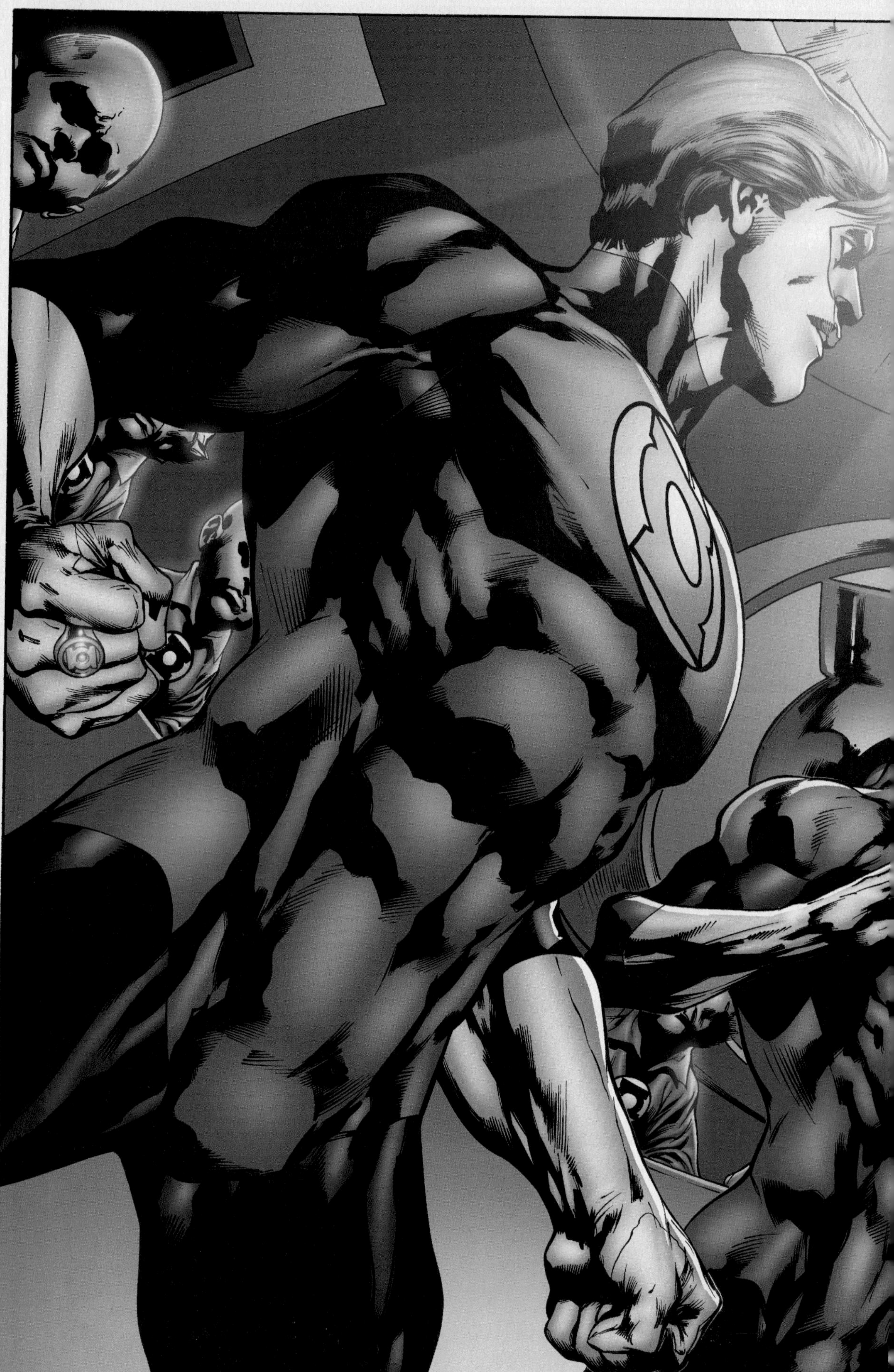

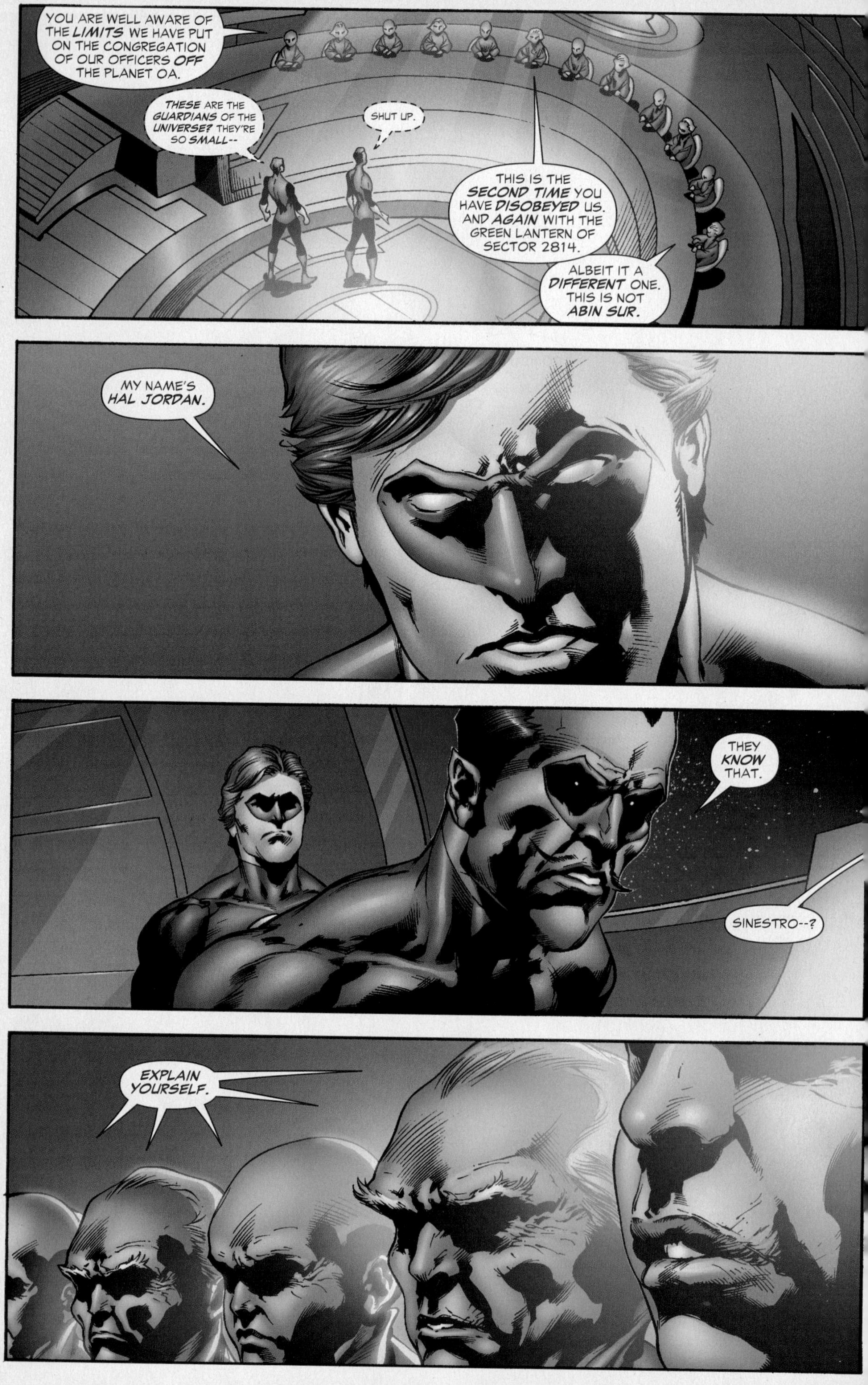
YOU ARE WELL AWARE OF THE LIMITS WE HAVE PUT ON THE CONGREGATION OF OUR OFFICERS OFF THE PLANET OA.
THESE ARE THE GUARDIANS OF THE UNIVERSE? THEY'RE SO SMALL--
SHUT UP.
THIS IS THE SECOND TIME YOU HAVE DISOBEYED US. AND AGAIN WITH THE GREEN LANTERN OF SECTOR 2814.
ALBEIT IT A DIFFERENT ONE. THIS IS NOT ABIN SUR.
MY NAME'S HAL JORDAN.
THEY KNOW THAT.
SINESTRO--?
EXPLAIN YOURSELF.

I WAS SIMPLY ASSISTING THIS OFFICER IN *LOCATING* AND *ARRESTING* THE *KILLER* WHO ENDED THE LIFE OF ABIN SUR.

ATROCITUS OF THE FIVE INVERSIONS.

AND BEFORE YOU SO *ARROGANTLY* RIPPED ME AWAY FROM THAT BACKWARDS BALL OF *DIRT*, I HAD HIM IN *CUSTODY*.

WE ARE WELL *AWARE*.

ATROCITUS WAS *TETHERED* TO YOUR RING.

THIS *TERRORIST* WILL BE RETURNED TO YSMAULT WHERE HE WILL CONTINUE HIS *SENTENCE*--

--AN *ETERNITY* OF IMPRISONMENT.

HOWEVER, THIS ARREST DOES NOT *EXCUSE YOU* FROM BREAKING OUR TERRITORIAL EDICT, SINESTRO.

GREEN LANTERNS MUST ONLY OPERATE IN THEIR *RESPECTIVE* SECTORS. THEY MUST PATROL *INDEPENDENTLY*. THEY MUST *FLY* ON THEIR OWN--

WHY?

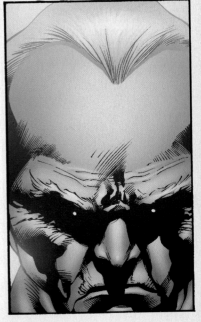

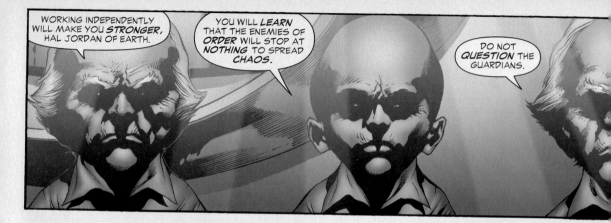

WORKING INDEPENDENTLY WILL MAKE YOU **STRONGER,** HAL JORDAN OF EARTH.

YOU WILL **LEARN** THAT THE ENEMIES OF **ORDER** WILL STOP AT **NOTHING** TO SPREAD **CHAOS.**

DO NOT **QUESTION** THE GUARDIANS.

WHY?

WE HAVE LIVED FOR **BILLIONS** OF YEARS.

WHAT WE DO, WE DO FOR THE **WELL-BEING** OF THE **ENTIRE** UNIVERSE.

LIKE THE **MANHUNTERS?**

JORDAN--

THE ANDROIDS THAT DID OUR JOB BEFORE THEY WENT "**GLITCHY**" AND SLAUGHTERED **EVERY** LIVING BEING IN SECTOR 666 BUT THE FIVE INVERSIONS--?

THEY ARE **LIES** FROM ATROCITUS--

IT **WASN'T** ATROCITUS THAT TOLD US ABOUT THE **MASSACRE.** IT WAS **ABIN SUR.** A MESSAGE--

MORE FABLES TO INSTILL **FEAR** AMONG YOU.

INSTILL FEAR IN **US?** YOU KNOW WHAT **I** THINK?

I THINK **YOU'RE** AFRAID.

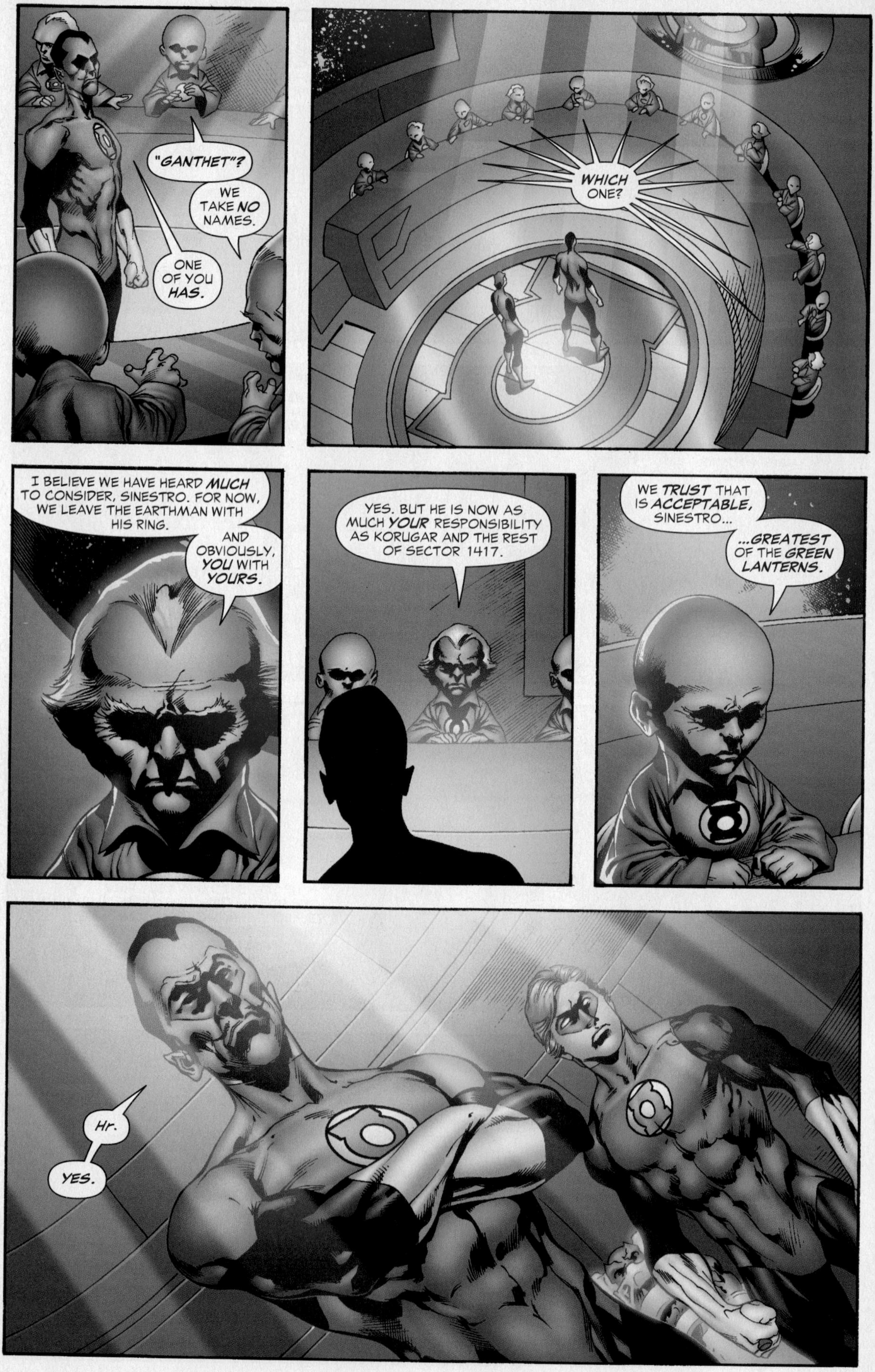
"GANTHET"?
WE TAKE NO NAMES.
ONE OF YOU HAS.
WHICH ONE?
I BELIEVE WE HAVE HEARD MUCH TO CONSIDER, SINESTRO. FOR NOW, WE LEAVE THE EARTHMAN WITH HIS RING.
AND OBVIOUSLY, YOU WITH YOURS.
YES. BUT HE IS NOW AS MUCH YOUR RESPONSIBILITY AS KORUGAR AND THE REST OF SECTOR 1417.
WE TRUST THAT IS ACCEPTABLE, SINESTRO...
...GREATEST OF THE GREEN LANTERNS.
Hr.
YES.

"THAT IS ACCEPTABLE."

HNNN!!

FSSSSSS

I *DID* DO IT.

YOU *DIDN'T* DO IT.

I *DID*.

NO ONE CAN BREAK THROUGH YELLOW, JORDAN. NOT EVEN SINESTRO.

I *CAN--*

YOU ONLY TRIED LIKE *TWENTY* TIMES, HUMAN! YOU CAN TRY ANOTHER *THOUSAND* AND IT WON'T MAKE A DIFFERENCE.

I BELIEVE HIM.

YOU, TOMAR-RE? YOU ALWAYS HAD FAITH *FAR* TOO READILY.

I SUPPOSE THAT IS ONE THING ABIN TAUGHT ME THAT HE NEVER TAUGHT YOU.

I SUPPOSE...

...I MUST *GO.*

I DO NOT HAVE TIME FOR ANY MORE *GAMES*...

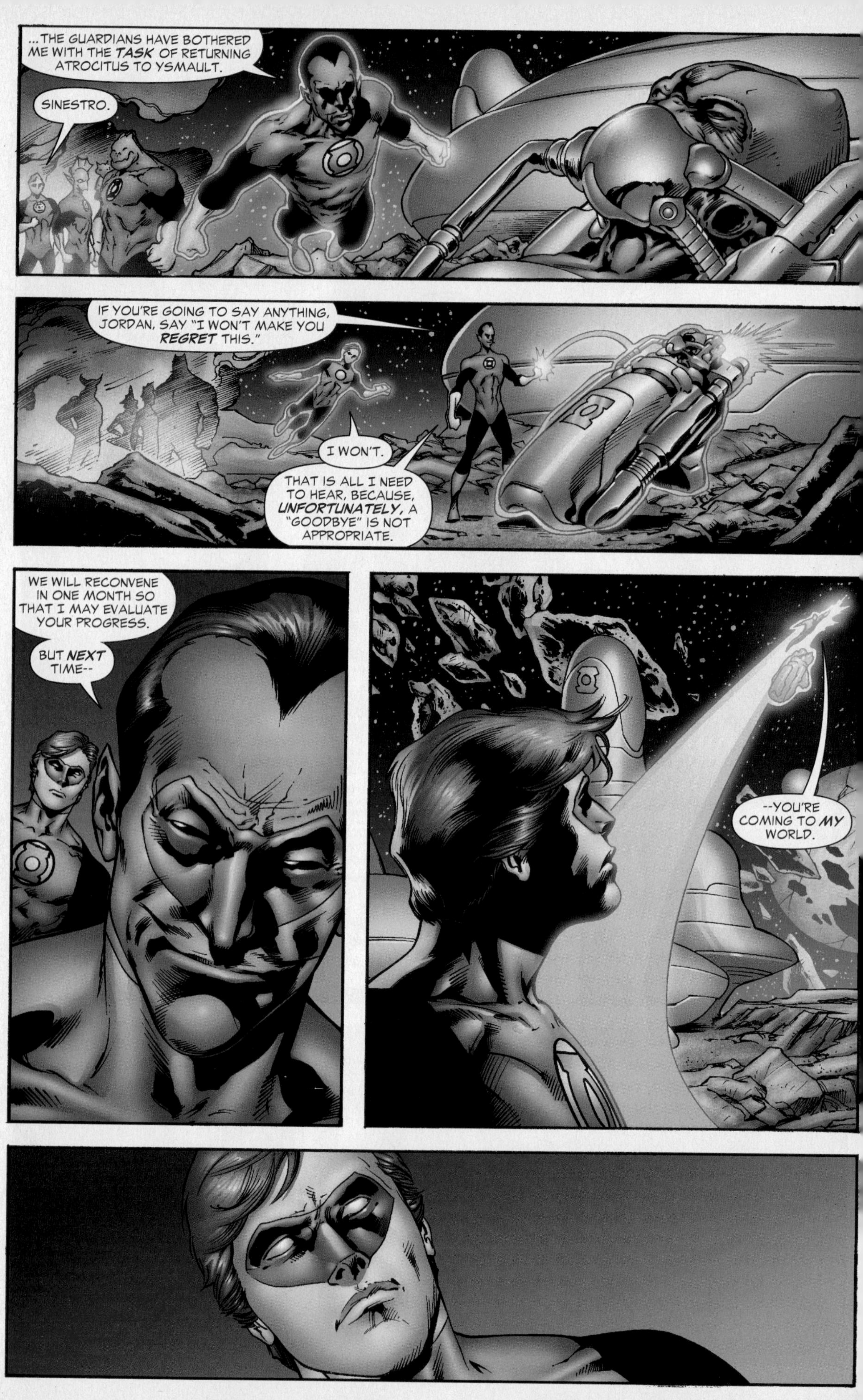
...THE GUARDIANS HAVE BOTHERED ME WITH THE TASK OF RETURNING ATROCITUS TO YSMAULT.
SINESTRO.
IF YOU'RE GOING TO SAY ANYTHING, JORDAN, SAY "I WON'T MAKE YOU REGRET THIS."
I WON'T.
THAT IS ALL I NEED TO HEAR, BECAUSE, UNFORTUNATELY, A "GOODBYE" IS NOT APPROPRIATE.
WE WILL RECONVENE IN ONE MONTH SO THAT I MAY EVALUATE YOUR PROGRESS.
BUT NEXT TIME--
--YOU'RE COMING TO MY WORLD.

"FERRIS IS LETTING *YOU* FLY?"

"IT'S NOT LIKE SHE HAD MUCH OF A CHOICE, TOM."

I GUESS NOT.

BUT BEING THE ONLY PILOT--

FOR NOW.

BEING THE ONLY PILOT, YOU'RE GOING TO BE LOGGING A *HELLUVA* LOT OF *FLIGHT TIME.*

THAT'S WHAT I'M HOPING.

I STILL DON'T GET WHY YOU WANT TO FLY A *PLANE* WHEN YOU'VE GOT THAT *MAGIC* RING.

THE RING'S NOT *MAGIC.* THE PLANES ARE.

SPEAKING OF. WHICH ONE AM I TAKING UP TODAY?

THAT ONE OVER THERE.

FWUMP

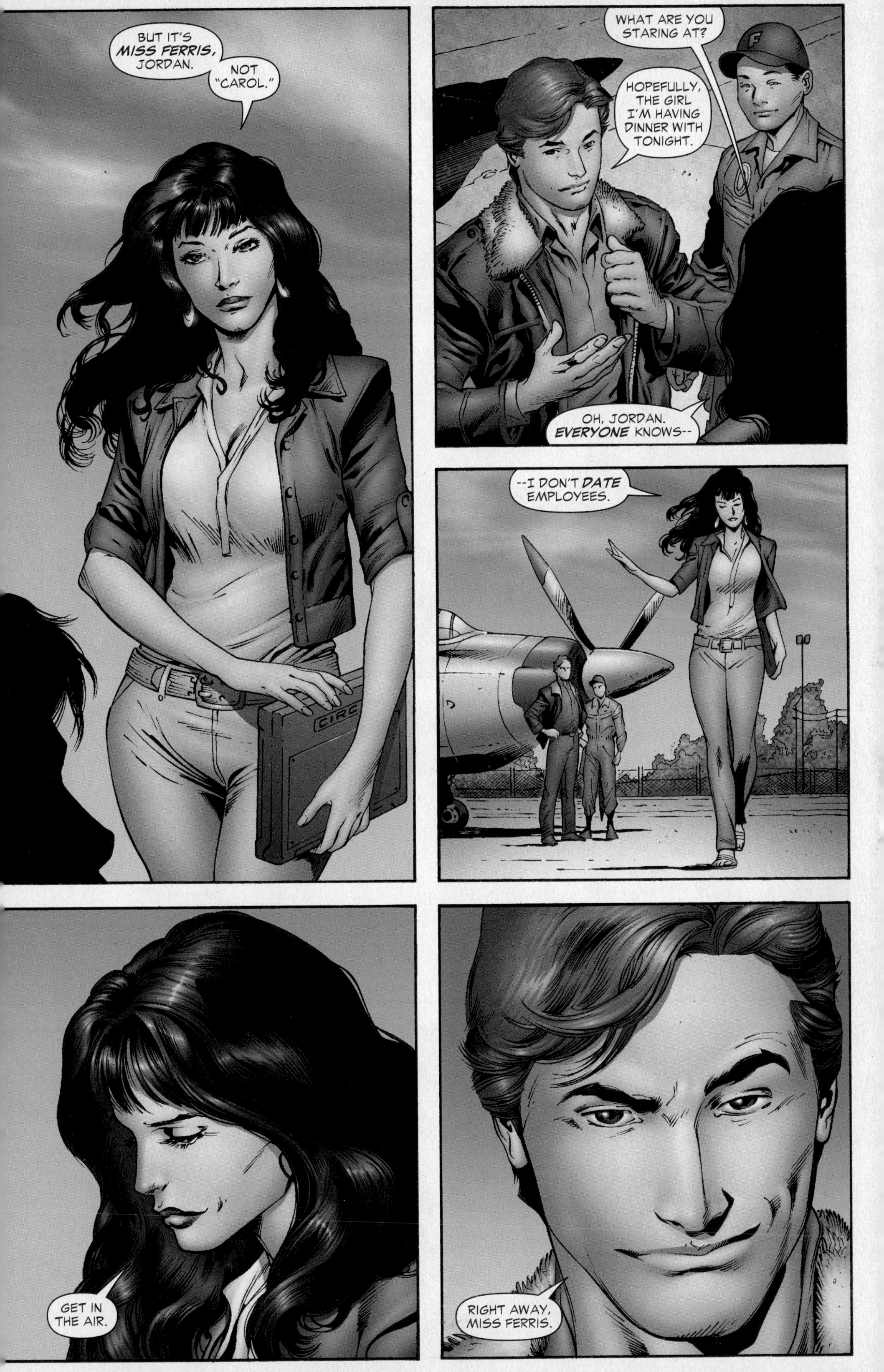
BUT IT'S *MISS FERRIS,* JORDAN.
NOT "CAROL."
WHAT ARE YOU STARING AT?
HOPEFULLY, THE GIRL I'M HAVING DINNER WITH TONIGHT.
OH, JORDAN. *EVERYONE* KNOWS--
--I DON'T *DATE* EMPLOYEES.
GET IN THE AIR.
RIGHT AWAY, MISS FERRIS.

...REPORTS OF MORE **STRANGE LIGHTS** IN THE SKY ARE POURING IN.

COAST CITY HOSPITAL
C C H

U.F.O.'S? SECRET AIR FORCE TEST FLIGHTS? OR ARE THESE RUMORS OF A GLOWING GREEN **MAN** TRUE?

IS THE **GREEN LANTERN** REAL?

WITH THE RECENT APPEARANCE OF **SUPERMAN** IN METROPOLIS, COULD COAST CITY HAVE ITS VERY OWN PROTECTOR? AN EMERALD WARRIOR--?

KLANK

KLK

CHRIST.

I D-D-DIDN'T DO ANYTHING **WRONG**.

STAND **UP**. STAND UP AND GET AWAY FROM THAT--

FWAYEE!

FWANGSSH

IT'S OKAY. DEAD IS G-G-GOOD.

DEAD IS **GOOD**.

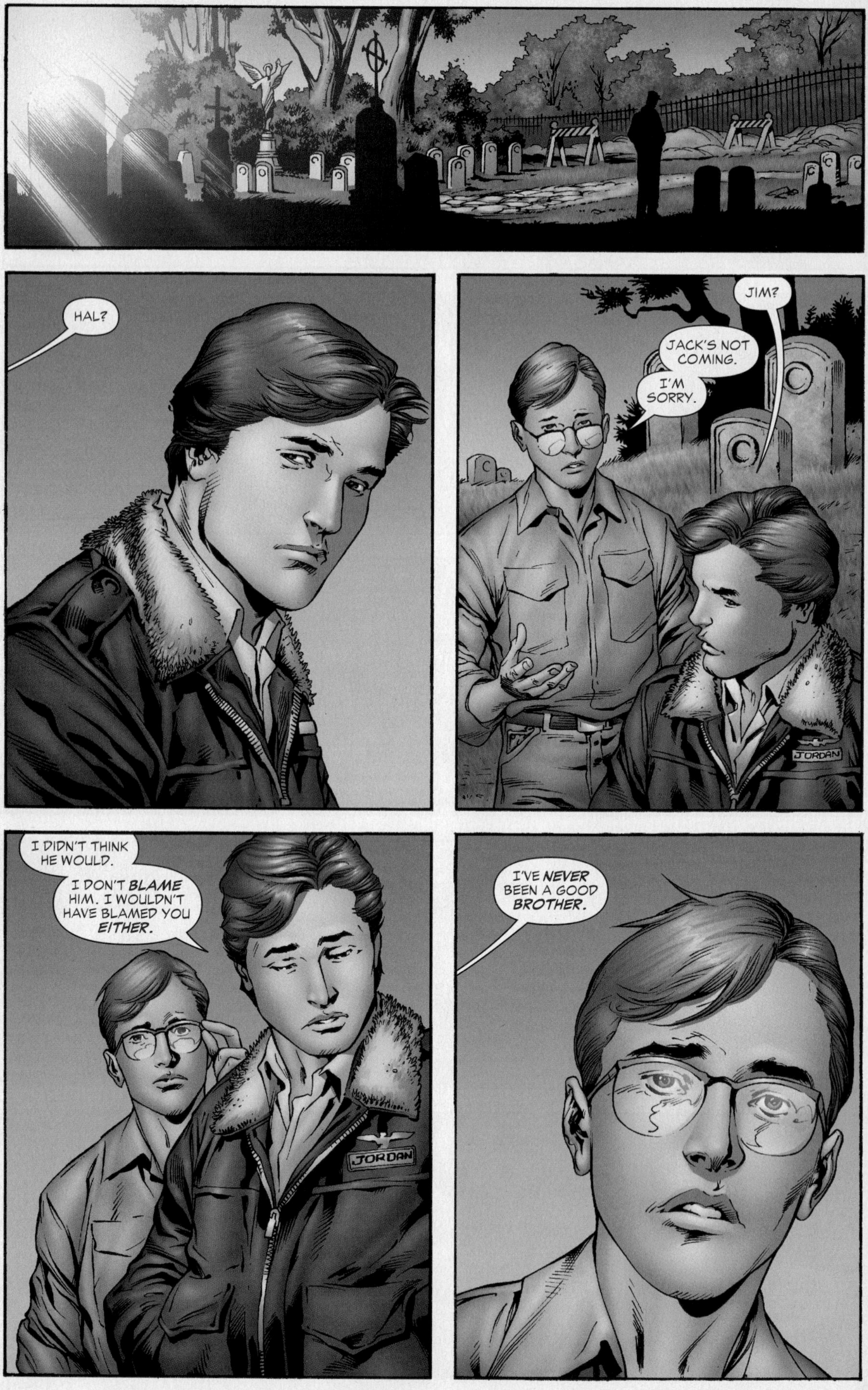

HAL?
JIM?
JACK'S NOT COMING.
I'M SORRY.
I DIDN'T THINK HE WOULD.
I DON'T BLAME HIM. I WOULDN'T HAVE BLAMED YOU EITHER.
I'VE NEVER BEEN A GOOD BROTHER.
JORDAN
JORDAN

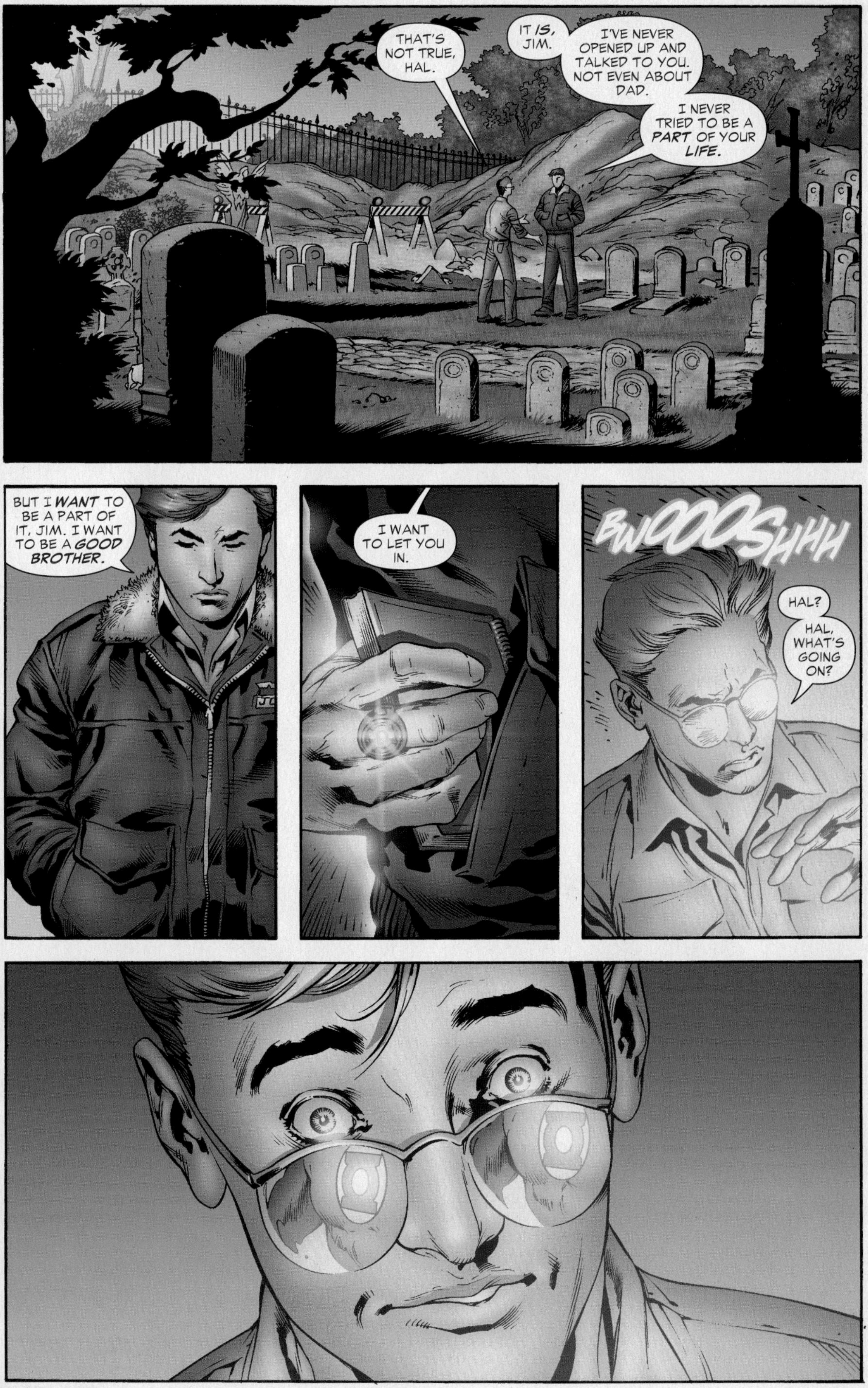
THAT'S NOT TRUE, HAL.
IT *IS*, JIM.
I'VE NEVER OPENED UP AND TALKED TO YOU. NOT EVEN ABOUT DAD.
I NEVER TRIED TO BE A **PART** OF YOUR **LIFE.**
BUT I **WANT** TO BE A PART OF IT, JIM. I WANT TO BE A **GOOD BROTHER.**
I WANT TO LET YOU IN.
BWOOOOSHHH
HAL?
HAL, WHAT'S GOING ON?